Volunteer Tourism in the Global South

This book explores the increasingly popular phenomenon of volunteer tourism in the Global South, paying particular attention to the governmental rationalities and socio-economic conditions that valorize it as a noble and necessary cultural practice.

Combining theoretical research with primary data gathered during volunteering programmes in Guatemala and Ghana, the author argues that although volunteer tourism may not trigger social change, provide meaningful encounters with difference, or offer professional expertise, as the brochure discourse and the scholarly literature on tourism and hospitality often promises, the formula remains a useful strategy for producing the subjects and social relations neoliberalism requires. Vrasti suggests that the value of volunteer tourism should not to be assessed in terms of the goods and services it delivers to the global poor, but in terms of how well the practice disseminates entrepreneurial styles of feeling and action. Analyzing the key effects of volunteer tourism, it is demonstrated that far from being a selfless and history-less rescue act, volunteer tourism is in fact a strategy of power that extends economic rationality, particularly its emphasis on entrepreneurship and competition, to the realm of political subjectivity.

Volunteer Tourism in the Global South provides a unique and innovative analysis of the relationship between the political and personal dimensions of volunteer tourism and will be of great interest to scholars and students of international relations, cultural geography, tourism and development studies.

Wanda Vrasti is Humboldt Foundation Postdoctoral Fellow at the Social Studies Institute, Humboldt University, Berlin, Germany.

Interventions
Edited by
Jenny Edkins, Aberystwyth University and Nick Vaughan-Williams,
University of Warwick

As Michel Foucault has famously stated, "knowledge is not made for under-standing; it is made for cutting." In this spirit The Edkins - Vaughan-Williams Interventions series solicits cutting-edge, critical works that challenge mainstream understandings in international relations. It is the best place to contribute post-disciplinary works that think rather than merely recognize and affirm the world recycled in IR's traditional geopolitical imaginary.

Michael J. Shapiro, University of Hawai'i at Mãnoa, US

The series aims to advance understanding of the key areas in which scholars working within broad critical post-structural and post-colonial traditions have chosen to make their interventions and to present innovative analyses of important topics.

Titles in the series engage with critical thinkers in philosophy, sociology, politics and other disciplines and provide situated historical, empirical and textual studies in international politics.

Critical Theorists and International Relations
Edited by Jenny Edkins and Nick Vaughan-Williams

Ethics as Foreign Policy
Britain, the EU and the other
Dan Bulley

Universality, Ethics and International Relations
A grammatical reading
Véronique Pin-Fat

The Time of the City
Politics, philosophy, and genre
Michael J. Shapiro

Governing Sustainable Development
Partnership, protest and power at the world summit
Carl Death

Insuring Security
Biopolitics, security and risk
Luis Lobo-Guerrero

Foucault and International Relations
New critical engagements
Edited by Nicholas J. Kiersey and Doug Stokes

International Relations and Non-Western Thought
Imperialism, colonialism and investigations of global modernity
Edited by Robbie Shilliam

Autobiographical International Relations
I, IR
Edited by Naeem Inayatullah

War and Rape
Law, memory and justice
Nicola Henry

Madness in International Relations
Psychology, security and the global governance of mental health
Alison Howell

Spatiality, Sovereignty and Carl Schmitt
Geographies of the nomos
Edited by Stephen Legg

Politics of Urbanism
Seeing like a city
Warren Magnusson

Beyond Biopolitics
Theory, violence and horror in world politics
François Debrix and Alexander D. Barder

The Politics of Speed
Capitalism, the state and war in an accelerating world
Simon Glezos

Politics and the Art of Commemoration
Memorials to struggle in Latin America and Spain
Katherine Hite

Indian Foreign Policy
The politics of postcolonial identity
Priya Chacko

Politics of the Event
Time, movement, becoming
Tom Lundborg

Theorising Post-Conflict Reconciliation
Agonism, restitution and repair
Edited by Alexander Keller Hirsch

Europe's Encounter with Islam
The Secular and the Postsecular
Luca Mavelli

Re-Thinking International Relations Theory via Deconstruction
Badredine Arfi

The New Violent Cartography
Geo-analysis after the aesthetic turn
Edited by Sam Okoth Opondo and Michael J. Shapiro

Insuring War
Sovereignty, security and risk
Luis Lobo-Guerrero

International Relations, Meaning and Mimesis
Necati Polat

The Postcolonial Subject
Claiming politics/governing others in late modernity
Vivienne Jabri

Foucault and the Politics of Hearing
Lauri Siisiäinen

Volunteer Tourism in the Global South
Giving back in neoliberal times
Wanda Vrasti

Cosmopolitan Government in Europe
Citizens and entrepreneurs in postnational politics
Owen Parker

Studies in the Trans-Disciplinary Method
After the aesthetic turn
Michael J. Shapiro

Volunteer Tourism in the Global South

Giving back in neoliberal times

Wanda Vrasti

LONDON AND NEW YORK

First published 2013
by Routledge
2 Park Square, Milton Park, Abingdon, Oxon, OX14 4RN

Simultaneously published in the USA and Canada
by Routledge
711 Third Avenue, New York, NY 10016

Routledge is an imprint of the Taylor & Francis Group, an informa business

© 2013 Wanda Vrasti

The right of Wanda Vrasti to be identified as author of this work has been
asserted by her in accordance with the Copyright, Designs and Patent Act
1988.

All rights reserved. No part of this book may be reprinted or reproduced or
utilised in any form or by any electronic, mechanical, or other means, now
known or hereafter invented, including photocopying and recording, or in
any information storage or retrieval system, without permission in writing
from the publishers.

Trademark notice: Product or corporate names may be trademarks or
registered trademarks, and are used only for identification and explanation
without intent to infringe.

British Library Cataloguing in Publication Data
A catalogue record for this book is available from the British Library

Library of Congress Cataloging in Publication Data
Vrasti, Wanda.
　Volunteer tourism in the global south : giving back in neoliberal times /
Wanda Vrasti.
　　p. cm. – (Interventions)
　Summary: "This work explores the increasingly popular phenomenon of
volunteer tourism in the Global South, paying particular attention to the
governmental rationalities and socio-economic conditions that valorize it as
a noble and necessary cultural practice"– Provided by publisher.
　Includes bibliographical references and index.
　1. Volunteer tourism–Developing countries. 2. Volunteer tourism–
Economic aspects–Developing countries. 3. Volunteer tourism–Social
aspects–Developing countries. 4. Volunteer tourism–Government policy–
Developing countries. I. Title.
　G156.5.V64V73 2012
　338.4'791091724–dc23
　　　　　　　　　2012004351

ISBN: 978-0-415-69402-5 (hbk)
ISBN: 978-0-203-10445-3 (ebk)

Typeset in Times New Roman
by Taylor & Francis Books

Contents

	Preface	viii
1	Introduction	1
2	The self as enterprise	28
3	Multicultural sensibilities in Guatemala	56
4	Entrepreneurial education in Ghana	86
5	Conclusion: international political life	119
	Bibliography	138
	Index	152

Preface

The story behind this book is a personal one. The summer after I earned my Masters degree I went on a backpacking trip to Morocco. It was the first time I ventured beyond the familiar surroundings of the Western world. Fresh out of courses on post-structural and postcolonial theory and heavily equipped with a critical awareness of the importance of difference and 'letting subaltern voices speak', I was hoping for a transformative tourist encounter that would neither be tainted by colonial residues nor give in to lofty liberal aspirations. What happened instead was I became, in the words of Jamaica Kincaid, an ugly person, tired, angry and frustrated. In the three weeks I spent trekking down the Moroccan coast I was repeatedly hassled, mocked, scammed, stared and shouted at. I resented being treated like a walking dollar sign or a sex object. But, instead of approaching these tensions with light-hearted tolerance and sympathy, like most of the other Western backpackers I met, I chose to retaliate: I refused to give up on my Western dress (to the chagrin of many local bus and cab drivers), became distrustful of local men and haggled for minuscule sums of money that I could have easily done without. I realized then that I had no idea how to engage with locals beyond the protocols of cultural relativism and political correctness. The brand of critical theory I picked up in graduate school taught me quite well that neither multiculturalism, with its apolitical celebration of cultural diversity, nor modernism, with its insistence on universal (read: European) values of progress, rationality and civility, could be satisfactory models for an ethical encounter with difference. What critical theory did not teach me was how to resolve the heightened contradictions and traumatic encounters tourism threw in my face. All these theories and the traumas kept piling up!

It was during this trip that I first learned about volunteer tourism – a steadily growing sector of the tourism industry directed mostly at young adults (ages 18–25) looking to spend their holidays doing charitable work in impoverished parts of the world. I knew right away that this research topic could supply the kind of passion and curiosity needed to push through a PhD course. It had clear affinities with questions that had preoccupied me since the beginning of my graduate studies, questions regarding colonialism, cosmopolitanism, modern narratives of labour and leisure, neoliberal strategies of government, post-Fordist transformations of work and flexible citizenship practices. Plus, it would allow me to make sense of my own nervous conditions surrounding touristic forms of encounter. This is not to say that I did not have my reservations, even outright revulsion, concerning volunteer tourism. I was particularly suspicious of the anti-modernist fantasies of localism and traditionalism that motivated volunteers to pay exorbitant sums of money to 'make a difference' in the lives of the global poor. There was something disturbing about the moral consensus surrounding charitable and multicultural sensibilities in advanced liberal democracies that I could not quite put my finger on, but which I wanted to explore in more detail. While most of these gut reactions did not prove to be wrong, they did become more theoretically sophisticated. In the three years I spent alternately doing volunteer work in the Global South and writing about it, it never ceased to amaze me that this relatively minor practice repeatedly unsettled both the theories I was trained in and the politics I believed in. Though I do not offer a firm answer as to whether people should enrol in volunteering trips or give advice about how tourists can ethically engage cultural difference, I hope those who read this book will at least be mesmerized by the complex snapshot volunteer tourism provides of the tensions and contradictions of the times we live in.

This book could not have been completed without the generous guidance and continuous support of my supervisory committee. Peter Nyers was the first to encourage my interest in tourism and, with humour and patience, did a wonderful job of assuaging any fears I might have had over the years about this not being a 'proper' international relations topic. William Coleman, with his distinctive penchant for scholarly rigor, made sure to always ask difficult questions that would keep me on my toes and temper my fondness for extrapolation and exaggeration. With Imre Szeman I shared an almost sardonic brand of intellectual scepticism for all fantasies of caring capitalism and moral righteousness. Our conversations helped me turn the original suspicions I had of volunteer tourism from gut-feeling into theorizing. I am also indebted to my former professors and colleagues at McMaster University, Marshall Beier, Catherine Frost, Bill Rodman, Diane Enns, Jean-Michel Montsion, Alina Sajed, Heather Johnson, and Mark Busser. Whether they introduced me to theories of international relations, cultural anthropology, and modern political thought, or simply helped me bounce around ideas, avoid dead-ends, and garner motivation to complete this project, they always made me feel at home in the intellectual community of our department and discipline. I would also like to thank the 'Interventions' editorial team at Routledge, Nick Vaughan-Williams, Jenny Edkins and Nicola Parkin who showed such wholehearted confidence in this project and the two anonymous reviewers who offered insightful comments for polishing up the manuscript. Finally, I am particularly grateful to the two volunteer tourism organizations that allowed me to join their programs, Volunteer Peten and Projects Abroad, along with the numerous volunteers I have met and befriended on these trips. This project would have been impossible without their enthusiastic participation, confidence and friendship.

x *Preface*

The exotic trips and copious writing stints leading up to this book were generously funded by the Social Sciences and Humanities Research Council of Canada, the Political Science Department and the Institute on Globalization and the Human Condition at McMaster University, and the Alexander von Humboldt Foundation. Earlier versions of certain fragments of this manuscript have appeared in *Millennium: Journal of International Studies*, *Theory & Event* and *Review of International Studies*. The editors of these journals were gracious enough to allow me to reproduce, albeit in modified form, some of the material here. Overall, the ideas presented in this book have been greatly improved thanks to a number of journal editors and anonymous reviewers as well as conference participants over the years, in particular, Debbie Lisle, Nicholas Kiersey, Naeem Inayatullah, David Blaney, Jodi Dean, David Chandler and Vanessa Pupavac.

Finally, this project goes out to my family and friends, in particular the Romanian diaspora in Kitchener and the Kottbusser Damm ex-pats in Berlin, who have always helped me find the right balance between writing and slacking. Special thanks go out to Nicolas Rode, who was with me in Morocco when I had my first tourist trauma and who was also there during my field trip in Guatemala, witness to every moment of intercultural despair, intellectual confusion and plain boredom. Thank you for being so much more wherever-you-go-there-you-are than me.

1   Introduction

The history of volunteer tourism (short 'voluntourism') is older than the term suggests. As a commercial practice volunteer tourism only gained currency over the past couple of decades, but 'the idea of combining voluntary service with travel' (voluntourism.org) is far from new. While its institutional roots can be found in the British Volunteer Service Overseas (VSO) established in 1958 and the US Peace Corps set up in 1961, the first organizations to send private citizens to the Third World for 'unofficial' aid and development work, the desire to explore the frontier of industrial modernity for charity and self-betterment is older. It can be traced back to the itineraries of colonial missionaries and educators as well as the nineteenth-century Grand Tour, which I will have more to say about later. But whereas these practices were informed by thinly veiled imperialist motivations and Eurocentric beliefs, volunteer tourism espouses a more recent cosmopolitan vision, reflected also in the rise of sustainable tourism, corporate social responsibility and ethical consumption over the past few decades. Underlying volunteer tourism is a multiculturalist appreciation for cultural diversity, a romantic reverence for nature and tradition and what seems to be a genuine desire to help but also learn from other cultures and people. On top of these noble sensibilities, volunteer tourism also benefits from being anchored in the latest (post-Fordist) forms of education and production, such as study abroad initiatives, continuing education, mandatory service programmes and internships. All of these help make this holiday option seem like sensible investment in the future. So while the idea of volunteer tourism is not unprecedented, its adaptation to contemporary emotional regimes and economic injunctions grants this combination of tourism and aid work unprecedented popularity and profit.

For the first time, during the 1990s, overseas charity work was packaged as an all-inclusive commodity and sold off to conscious consumers (mostly young adults aged 18–25) through travel agencies, for-profit organizations and educational institutions. With 1.6 million participants per year, volunteer tourism is quickly becoming the fastest growing sector of the travel industry (Guttentag 2009: 538). A Travelocity poll from 2007 predicted that the number of Americans planning to take volunteering trips abroad over the next couple of years would increase from 6 per cent to 11 per cent. The Travel Industry

2   *Introduction*

Association of America (TIA) is even more confident, forecasting a 28 per cent rise in demand as far back as 2006 (Dalton 2008). In the UK, where the gap year is a far more institutionalized rite of passage, a University of London review from 2004 counted as many as 800 organizations offering volunteering services abroad (Ward 2007). Although not all volunteer tourism providers are for-profit, travel titans such as Travelocity, Cheaptickets, First Choice Holidays, GAP Adventures and Travel Cuts have recently jumped on board, crowding out or joining forces with not-for-profit organizations, such as Habitat for Humanity and United Way (Dalton 2008).

Volunteer tourism in the developing world, which is the focus of this study, represents only a fraction of the gap year industry: it accounts for 10,000 participants a year and rising (Simpson 2005: 448). Although reliable statistics on for-profit voluntourism in the Global South are painfully absent (the few that exist offer widely dissimilar figures and should, therefore, be viewed with caution), there can be no doubt about the rising popularity of this trend (Guttentag 2009: 538). No longer is overseas charitable work limited to eccentric dropouts, skilled humanitarian personnel and state-sanctioned development initiatives. Middle-class young adults from Western countries, eager 'to undertake holidays that might involve … alleviating the material poverty of some groups in society, the restoration of certain environments or research into aspects of society or environment' (Wearing 2001: 1), now has a variety of organizations, placements and destinations to choose from.

At first glance, there are at least two possible explanations for the growing popular success and moral appeal of this form of travel. First, volunteer tourism presents itself as an alternative to and critique of mass tourism and its notoriously destructive effects. Phrases like 'giving back to the community' and 'making a difference in the world' that litter the brochure discourse are meant to tickle the post-materialist and anti-modernist sensibilities of the Western ethical consumer looking to demonstrate their superior social capital by 'travelling with a purpose'. In addition, the institutionalization and professionalization of this practice have turned volunteer tourism into a 'standard requirement for higher education and career development' (Simpson 2005: 448). For students and young graduates eager to distinguish themselves in an increasingly precarious and competitive economic climate, the promise of gaining exotic cultural knowledge and professional expertise outside of the classroom is particularly relevant.

As we shall see, there is ample evidence for both interpretations throughout this book, but these stories alone cannot explain the root of this seduction. We still need to ask: where does this yearning for travelling with a (humanitarian) purpose come from? Why is an escape from modern society pleasurable and even desirable? What is it about the present moment that requires individuals, especially young adults, to organize their lives, even their spare time, around imperatives of cosmopolitan sensibilities and personal responsibility? And why have these imperatives become shorthand for entrepreneurial action expected from good neoliberal subjects? Together, these questions betray a deeper curiosity

Introduction 3

about the kinds of political subjects and social relations volunteer tourism produces and about whether these consolidate or deviate from already existing formations of power. The approach adopted in this book combines the typically Foucauldian preoccupation with subject formation with a more Marxian inquiry into the duplicitous effects of self-making. It pays special attention to the ways in which even the most well-intentioned attempts at making ourselves into 'the moral subjects of our own actions' (Foucault cited in Nelson 2009: 130) can be used to strengthen the logic of capital. At the same time, the question resonates with the postcolonial critique of Orientalist forms of representation and cultural fantasies that allow some people to affirm their sense of self by taking a detour through other people's version of everyday life.

I knew from the very beginning of this project that I did not want to treat volunteer tourism as a sub-section of the tourism industry. I did not want to provide a technical assessment of the effectiveness of volunteer tourism or formulate recommendations for enhancing the day-to-day operations of voluntourism organizations. Static approaches such as these are responsible for most of the lifeless sociological analyses that currently dominate the field of tourism studies (Franklin and Crang 2001; Hutnyk 2006, 2007). It was also not my ambition to unveil the hidden motives or underlying nature of individual volunteers. The question of whether volunteers are hypocritical or selfless figures lies in the territory of social psychology and does not concern me. Whether volunteers believe in the normative desirability of their actions (which I believe most of them do) or participate solely to boost their résumés does not do anything to change the fact that this practice carries with it a certain moral and material weight. The approach I have chosen instead situates the increasingly popular phenomenon of volunteering in the Global South at the intersection between subjectivity, biopolitics and capital in neoliberal governmentality. It uses volunteer tourism as an opportunity to explore what about the present moment requires individuals, especially young adults, 'to bring [themselves] to labour in an enterprising fashion' (Kiersey 2009: 381), and why this ethos of entrepreneurship relies in equal measure upon economic rationalizations and emotional dictums.

Drawing upon ethnographic material gathered during two volunteering programs in Guatemala and Ghana, I argue that, notwithstanding its practical and ethical deficiencies, volunteer tourism is not a bait and switch strategy that tricks volunteers into paying large sums of money with nothing to offer in return. Even if voluntourism does not result in the kinds of social change, authentic encounters with difference and professional expertise volunteers are led to expect (and enticed to purchase), even if volunteers constantly complain about 'not feeling needed' either because the local population is not 'poor enough' to require foreign assistance or their placements are not well-structured enough to endow them with any meaningful work experience, volunteer tourism still fulfils its promise in different ways. Whether it is by allowing tourists to demonstrate their superior social capital through ethical forms of consumption (as was the case in Guatemala) or by helping them

4 *Introduction*

develop various affective and entrepreneurial competencies needed to navigate the challenges of flexible capital (as in Ghana), volunteer tourism helps young adults from the Global North assume a type of political subjectivity that, in its fidelity to neoliberal injunctions, embodies a new normative ideal. In other words, the effectiveness of volunteer tourism should not to be assessed in terms of the goods and services it delivers to the global poor or the emancipatory alternative it presents to liberal modernity, but in terms of how well it helps (re)produce subjects and social relations congruent with the logic of capital in seemingly laudable and pleasurable ways.

To take issue with a model of action so seeped in noble intentions and transformative ambitions may seem like a callous, even misanthropic gesture. (As someone once said to me after I had explained the subject of my dissertation: 'Your thesis is mean'.) Because volunteer tourism is thought to be a spontaneous act of kindness in response to other people's needs and suffering, it becomes a standard of reference for what it means to be good, ascribing value (in the form of human and social capital) to anyone involved in this practice. Stories about building houses in Latin America or distributing medical supplies in Africa have come to occupy a (suspiciously) firm moral grounding that *demands* applause. But it is precisely because voluntourism enjoys such unabashed support that we should interrogate its claims, strategies and ambitions. In other words, it is less the novelty or magnitude of volunteer tourism that should trouble us, but the virtuous place it occupies in our collective imaginary, from self-righteous participants, enthusiastic parents, educators, employers, all the way to the congratulatory coverage in popular and scholarly publications. This line of inquiry goes back to critical theory's original intent, which is not about providing expert solutions to predetermined problems (such as, how to address the technical problems of voluntourism to make this a more transparent and accountable industry) but about interrogating our received notions of order, progress and justice together with the power relations that allow them to pass as normative truth (Foucault 1980; Cox 1983).

In what follows I offer an introduction to this project and the study of volunteer tourism in general, starting with a review of the literature, a section on ethnographic methods, some preliminary thoughts on theory, a note on the contribution to international relations research and finally a chapter outline of the book.

The seductions and discontents of volunteer tourism

None of the conclusions about volunteer tourism I advance in this book were apparent from the start. I meandered through promotional literature, scholarly apologias and critiques of volunteer tourism as well as ethnographic surprises, theoretical reflections and several editing stages. My initial thoughts about volunteer tourism were shaped by the brochure discourse, in particular voluntourism.org, a sprawling web platform meant to 'educate, empower and engage' tourists, NGOs, tour operators, communities and corporations to embrace this practice. Volunteer tourism, the website boasts, represents the blending of your favourite passions and, perhaps, pastimes. History, culture, geography, environment and the recreation of exploration meet the inspiration of your voluntary efforts in serving a destination and its residents. Body, mind and soul respond to the awakening of thoughts, feelings, emotions, via a labour of gratitude that is offered as a part of your overall itinerary. VolunTourism provides you with perspective and balance. You are able to utilize your 'six' senses and interact with your destination in ways that had previously existed beyond your capacity of expectation. This is travel that unites your purpose and passion and ignites your enthusiasm in ways unimaginable.

(Clemmons 2009)

According to the website, volunteer tourism contains benefits for all stakeholders involved: it allows tourists to travel beyond 'the boundaries of the brochure', host communities to share their cultural richness with others, NGOs to generate revenue in a sustainable way, tour operators to differentiate their product in a 'responsible' manner, hotels and suppliers to 'green' their operations and reduce costs, corporations to demonstrate their commitment to social responsibility, build employee morale and provide innovative training for their staff and educators to enhance their classroom experience. Volunteer tourism offers something for everyone. It is a win-win situation, for volunteers especially, who get to explore new depths of their own personas while making a charitable contribution to the world. For the first time, the personal and the global, the pleasurable and the altruistic and 'the joy and fulfilment associated with them, [can] be synergized and harmoniously blended into one consumable opportunity' (ibid.).

The Lonely Planet guide *Volunteer: A Traveller's Guide to Making a Difference Around the World* (2007) adopts a slightly more tempered tone. Well-aware of the common charge that voluntourism is 'part of a long tradition of people from the West setting off to help or change the countries of the Global South and have adventures while they do it', the Lonely Planet authors stress the continued need for individual responsibility. '[W]hether international volunteering is the new colonialism or not is, in large part, down to the attitudes of you, the volunteer and the organization you go with' (ibid.: 10), which is why the book spends much of its time charting the vast and somewhat confusing spectrum of volunteer organizations to help readers pick not only the most 'responsible' tour provider but also the best-suited placement for their personality. Still, time and time again it is made clear that the success of the experience depends on 'personal attitude'. Volunteers are encouraged to show open-mindedness and humility towards local culture and people. They should acknowledge that, although voluntourism implies a commitment to humanitarian aid and assistance, host communities are not passive recipients of foreign altruism, but also have a lot to offer in terms of cultural wisdom, foreign languages, technical skills and exotic adventures. Being grateful for their hospitality and respectful of their culture can go a long way to ensure that volunteer tourism remains an equitable encounter.

6   *Introduction*

The growing scholarly literature on volunteer tourism coming out of leisure and hospitality studies oscillates between these two options: it is either openly celebratory of the transformative potential of volunteer tourism or it claims that this potential, even if not entirely altruistic, can be realized with some minor technical adjustments. As Wearing and Neil put it: 'Living in and learning about other people and cultures, in an environment of mutual benefit and cooperation, a person is able to engage in a transformation and development of the self' (2001: 242). Overseas volunteering is understood as a morally admirable encounter between hosts and guests that breaks with the vacuity of mass tourism to foster cultural exchange, social transformation and personal development (Wearing 2001, 2002; McGehee and Santos 2005; Wearing *et al.* 2008). There is now also a growing number of empirical case studies dealing with the 'mutually beneficial' impact of volunteer tourism in Australia (Higgins-Desbiolles 2009), Thailand (Broad 2003), Indonesia (Galley and Clifton 2004), South Africa (Stoddart and Rogerson 2004), Costa Rica (Campbell and Smith 2006) and Latin America (Söderman and Snead 2008) to confirm these exuberant conclusions. Even in those rare instances when leisure and hospitality scholars notice the structural inequality foundational to voluntourism, they insist that with better industry regulations in place this problem can be smoothened out. Invariably, the commitment behind this research is to fine-tune the tourism industry by making volunteer organizations more accountable and sustainable, designing more effective placements, taking into account local needs and priorities, increasing the transparency of payment schemes and improving industry credibility (Guttentag 2009; CBC Radio One 2009). It rarely questions the ethico-political rationalities that make overseas volunteering necessary and valuable in liberal capitalist societies.

There are both disciplinary and technical reasons for this limited understanding of voluntourism. On the disciplinary front, international volunteering restores the field's confidence in the transformative powers of travel, allowing management and hospitality studies to continue its unholy alliance with the tourism industry. On the technical front, the discipline's behavioural orientation precludes any serious engagement with the political implications and subjective complexities of volunteer tourism.

Package tourists have long been ridiculed as self-absorbed, hedonistic masses, with no understanding of local culture, no consideration for natural surroundings and no individuality beyond that which is sold to them through advertising and mass consumption (Butcher 2003). Especially in anthropology and sociology, which have made a business out of disparaging this type of travel (Crick 1989), mass tourism is considered a sad statement on modern existence. Dean MacCannell (1973), the cheerleader of tourism sociology, for instance, explains that while the ambition of modern mass tourism is to give people access to the 'backstage', an unedited version of local everyday life, so as to help them make up for the alienated condition of modern life, in reality all tourists get to see is a *mise-en-scène* of local culture. The inaccessibility or constant deferral of authenticity in tourism is indicative of a larger semiotic aporia: for something to be perceived as authentic it must be marked as such; yet, in this act of marking, the real is instantly pushed further into the distance, never to be reached (Frow 1997). It also speaks to a programmatic difficulty in tourism: local tourism providers often willingly refuse to invite their customers to the 'backstage' as a way of resisting the complete commodification of local life forms. All in all, conventional travel seems to be better at mirroring the afflictions of Western modernity (the sense of historical decline, personal fragmentation, moral disintegration and loss of personal freedom) than at alleviating them (ibid.: 80).

Compared to mass tourists, who constantly fall for these tricks, volunteer tourists (or responsible tourists in general) are savvy, resourceful, sophisticated, cultured, sensitive, spontaneous, adventurous and creative (Butcher 2003: 21–22). In making the eradication of global poverty and environmental degradation their *raison d'être*, volunteer tourists avoid the disappointments of mass tourism and recover a sense of purpose and personal meaning. In choosing intimate cultural encounters over manufactured tourist experiences, they critique the conformism of modern society and the homogenizing effects of globalization. Instead of mass consumption, all-inclusive resorts and ecological destruction, they turn to the rural, authentic, unspoiled, traditional and non-Western other for spiritual regeneration and self-critique. Volunteering gives these tourists access to what mass tourism always aspired to but never delivered: an unedited version of other people's version of the everyday, an Eden lost to the West in the process of modernization (MacCannell 1973; Cohen 1979; Badone 2004; Bruner 2005). In volunteer tourism, the disease, poverty and pollution afflicting the Global South are not hidden from sight. On the contrary, these 'disturbing' realities are what constitute a large part of the appeal and justify the cost of volunteering trips, which can be two or three times the value of classic relax-and-escape packages (Ward 2007). Because overseas volunteering is a small-scale, low-impact form of travel that places community development above profit making, Western tourists (who can afford the trip) are given the opportunity to overcome the proverbial modern alienation and apathy by 'making a difference' in the lives of local people (Wearing 2001).

Volunteer tourism also impresses through its promise to resuscitate the nineteenth-century ideals of the Grand Tour where genteel young men embarked on long exploratory trips as part of their studies. The purpose of the Grand Tour was one of education, exploration and sensibilization to the manifold realities of a growingly interconnected world. It was also a way for young men from the upper classes to gain social status and demonstrate a certain sense of maturity and masculinity (Wearing 2002: 243). While modern-day successors of the Grand Tour traveller still exist (backpackers, nomads, pilgrims, drifters and dropouts), mass tourism, beginning with Thomas Cook's pioneering efforts in affordable tourism for the bourgeois masses in the 1840s, is usually said to have destroyed the Golden Age of travel. Sprawling tourist infrastructure has spoiled natural surroundings and traditional cultures, while swelling tourist

8 *Introduction*

hordes have made authentic cultural encounters nearly impossible. By putting *travail* back into travel (Lisle 2010) volunteer tourism will hopefully recover some of these mythical connotations. The fact that this romantic longing for the bygone era of aristocratic travel contains an elitist discontent with the democratization of tourism does not seem to upset this logic (Butcher 2003: 23). Those who dispose of the 'discretionary time and income to travel out of their sphere of regular activity to help others in need' (McGehee and Santos 2005: 760) will broaden their cultural horizons and gain a sense of self-fulfilment. Those who do not fall by the wayside.

From a technical perspective, the narrow understanding of voluntourism we receive from leisure and hospitality studies speaks to the broader epistemological and methodological parochialisms of the discipline. Most tourism research adopts a behaviourist approach that privileges volunteers' motivations, attitudes and experiences over the larger power relations and socioeconomic conditions that make this encounter possible in the first place. It is commendable that tourism research makes an effort to include individual 'voices' (tourist and local), but when all voices are treated equally, regardless of their social position and background, this empiricist commitment becomes futile (Bayart 2008: 199). Just because volunteers are enthusiastic about and satisfied with their chosen holiday does not mean that the practice as a whole is unproblematic or progressive (Guttentag 2009: 540). We also need to probe the discursive and historical conditions that allow some to take a cheap holiday in other people's lives. Yet leisure and hospitality studies are mostly reluctant to pursue this line of inquiry. Instead, they prefer to approach tourism in purely technical terms, as a set of transactions between hosts and guests to be assessed in terms of returns, customer satisfaction, best business practices and regulatory codes of conduct (Hutnyk 2004).

In addition, tourism studies have a history of cutting up fluid tourist practices into static and discreet typologies that correspond neatly to niches in the industry, such as all-inclusive tourism, sex tourism, ecotourism, heritage tourism, responsible tourism, volunteer tourism and so on. This so-called 'trinketization of tourism' is part of a larger move in tourism studies to reduce 'all life to mere commodities' (Hutnyk 2007) and is indicative of the discipline's uncomfortable proximity and subservience to market research (Allon *et al.* 2008: 75). Tourism sociologists complain that the descriptive and business-friendly tone of this literature has produced 'a tradition of flatfooted sociology and psychology', which is more concerned with providing empirical support and technical advice to the travel industry than 'indulging' in critical theory (Franklin and Crang 2001: 6). Not surprisingly, then, much of the academic discussion on volunteer tourism 'ignore[s] politics, commodification, inequality and exploitation at the very moment that these matters are the very basis of the possibility of "third-world" tourism in the first place' (Hutnyk 2006).

One criticism leisure and hospitality research has taken seriously with regards to voluntourism is the 'hypocrisy charge'. What if volunteers are not entirely selfless souls, but participate only for personal and professional gain?

Introduction 9

Media attacks on volunteer tourism have done a lot to spread these fears in the public mind. For instance, a *Maclean's* article aptly entitled 'Helping the World. And Me: Is Volunteer Tourism about Saving the World or Enhancing a Résumé?' notes that 'what inspires idealistic twenty-something-year-olds to lend a [helping] hand often has less to do with philanthropy and more to do with "personal gain"', be it in the form of course credit or professional credentials (Mendleson 2008). An on-going Dalhousie University study on the implications of voluntourism observes that the most-cited reasons interviewees give for participating in volunteering trips are skills acquisition and career development (ibid.). Responses to this charge are divided. Some choose to dismiss it altogether, seeing egoism as a universal trait of human nature: 'I think most people would be lying if they didn't say there was some selfishness in why they were going [to volunteer]' (Wearing 2001: 70). Others argue that self-interest, although not the best of human traits, can be excused as long as voluntourism continues to attract a growing number of followers and effect positive social change (Söderman and Snead 2008). Whatever the response, the 'hypocrisy charge' implies the wilful distortion of an otherwise noble intention. It does not dispute the moral desirability of volunteer tourism. It does not question its structural or discursive organization. It only suggests that a few bad apples have co-opted volunteering for their own benefit and urges us to fine-tune the industry's recruitment and supervisory mechanisms to better distinguish those who sign up for selfish reasons (to enhance their résumé, gain social capital, follow a popular trend) from those who enrol for noble ones (to explore another culture, learn another language, provide much-needed assistance, develop new skills, go on an alternative kind of holiday or fulfil a life-long dream).

A much more serious charge is the idea that no matter how pure or corrupt the intentions, volunteer tourism always benefits travellers far more than it does host communities. Recent media coverage suggests that volunteer tourism is a form of 'new age colonialism' (Lonely Planet 2007: 10) that works to inflate volunteers' sense of self-esteem and alleviate their guilty conscience at the expense of locals, whose needs remain unaddressed, whose jobs are replaced by unskilled volunteers and who are condemned to perform low-wage service work for the enjoyment of Western tourists (Birrell 2010; Richter 2010).

> The desire to engage with the world is laudable, as is the desire to volunteer. But we need to tread more carefully. Unless we have time and transferrable skills, we might do better to travel, trade and spend money in developing countries. The rapid growth of 'voluntourism' is like the rapid growth of the aid industry: salving our own conscience without fully examining the consequences for the people we seek to help. All too often, our heartfelt efforts to help only make matters worse.
>
> (Birrell 2010)

A slightly more vitriolic accusation suspects tourists of using volunteering only to rank themselves against other travellers on the backpacker circuit in

10   *Introduction*

ways that are so vain and petty that they do not even deserve to be included under the category of social capital. Exceptional volunteering tales like, 'I was in Malawi to set up a creative writing program. For orphans. *In jail*', become a rare asset that can be exchanged for status, authority and even sex (MacKinnon 2009). The more sordid the placement, the greater its aura.

These are not new accusations. Critical scholarship on tourism has always operated on the assumption that travelling to the Global South helps white middle-class subjects assert their autonomy, magnanimity and superiority over the backward locals and the less educated and mobile working classes at home. Tourism, whether during colonial or contemporary times, whether done with the blessing of empire or for charitable reasons, has always been fraught with Orientalist sensibilities. Continuing an argument first launched by Edward Said (1979), English and cultural studies have taken to analyzing the discourse of travelogues in search of the continuities between colonial rule and travel (Mills 1991; Pratt 1992; Grewal 1997; Ghose 1998). For postcolonial theory, in particular, travel writing has become an easy target to demonstrate the violent and exclusionary effects of colonial forms of knowledge and power. As one commentator notes, travel writing is 'the most recent darling of the trendy humanities and lit-crit set, who scour travel books, both well known and hopelessly obscure, for evidence of postcolonialism, postimperialism, patriarchy and other evils' (Wilson cited in Lisle 2006: 18). But just because this has become a fashionable trend does not mean that the disparaging conclusions they reach are incorrect. The criticism, it seems, is rather directed at the one-dimensionality of the analysis, which is overly concerned with matters of representation and textuality. That is why the few studies that take a more empirical approach to the topic are a welcome addition.

Nancy Cook's (2005, 2007, 2008) and Barbara Heron's (2007) research on aid workers in the developing world confirms that the aim of transnational philanthropy is not to spread development and cross-cultural understanding, but to endow Western subjects with the 'cultural competencies' (tastes, values, sensibilities and experiences) necessary to perform a 'white', 'bourgeois' and 'enlightened' type of subjectivity (Heron 2007: 29). This is especially true for white women who use charity and philanthropy towards colonial subjects and the domestic poor as a way to carve out a space for themselves in the public sphere and assert their equality vis-à-vis white men (Cruikshank 1999). Kate Simpson (2004, 2005) finds a similar dynamic in volunteer tourism. Despite the language of 'making a difference' and 'broadening horizons', volunteer tourism is not about promoting either development or enlightenment, but rather about cultivating a 'professional, self-governing, careerist persona' (Simpson 2005: 447). This is achieved by cementing already existing stereotypes and dichotomies between mobile, flexible and worldly tourists and poor-but-happy locals. John Hutnyk, in his study of charity workers in Calcutta, takes this point even further. Volunteer tourism, he argues, is 'the soft side of an otherwise brutal system of exploitation' in that it maintains the 'Third World' as the disempowered recipient of our discretionary aid and benevolence (Hutnyk

1996: ix). The most vocal critic of volunteer tourism, however, remains Ivan Illich. In an unapologetic speech delivered to a room full of soon-to-be volunteers in Mexico he argues that 'good' volunteers are the hypocritical ones because they prefer to ignore the forms of inequality that give them the right 'to impose [their] benevolence' on the developing world (Illich 1968: 4). According to Illich, if we conducted an *honest* evaluation of volunteering programs, something all organizations should periodically engage in, the political amnesia informing this type of travel as well as its utterly unredeemable nature would become painfully evident. Compared to the mostly 'stale, tired, repetitive and lifeless' study of tourism (Franklin and Crang 2001: 5), critical approaches such as these help politicize transnational travel by demonstrating how everyday practices usually imagined as trivial or private are in fact key sites of producing and disseminating political meanings, from cosmopolitan visions to imperialist impositions.

In international studies, a discipline that claims to study precisely this global distribution of power, the discussion on global tourism is still sparse. Much like anthropology, sociology and geography, international relations (IR) 'can barely disguise [its] contempt' for tourism (Crick 1989: 308). This has a lot to do both with the methodological and the thematic requirements of tourism research. Researchers fear that going into the field and spending extended periods of time in the proximity of tourists will cloud their powers of judgement and jeopardize their professional credibility. As Malcolm Crick explains, tourism is a 'cracked mirror in which we can see something of the social system which produces [field workers] as well as tourists' (Crick 1985: 78). If academic work is governed by a bourgeois value system that maintains a strict separation between work and leisure, researchers who act like tourists risk violating this code and compromising their claims to disciplinary authority and, implicitly, public funding. This is particularly true for people doing ethnography.

Ethnographers have always competed with tourists over the authenticity and credibility of the reports they bring back from foreign lands (Badone 2004: 186). To demonstrate their professionalism, field workers must act like heroic figures in search of legitimate (read: scientific) knowledge, not slackers indulging in journeys of self-discovery and questionable public conduct. These methodological concerns, which feature prominently in all social science disciplines, are further exacerbated in the case of international relations, a discipline so preoccupied with questions of inter-state security and so deeply entrenched in the legacy of rational positivism that ethnographic research on the quotidian aspects of life is bound to arouse suspicion.

These obstacles notwithstanding, the past decade has witnessed the publication of a handful of IR studies dealing with transnational tourism in relation to state building (Hazbun 2008), global political economy (Chin 2008), national identity and global development (Clancy 2001, 2009). This book shares the closest affinity to Debbie Lisle's study of *The Global Politics of Contemporary Travel Writing* (2006). Lisle starts from the assumption that travelogues are revelatory of global politics in the same way that government documents or

12 *Introduction*

media reports are. They shape and consolidate our understanding of other people and places in ways that are far from benign. According to Lisle travel writing is dominated by two main approaches to identity and difference, and she takes issue with both. The colonial approach, she argues, assesses cultural differences from a Eurocentric gaze, whereas the cosmopolitan view celebrates global diversity from an equally European belief in recognition, tolerance and multiculturalism. The first seeks to erase difference by imposing universal liberal values onto people in extreme positions of inequality; the second neglects or trivializes difference to overlook the persistence of global poverty and injustice. Both gazes, in one way or another, 'mimic the "previous sensibilities" of Empire' (ibid. 5). What Lisle has to say about travelogues is also true for volunteers. Just like travelogues are historically linked to imperial adventures, so volunteers, as amateur anthropologists in foreign lands, reproduce problematic representations of difference with concrete political implications. They either disparage the other, legitimizing centuries of foreign intervention and dispossession, or they romanticize local populations, refuting their claims to material redistribution and social justice.

Still, in what follows, I want to encourage a more ambivalent reading of voluntourism, which acknowledges the continuity between volunteer tourism and colonial forms of knowledge, power and domination, but which also respects the novel and fluid elements of this experience. There is a lot more uncertainty and contingency found over the course of a volunteering trip than in a fixed literary text. Ethnography can capture the temporal fluctuation of voluntourism in ways that discursive readings of travel narratives cannot.

Ethnography: journey and method

From the very start I wanted this to be an ethnographic project. Both the sycophantic appraisals found in leisure and hospitality studies and the critical accusations of neo-colonialism fail to capture the complex logic of volunteer tourism, which I understand as an *innovative* strategy of government reflective of contemporary transformations in capitalist production, consumption and citizenship practices. To the extent that volunteer tourism offers us a glimpse into neoliberal strategies of subject formation, I was hoping to tell a story that extended far beyond international volunteering into an anthropology of the present, or a biopsy of neoliberal rationalities of government. While I had no shortage of grand scholarly ambition, I did not have a clear hypothesis to guide me through the project. All I had was a vague idea about the compassionate pretences of volunteer tourism collected from travel guides and promotional brochures. The project became ethnographic almost by default because ethnography is the process (and the outcome) of recreating the world of meaning experienced during fieldwork without aiming for scientific objectivity and replicability. With its method of 'deep hanging out' (Madison 2005) and commitment to self-reflexivity, ethnography would allow me to embark on a double rite of passage: that of a tourist entering the 'secrets' of another culture and

Introduction 13

that of a field worker penetrating the 'inner sanctum' of a disciplinary tradition (Badone 2004: 184). But, at the time, I had little idea about where this would take me or the surprises, false expectations and changes of heart involved in getting there.

My interest in ethnography did not come out of thin air. In the social sciences, feminist, postcolonial and Marxist writers began importing ethnographic methods and materials during the 1980s. Gathering spoken and performative repertoires of people 'on the ground' became the preferred method of research for scholars interested in the political value of the subaltern, the personal and the everyday. Much of the infatuation with ethnography can be explained in terms of its promise to access the 'really real' (Behar 2003: 16), let the subaltern speak and produce innocent knowledge outside the constraints of theory and representation (Scott 1992: 44). The hope was that ethnography, with all its participatory and experiential qualities, would capture a more accurate and relevant version of social reality and communicate it in a jargon-free style. This is a noble ambition. Who would not want to write 'stories about real people in real places' (Behar 2003: 16) that cross academic walls and help spur political change? But this 'ethnographilia' also betrays a century-old quest for authenticity and real-world applicability haunting the social sciences and humanities. It lies at the root of many misguided attempts to 'write from the heart' without much theoretical depth or political weight (Vrasti 2008).

Strangely enough, just as ethnography was 'being widely appropriated as a liberating method' in fields such as cultural studies, social history and political science, 'its authority [was and still is] seriously challenged from both within anthropology and outside' (Comaroff and Comaroff 1992: 7). During the 1980s, anthropology was undergoing a *crise de conscience* of its own, triggered in equal measure by the (re)discovery of the discipline's colonial roots and growing scepticism about ethnography being the 'idiom in which [reality] prefers to be described' (Geertz 1988: 140). Critical anthropologists were pointing out that ethnography cannot create a perfect correspondence between reality and its textual representation. Interviews and verbal testimonies cannot guarantee access to some unadulterated version of reality. Rather, all ethnography 'is from beginning to end enmeshed in writing', as James Clifford famously pronounced (1983: 120; *see also* Clifford 1988, 1986a, 1986b; Fabian 1983, 1991; Rosaldo 1986, 1993; Behar 1996). This meant that it was the ethnographer, with the help of narrative strategies like unobtrusive observation, theoretical abstraction and professional jargon, that was producing the veracity and authority of the text – not the 'indigenous' voices and events from the field (Marcus and Cushman 1982: 31–37). This tight editorial control, which was seen as a continuation of anthropology's uncomfortable relation with colonial forms of domination, had to be unsettled by bringing in different voices, more transparent writing and self-reflexive theorizing.

I was not really interested in pursuing either one of these avenues. I was neither convinced by the idea that ethnography could offer a window onto reality, nor did I want to experiment with the deconstructivist promises of the

14 *Introduction*

genre. Gradually, it seemed less important to me that ethnography unsettles the spatio-temporal foundations of textual representation and disciplinary knowledge. If initially I had been sympathetic to this project (Vrasti 2008), over the course of my field work I would discover a more pragmatic use for ethnography. I began to see ethnography as a strategy for navigating the ambiguities of researching a trend I found both fascinating and problematic, living with people who would become my friends and the target of my critique, amidst cultures I could not fully understand or appreciate.

Constraints of funding and time limited my research to only two commercial voluntourism projects: one with a small nature conservation organization called Volunteer Peten in Guatemala, the other with a large and fairly renowned voluntourism agency, named Projects Abroad, teaching English in Ghana. Since I was going to write a touring ethnography of volunteer tourism, I wanted to respect the inevitable messiness of independent travel. I planned for flights, visas and vaccines, but left lots of room in my luggage for chance encounters and changes of heart. I left home in fall 2008, hoping to find the compassionate subject eager to 'give back' and 'do something useful on vacation' the brochure discourse seemed directed at. My guiding assumption was that there had been a significant shift in the logic of neoliberal governmentality from the (wo)man of reason to the (wo)man of feeling, from the *homo oeconomicus* guided exclusively by market rationality to a more complex figure that complemented utility calculations with Romantic sensibilities and bohemian values. I originally thought the sacrificial, charitable and even heroic acts young middle-class adults were encouraged to perform on volunteering trips to the Global South would help demonstrate the incorporation (or instrumentalisation) of affectivity under neoliberal rule. But, as is often the case with ethnography, knowledge rarely awaits us in the field. If it does, it is a different type of knowledge than we expected.

During my travels to Guatemala and Ghana, where I conducted some 30 interviews with volunteers and staff members, I found little evidence to substantiate the stories of sacrifice and compassion advertised in brochures. Instead, I would repeatedly hear volunteers complain about 'not feeling needed' and experience the sentiment myself. The places we lived in (San Andres, Guatemala and Ho, Ghana) did not resemble the photogenic poverty shots many of us had seen on charity infomercials and fundraiser posters. There were no visible signs of starvation or malady and locals did not seem to need or appreciate our assistance. There was constant frustration about the poor organization of volunteer placements, which were either unresponsive to local needs or poorly tailored to volunteers' professional skills. All in all, we often felt useless, bored and, even somewhat, deceived. On average, it only took volunteers a couple of weeks to give up on their compassionate ambitions of 'making a difference in the world' and start slacking. We would travel on weekends, hang out in bars and at expat hotel pools and spend several hours every day in internet cafes.

Initially, I feared that I had picked the wrong research sites. I could not understand how care and compassion could be missing from a practice that depended on these very emotions for its success. It took me some time to realize that whatever the technical or ethical difficulties of volunteer programs, these do not necessarily detract from the appeal of the voluntourism experience. Most volunteering programs are poorly structured, unaccountable to local needs and simply chaotic, yet they continue to succeed, not only in the commercial sense, but also in endowing volunteers with a sense of personal meaning, self-esteem and worldliness. There is a distinction to be made between the volunteering *organization*, whose role is simply to sell a product that grants tourists access to a locale they would otherwise not dare to travel to on their own, and the volunteering *experience*, which includes encounters and events far beyond this narrow commercial exchange. Just because the placements at Volunteer Peten and Projects Abroad did not allow volunteers to demonstrate their compassion and good will, does not mean that my initial suspicion of volunteer tourism being an indication of a new turn in neoliberal governmentality towards affect and sociality is incorrect. As both trips would prove, volunteers had no trouble finding alternative ways to demonstrate their emotional capacities and entrepreneurial competencies.

In Guatemala, volunteers affirmed their cosmopolitanism by showing their appreciation for the local culture and people. If San Andres was not 'poor enough' to allow volunteers to demonstrate their compassion, at least it was slow, quaint and remote enough to let volunteers develop a cultural sensibility of the liberal multiculturalist sort. Because San Andres could conceal its lacks so very well, the place came to serve as a 'supply point' of desire for Western tourists and a backdrop for their sentimental education (Ahmed 2006: 115). Even if the work itself was not rewarding, living in a distant rural town with strong familial bonds and an unhurried pace of life still allowed white middle-class tourists to escape the conformity of consumer capitalism and experience life outside the estrangement of modern society.

In Ghana things were somewhat more complicated because racial tensions stood in the way of any such coalitions of sympathy. Volunteers felt exhausted and harassed by the scrutinizing gaze of locals, which they perceived as 'reverse racism'. But here too volunteering or simply living in exotic, dangerous 'Africa' functioned like a seal of maturity, bravery and self-sacrifice. Living in a radically different culture, without local language skills, modern amenities or the comfort of loved ones, students and graduates acquired the immaterial skills (communication, cooperation, leadership skills, problem solving) needed in the new economy. Phrases like 'expand your horizons', 'fulfil your potential' or 'come back a changed individual' may sound like empty platitudes, but, in fact, they express the sincere pedagogical ambition of volunteer tourism. In both instances, then, volunteer tourism acted as a successful and seductive strategy of government in its ability to produce subjects and social relations congruent with the exigencies of cognitive capitalism.

I could have never told this story without the help of ethnography, which is particularly well-suited to capturing the inherent fluidity of travel. What seems to be a fairly clear-cut sub-section of the tourism industry is, in fact, a

16 *Introduction*

peripatetic practice that combines experiences of holiday and dwelling, citizenship and touristic practices, work and leisure in new and exciting ways (Allon *et al.* 2008: 14). That is why, instead of talking about volunteer tourism as a self-contained, empirically observable practice, as in most tourism and hospitality studies, we are better off thinking about volunteers drifting along a continuum from 'travelling' to 'dwelling' in search of meaning and self-esteem in the global arena (Hutnyk 1996; Allon *et al.* 2008: 86–87; Ong 1999: 6). Also, a politically engaged study of volunteer tourism is one that does not simply describe volunteer tourism, but also connects it to other itinerant sites (consumption patterns, labour markets, universities) and identities (employers, educators, local populations) to show how it operates as part of larger socio-economic and cultural circuits. Ethnography, with its mix of experience and interpretation, empirical observation and theoretical abstraction, sensorial proximity and intellectual astuteness (Clifford 1988), helped me make these connections explicit in a way that other social science methods, both positivist and constructivist, often cannot either because they are too concerned with scientifically representing empirical reality or because they absolve themselves from this responsibility altogether.

What is true of tourism can also be said of subjectivity: it is an inherently elusive category that escapes perfect representation. Subjectivity is never complete; it is a constant field of struggle between power and resistance: both are present at all times. Several accounts have already tried to capture the complexities of neoliberal subjectivity, with an eye to both its entrepreneurial and affective injunctions, most notably David Brooks (2000) and Richard Florida (2002). Yet instead of exploring the temporal unfolding of subject formation, these authors have used behavioural trivia and pop-psychological observations to present us with an already formed subject, an individual so set in their ways and so secure in their position that it can only be an inanimate prototype. Ethnography proved crucial for charting the temporality of subject making over the course of a volunteering trip, from fantasies of care and compassion to boredom and disillusionment and, finally, to the development of multicultural sensibilities and other affective competencies useful for cognitive capitalism. It revealed not only the ways in which volunteers' charitable impulses and cosmopolitan sensibilities get co-opted by dominant discourses of rule, but also how volunteers resort to boredom and frustration to contradict the brochure discourse and reject the institutional organization of volunteering to stage more self-directed encounters with difference. The latter should be regarded as instances of resistance even if ultimately they get channelled back into the logic of neoliberal governmentality.

But it is not just volunteers who travel, crossing continents and shifting subject positions. Research travels as well. The project travelled through various stages of research, from literature review to field work, back through libraries, field notes, committee meetings, conference presentations, successive writing and endless editing stages to see the light of day. Some of these travels were filled with false expectations and dead ends; others were full of epiphanies and

Introduction 17

surprises. In all cases, the road research travels from thesis to theory is unpredictable and filled with doubt and anxiety. Telling this story in a way that remains loyal to the windy road knowledge travels before it reaches the reader's eye is the primary task of ethnography.

I am not talking here about ethnography's promise to 'liberate [academics] from the pedantic, technical discourse of their disciplines' (Foley and Valenzuela 2005: 224). Rather, what I am referring to is the idea of ethnographic writing as *improvisation* (Cerwonka and Malkki 2007). Throughout this book I use ethnography less as a method for gathering information through interviews and participant observation (although this is clearly part of the process) than a textual strategy for building theory from the disparate events, statements, experiences, dilemmas and surprises I encountered during my travels, but also at home, at my desk, in libraries, at conferences and during seminars. Ethnographic improvisation, then, is a logistical answer to the problem of managing conflicting and overlapping information, commitments and social roles. It requires constant travelling back and forth between the part and the whole, experience and text, fieldwork and theory until we finally find a persuasive way to piece these two seemingly distinct registers together (Cerwonka 2007: 15, 19).

Making this improvisational work public is not just an exercise in honesty, but also a challenge to what is formally known as 'method' – how it is taught, practised and written up. We are taught in methodology courses that research is the result of a linear accumulation of knowledge. But the answers to our research questions rarely await us 'in the field'. Often we return home more confused than we were in the first place. It is neither experience nor interpretation, neither methodological virtuosity nor theoretical skill that makes research work, but improvisation (Cerwonka and Malkki 2007). This has nothing to do with 'weak' research design or self-indulgent solipsism. There is as much reflection as there is spontaneity involved in the task of writing ethnography, which after all is nothing but the selective retelling (gathering, sorting, arranging, reformulating and forgetting) of fieldwork events with the double aim of theoretical persuasiveness and sensorial accuracy (van Maanen 1988). A text that is aware of 'the subtle forms of knowledge found in ineffable moments of intuition and epiphany' (Behar 2003: 23) only acquires a more credible voice: nothing can be left out of ethnography without, automatically, taking something away from theory.

But a more honest ethnography is not necessarily a more accurate representation of reality. Not only does writing always distort reality, as post-structuralism teaches us, but, without being filtered through theory, ethnography remains little more than a storytelling device. Only very late in my research did I realize that while I aspired to recreate the dramatic milieu of everyday experience through ethnography, indeed to correct the dehumanized (people-less, story-less and emotionless) view of reality social science research gives us, without the import of theory, especially the dense, continental kind, I would not be able to explain the material and symbolic conditions that make volunteer tourism a desideratum for neoliberal subjectivity. Ethnography, unfortunately, cannot

18 *Introduction*

single-handedly offer a critique of volunteer tourism because it lacks an explicit political orientation beyond its rather recent commitment to transparency, polyphony and deconstruction. These are worthwhile objectives to have (especially in my case where I was not the only ethnographer in the field: all volunteers are anthropologists eager to understand the local culture without spoiling it), but without a larger political ambition even the most ethically conscious texts cannot help but remain mired in the technical or the anecdotal. Verbal testimonies, everyday actions and local colour, no matter how evocatively reproduced, cannot speak for themselves: they only provide a picture of the subjects and social relations present in volunteer tourism, not an analysis of their historical, political and material conditions of possibility. This is particularly dangerous in the case of volunteer tourism where, as Jean-Francois Bayart puts it, 'the question of subjectivation is too serious to be left up to the subjects' (2008: 199). In other words, no matter how urgent the ethical demands of textual representation, we cannot allow the spoken repertoires of our research subjects to sideline the material and discursive strategies involved in producing a neoliberal social field (Ferguson 2006: 19).

To make ethnography amenable to the study of the distribution, reproduction and contestation of power I decided to place it in conversation with Foucault's archaeological method. The archaeological method, also known as 'analytics of government' (Rose 1999: 15–20; Dean 1999: 20–27), is interested less in describing the 'general principles of reality' than in identifying the rationalities that make that reality acceptable and the fissures that could transform it (Foucault 2002: 201). Its purpose is to unearth the conditions that make certain judgments possible and foreclose others, the rules and forces that make certain utterances and performances coagulate into a regime of truth and outlaw others as instances of illegality and abnormality (Butler 2003: 4). Different from historical methods, archaeology does not dig up chronological events and personalities to explain how the past became the present. Rather, it interrogates the rationalities through which the present became materially and historically possible in the first place (Gordon 1980: 242). Archaeology does not explore the essence of things and, as such, is allergic to concepts that historical, sociological, economic and political analyses take as a given (state, sovereignty, civil society, people, capital, etc). Instead, it 'examines the conditions under which regimes of practices come into being, are maintained and are transformed' (Dean 1999: 21). Foucauldian archaeology allows us to analyze the discursive repertoires of volunteer tourists in a way that goes beyond the psychological and sociological appearances of tourism explored in leisure studies and beyond the 'ascribed/described/pronounced subjectivities' highlighted in post-structural and postcolonial analyses (Hutnyk 2007). It allows a 'not so fashionable materialist analysis' of the power relations that make volunteer tourism a necessary and commendable enterprise (ibid.).

Overall, then, I adopt a dialogical method that switches between the narrative testimonies and experiences of volunteers and a critical analysis of the governmental strategies involved in their subjectivization. One cannot function without the other. The minute detailing of everyday practices and lived experiences is purely descriptive unless it takes into account the regulatory effects of political institutions, economic regimes and programs of governmentality. By corollary, an analytics of governmentality without an element of human agency remains sterile and abstract (Ong 1999: 3–4). The former is particularly useful in making sense of the unwieldy strategies involved in producing subjects, while the latter helps capture the rules and forces that valorise certain subjects while delegitimizing others. This exchange also allows for theory to be brought back into the conversation without necessarily reproducing the anxieties around aloof and inaccessible scholarly texts. It helps demonstrate the power of critical theory to act as a hermeneutic guide to the present condition and our role in it.

In merging ethnography and archaeology, my writing has perhaps become much more theory driven than I had originally hoped. While this may seem like a betrayal of my initial ethnographic aspirations, I maintain that theory does not necessarily act as an alienating force. To inspire political action, social analysis does not have to keep scholarly erudition to a bare minimum, as many ethnographic aficionados propose. The 'all-these-theories-and-the-bodies-keep-piling-up' logic (Zalewski 1996) often does more to police the use-value of critical theory than advance politically progressive scholarship. While appeals to linguistic clarity are not without merit, the all-too-often concomitant notion that ideas themselves ought to be simple typically stems from populist anti-intellectualism. Making scholarly texts 'user-friendly' is, in fact, a lengthy and arduous task involving a great deal of political engagement, disciplined commitment and editing work.

We cannot reject critical theory off-hand simply on account of its textual density. Certainly, there are plenty of examples of 'bad' theory – exceedingly esoteric, methodologically flawed, poorly communicated and plain unconvincing theory. But, I would argue, these are less examples of theory than of 'theoreticism' – the dogmatic application of critical theory divorced from its historical context and lived surroundings. To quote Sylvère Lotringer (2009), 'anti-theory and theoreticism are two sides of the same coin. But, of course, it is the wrong coin'. In a slightly different vein, Fredric Jameson explains that 'what is socially offensive about "theoretical" texts like [his] own, is not their inherent difficulty, but rather the signals of higher education, that is, of class privilege, which they emit' (cited in Kunkel 2010). The confinement of theory to the halls of the corporate university is indicative of a larger tendency in neoliberal capital to commodify dissent (Frank and Weiland 2002; Boltanski and Chiapello 2005). The knee-jerk reaction to this is to reject theory altogether for its elitist connotations. A much better strategy would be to recognize that theory is what makes the world around us intelligible and malleable, and try to rescue it from the claws of professionalism by democratizing theoretical literacy.

This is not always an easy task. Much of the language and ideas presented in this book, for instance, are not readily accessible to people outside the profession – a problem I assume full responsibility for. However, I found theory

20   *Introduction*

to be essential for understanding the duplicity and complexity of our current predicament, where radical aspirations for community, autonomy and human dignity are systematically placed in the service of market imperatives and disciplinary rule. Emancipatory politics that trades theory for 'speaking truth to power' is bound to produce more of the same. The road to hell is paved with uncritical intentions. My hope was that theory would help us understand how even pleasurable and empowering individuation strategies, like those employed in volunteer tourism, can make people complicit with unjust and violent conditions, and that this would encourage a more rigorous (self-)examination of our deepest emotional and political investments – a 'critical ontology of ourselves', as Foucault called it (1997c).

Governmentality, biopolitics, capital

Speaking of theory, most of the inspiration for this project comes from Michel Foucault's lecture series at the Collège de France, *The Birth of Biopolitics* (2008), where he argues that neoliberal government is neither the ideology of neo-conservative policy makers, nor a historical period characterized by the withdrawal of state authority in times of economic globalization. Rather, it is a set of power relations that extends the logic of market relations to the entire social field, from macroeconomic policies to public policy, education, labour, recreation and personal conduct. The market becomes both the power of formalizing state and society and the standard of truth against which these should be measured. The first order of business in neoliberalism, then, is to intervene in the social sphere to make sure that it contains forms of life, action and sociality appropriate for a flexible market economy. This objective does not necessarily require active planning and premeditation on behalf of state agencies and representatives. Something more complicated is at work here. The ideas (and ideals) of neoliberalism may originate in but also go beyond the institutional loci of government to extend across a variety of social spaces, from households to communities, local to transnational spaces, exceptional to mundane instances. This is what Foucault understood by governmentality: a 'model of social control' that does not rely upon the direct intervention of the state and its agencies of power, but on the ability of individuals to freely govern themselves in light of certain economically viable principles and axioms (McNay 2009: 57).

What this suggests is that subjectivity, our most intimate and private sphere of existence, does not lie 'outside' the purview of power, but is intensely governed (Rose 1991: 1). This 'growing inclusion of man's natural life in the mechanisms and calculations of power' (1998: 119) is what Agamben, following Foucault, defined as biopower. Autonomist Marxists like Michael Hardt and Antonio Negri (2004) later modified the term to suggest a mode of organization that subsumes all social life, including areas formerly external or ornamental to capitalism, to the logic of capitalist production. Whereas previous forms of capitalism extract value from turning raw materials into commodities, today's

Introduction 21

cognitive capitalism hinges on our collective penchant for language, communication, sociality and affectivity. The Marxist interpretation of Foucault (the 'Italian Foucault' in this case) takes seriously the claim that biopolitics is not just about regulating the beginnings and endings of life, but also about producing, sustaining and enriching the content of our lives. Biopolitics is present not only in exceptions to the law or violations of our human rights. It also harbours a distinctly normative ambition. On the one hand, biopolitics seeks to optimize the content of our lives by producing a healthy, productive and fulfilled workforce. On the other, it tries to align capitalism with certain normative principles borrowed from multiculturalism and identity politics, countercultural movements and associational life (community, communication, cooperation, charity, compassion, dignity, creativity). In effect, biopolitics comes to stand in for the social goal capitalism was accused of never having (Jameson 2000: 62).

Nowhere is the biopolitical ambition of neoliberal government more evident than in the strategies used to encourage subjects to give their lives an entrepreneurial shape. The so-called *homo oeconomicus* model of action, described by Foucault in *The Birth of Biopolitics* (2008), but also used in classical economics, urges individuals to make choices in terms of cost–benefit calculations, assume responsibility for their actions and treat all those around them as potential competitors in the struggle for human capital (McNay 2009: 63). As the example of volunteer tourism demonstrates, market rationality is a necessary but not exclusive condition to meet these requirements. The rational, rugged and ruthless entrepreneur championed in economic liberalism is sometimes at odds with the normative ambitions of biopolitics. Especially since the student and worker struggles of the 1960s and 1970s helped expose the alienating and authoritarian consequences of modernist structures of living and working, it no longer seems sufficient (or satisfactory) for individuals to navigate their social surroundings using only instrumental action to the exclusion of all other social and moral considerations. The new entrepreneur, invoked in management literature, self-help books, urban regeneration schemes and government initiatives of the 'Third Way', is not asked to dispense with economic rationality, only to complement it with what were once bohemian and counter-cultural dispositions. Instead of the rational, calculating and cold-blooded *American Psycho*, the good neoliberal subject of the twenty-first century is the rather schizophrenic figure of the compassionate entrepreneur, the happy workaholic, the charitable CEO, the creative worker, the frugal consumer and, last but not least, the volunteer tourist.

This shift in subjectivization strategies might look like cause for celebration: it seems to invite more meaningful, rewarding and humane forms of (inter) action. But it should in fact be reason for concern: a model of subject formation that takes its cue from the principles of economic entrepreneurship, even when entrepreneurship combines instrumental rationality with cosmopolitan sensibilities, introduces new selection criteria for political membership and economic security that in many ways are more stringent and more ambiguous than ever before. What this suggests is that political subjectivity, that is,

22 Introduction

the ability to make ourselves into subjects that can act meaningfully in the world, is in fact a scarce and unequally distributed good. Unlike Foucault, who saw subjectivity as a ubiquitous, inescapable process of meaning making, this approach suggests that governmentality is never about including or subjecting everyone equally. It is simply a standard of measurement to assess people's ability to live up to whatever governmental injunctions are deemed necessary, ordered and just in a particular historical moment. There is plenty of room for both pleasure and punishment in this story. Those who live up to historically sanctioned programs, strategies and technologies of government will come to enjoy full political and economic rights. The rest will suffer various degrees of exclusion and exploitation in the form of un- and underemployed, indentured labourers, undocumented migrants and so on.

In dedicating their time and money to helping the global poor, volunteers display precisely the types of qualities needed to assume a privileged subjectivity: an ability to operate in distant and diverse settings, a desire for social change and an interest in experimenting with one's self and the world around it. Meanwhile, the recipients of their charity are excluded from this exchange and the possibilities for mobility, development and self-determination it entails. They must remain passive victims or timeless objects of attraction to help volunteer tourists acquire social capital and entrepreneurial competencies when vacationing in their midst. The paradox of volunteer tourism is that, even when it takes place in the Global South, its merits are assessed according to norms and principles dominant in liberal post-industrial societies. It is 'at home' that the mobility, creativity and magnanimity volunteers display overseas are turned into desirable goods for an economy where credentials and expertise are no longer enough to secure employment, and for a political community where territorial belonging is no longer a sufficient condition for full membership.

Repopulating international relations

This book is written from a multi-disciplinary perspective that combines insights from anthropology, sociology, geography, cultural studies and political theory. Its disciplinary home, however, remains international relations. Volunteer tourism is a worthwhile topic of inquiry for international politics not necessarily because it is a transnational phenomenon with a range of implications for cross-border mobility, economic development, policy-making structures, global security and the environment, as others have already demonstrated (Hazbun 2008, Chin 2008, Clancy 2001, 2009). More importantly, global tourism provides us with a glimpse of the lived encounters that give shape to global identities and relations. I agree with Debbie Lisle (2006) when she argues that tourism is just as illustrative of global politics as government documents or media reportage because it informs and legitimizes the ways in which we understand and engage with other people and places.

As a traditionally state-centred discipline with positivist foundations, IR has usually ignored the fact that identity formation lies at the heart of our political engagement with transnational others. World politics needs to be recognized 'as a process of cultural interactions in which the identities of actors are not given prior to or apart from' seemingly mundane exchanges like those produced through international tourism (Anand 2007: 13). The price IR pays for this neglect is high. It dehumanizes the discipline, causing it to produce expertise that is often complicit with imperial intervention, policing and dispossession. It also produces sterile knowledge that students and the public at large find difficult to relate to. This is not to say that the contribution of this study consists only in filling a gap in the repertoire of international studies. To constantly try to make IR complete by adding new methods, topics of inquiry and theoretical approaches from the 'outside' will only further cement the discipline's ontological insularity from economics, sociology, history and philosophy (Walker 1993, Beier and Arnold 2005). Rather, the arguments in this book are meant to make an intervention in critical debates on subjectivity, power and resistance that stretch across various disciplines.

My ambition in studying volunteer tourism is to repopulate IR scholarship with the voices and actions of white middle-class individuals (the bourgeoisie so to speak), not so different, in terms of their economic background, education, values and tastes, from those populating the academic profession. There has always been a deeply ingrained belief, amongst the bourgeoisie especially, that despite their best intentions white middle-class people will never represent a revolutionary force in society. John Fowles once remarked that 'the bourgeoisie is the only class that genuinely despises itself, its material possessions and social position' (1969). They might donate money to charity, buy fair trade or handmade products, volunteer their time and even become politically active, but at the end of the day they lack the legitimacy and firsthand experience that working-class people, minorities and formerly colonized people have. Whatever the bourgeoisie does in the name of social change and justice it will only help liberal subjects consolidate their social capital and social mobility because, ultimately, the world is made for their inhabitation. This study of volunteer tourism certainly does not escape this line of argument, but at least it tries to counter bourgeois self-hatred with self-reflection. Where usually critical theory will erase the white middle-class subject from the picture, claiming it is already at the centre of cultural value and knowledge production (which is true), and try to replace it with the voice of the oppressed and marginalized, it seems to me it is still important we understand the conditions, both symbolic and material, that make the bourgeoisie the norm-setting class.

IR cannot be accused of having been blind to privilege. In its heyday, the discipline was deeply involved with the 'kitchens of power' (Hoffman 1977: 49, 58) and devoted most of its attention to studying (and influencing) the activities of politicians, bureaucrats and defence intellectuals. Individuals rarely appeared on the international stage, leaving sovereign states to assume the place and role of people. But when they did, it was mostly heads of state, military personnel and diplomats. It was only in the late 1980s, with the publication of a special issue of *International Studies Quarterly* (1990) on

24 *Introduction*

'Speaking the Language of Exile', that a dissident group of IR scholars began to make itself known. Foucault, particularly his theories on discourse, power and history, was quickly mobilized to denaturalize the disciplinarity of the field, especially its overwhelming focus on interstate problems of security and stability to the neglect of domination, inequality and symbolic violence. Amidst the rise of social constructivist epistemologies in the 1980s and 1990s, IR began to turn its attention to the ways in which global power affects people 'on the ground'. Suddenly, a newborn fascination with the lives and voices of marginal subjectivities (women, minorities, native peoples, colonial subjects, migrants and refugees) emerged. Almost overnight, the disciplinary onus (at least in critical quarters) shifted from privilege to persecution.

It is not my intent to belittle these emancipatory efforts, which have done a lot to repopulate global politics with new subjects and forms of agency. Without these interventions, the voices of women, colonial subjects, racial and sexual minorities would have never been heard in international studies. But there are also limitations to this approach. Instead of taking full advantage of the epistemic possibilities it has opened up, critical IR remains enthralled with exceptional and violent instances of power, already abundant in the post-9/11 era (foreign interventions, use of torture, extraordinary rendition, widespread surveillance and several other violations of civil rights). Critical security studies, for instance, assume global biopower manifests itself in the absence or in violation of democratic politics and citizen protections through spectacular instances of new imperialism and fascism (Dillon and Reid 2001, 2009; Shapiro, Edkins and Pin-Fat 2004; Jabri 2006; Reid 2006; Dillon 2007; Dillon and Neal 2008). 'They are more interested in how the liberal way of rule "kill[s] to make life live" than in how it uses capitalist principles to give expression to life's highest ambitions' (Vrasti 2011: 14). Similarly, feminist and postcolonial approaches tend to treat power as a pejorative force the principal goal of which is to dominate and distort our lives. We are dealing here with the remnants of a problematic (humanist) dichotomy between power and people, where the former is a corrupt and ignoble thing while the latter is a repository of autonomy, agency and authenticity. This approach fails to sufficiently distinguish between violence and power, or to consider the productive function of power.

As Foucault explains, violence is a force that destroys certain expendable bodies and objects, whereas power is a relation that organizes social life (communities, identities, education, housing, finance, labour, architecture and lifestyle choices) to help individuals articulate their identity and navigate their social landscape (Deleuze 1988). Power is both what presses upon the subject from the outside and the condition of possibility for the subject to exist, both what we oppose and what we depend on, subordinating and producing us at the same time (Butler 2005: 2). We find a similar 'normative' ambition in biopower. In its most mundane and habitual form, biopower is meant to optimize the health, prosperity and general well-being of the population in the name of economic growth. This is not to deny the violent sacrifices this project often requires in the form of sovereign police, racial discrimination and capitalist expropriation. But we should also acknowledge that the promise of achieving social cohesion and promoting the health and happiness of the populace usually takes a benign and benevolent aspect supported by rather than defiant of the law.

International relations has neglected these complexities because it prefers to focus on examples that fall 'outside' of the state, leaving the organization of our economies, cities, households and private lives to sociologists and anthropologists. This, I argue, is a missed opportunity. Now that international relations has acquired the necessary space and tools for this type of analysis, it needs to investigate the quotidian, seemingly trivial aspects of international political life to better understand how power, sovereignty and global governance function.

Following this impulse, this book explores how 'average' people attach themselves to power in inconspicuous, seemingly harmless ways. These are neither the elites usually credited with making global politics, nor the marginalized subjects critical theory has become so fond of, but white middle-class individuals. In doing so, this line of inquiry arrives at conclusions that upset the classic picture of subjectivity, agency and resistance critical theory usually presents us with. Volunteer tourism illustrates the famous Foucauldian lesson that power does not just violate or subjugate individual autonomy and agency, it also entices and nurtures them. Liberal capital allows young adults from the Global North to view their intervention as noble and necessary, acquire expertise and self-esteem during their travels and translate their enjoyment into entrepreneurial advantages. This realization that autonomy and agency can in fact lie at 'the heart of ... disciplinary control' (McNay 2009: 62) forces us to question our most cherished ideas about resistance. What possibilities for resistance still remain if agency, autonomy and subjectivity are already enlisted in the reproduction of power?

Because critical theory has had a tendency to focus on those for whom power has the most harrowing effects rather than on those who derive enjoyment and status from power, it could comfortably avoid this difficult question. But this is a dangerous omission: neglecting the ways in which the liberal bourgeoisie reproduces itself through material conditions, codes of conduct, tastes and sensibilities risks pushing the invisible centre of our political order further into oblivion and does nothing to undermine its power to shape what is desirable or normative. It only leaves us more mystified about the ways in which power manifests and reproduces itself in the first place. To counteract this omission, I have chosen to put the question of the subaltern on the back-burner of this study. Although the research took place in the Global South, this project remains an anthropology of home. It is mostly concerned with the experiences and subject formation practices of Western individuals travelling abroad, not their impact on host communities.

There were also ethical considerations for this choice. Both Ghana and Guatemala have a long history of white people coming through to inspect, study and take pictures of them. Arriving in these communities to 'help' locals protect their natural resources, bandage wounds and educate their children was an

26 *Introduction*

imposition I no longer cared to extend through personal interviews. Although I had a few informal conversations with locals about the effects of volunteering in their communities, I chose not to reproduce these testimonies. Locals were either sceptical of the overall usefulness of foreign assistance or they refused to recognize volunteers as proper 'workers', preferring to treat them as 'tourists' (read: consumers) instead. Publicizing these attitudes could have jeopardized the livelihoods of local people working with volunteers. Logistical obstacles, such as language barriers and difficult rapport, further added to this decision. This being said, subaltern figures are not entirely absent from this study. They are invoked indirectly through volunteers' humanitarian ambitions and narratives of encounter with local populations. It is through this mediated exchange that we come to grasp the power dynamics at the core of volunteer tourism.

Chapter outline

The second chapter explores the theoretical themes central to this project – the mutations of biopolitics, capital and subjectivity in neoliberal times, and treats volunteer tourism as a symptom of these. Foucault defined neoliberalism as a mode of government that extends the entrepreneurial form across the entire social field without directly manipulating individual freedom and autonomy. The success of this task depends on biopolitical interventions into the life of the population, not only in the form of exceptions and violence, but also by making society congruent with the logic of market rationality. In recent history this has involved the incorporation of dissident language and bohemian values into entrepreneurial conduct. While this has made capital accumulation seem more tolerable and political authority more subtle, the commodification of intellect, affect and sociality extends market logics into the realm of political subjectivity. Political rights and material benefits are distributed competitively depending on individual abilities to abide by the injunctions of neoliberal capital. Only those individuals who are able to respond opportunistically and creatively to the demands of capital stand to benefit from the present condition.

Chapter 3 traces my convoluted research travels through the Peten region of Guatemala. The volunteers I met there did not perceive the local community as poor or appreciative enough to justify the need for foreign assistance. As a result, they quickly lost interest in 'giving back' and 'making a difference', as I had initially expected and turned to alternative ways of demonstrating their affective capacities. They began sightseeing, getting to know the locals and learning about the indigenous culture. Yet the seemingly benign and benevolent coalition of sympathy volunteers crafted with the local population did more to reproduce the depoliticizing logic of multiculturalism than to initiate any meaningful encounter with difference. The experience in Guatemala, then, shows that in subsuming difference to the consumptive logic of capitalism, the emotional styles cultivated in volunteer tourism can only serve to validate the moral superiority of white middle-class subjects.

Introduction 27

In Ghana racial tensions made it difficult for volunteers to fall in love with local culture and people. Their white bodies were the constant subject of curiosity and admiration: the texture of their skin and hair was inspected, their table manners studied, their smoking habits scolded, even their pictures taken. Whiteness could no longer function as the absent centre of humanity (Ahmed 2006). To cope with these nervous encounters volunteers had to focus on the technical benefits of their volunteering experience: receiving professional training, living without modern amenities and travelling independently through Western Africa allowed volunteers to develop immaterial skills that would enhance their employability and work versatility in an increasingly competitive and precarious economic climate. Here volunteer tourism functioned as a new type of moral and technical education for young adults who want to learn how to operate in multicultural settings and globalized sites to better consolidate their professional future.

Together these ethnographic chapters examine two interrelated functions of volunteer tourism. While the experience in Guatemala functioned as a form of post-Fordist consumption, which allowed volunteers to affirm their flexibility, mobility and worldliness over less sophisticated consumers, the trip to Ghana taught volunteers to extend their human capital beyond professional expertise and academic credentials in ways congruent with post-Fordist modes of production.

Drawing on these two facets of voluntourism, the final chapter argues that the emotional and entrepreneurial strategies mobilized on these trips (re)produce hierarchical and uneven modes of political subjectivity. In both instances volunteers come to embody desirable resources, capacities and aesthetic sensibilities that help them expand their 'field of possibilities' (Foucault 2001: 343) and acquire a more advantageous form of political subjectivity. Meanwhile local populations remain stuck between the two poles of romanticisation and denigration. The book ends on a positive note. Reflecting on the most recent global economic crisis, I pose the possibility of entrepreneurially oriented acts of community and charity, like volunteer tourism, giving way to non-market-based experiments of living in common.

2 The self as enterprise

Overseas volunteering is generally considered to be a noble way of providing foreign assistance to the global poor. A rainforest in Brazil is being cut down, a rural school in Bangladesh does not have textbooks, sea turtles in Mexico are on the brink of extinction and children in Africa are starving. In all of these cases and many more like them, volunteers are urged to donate their time and resources to 'make a difference' in the lives of 'less fortunate' people. Although cohorts of volunteers sign up in the hope of 'helping out' and 'giving back', my research shows that there is little evidence to substantiate these stories of sacrifice and compassion. During my travels to Guatemala and Ghana, volunteers repeatedly complained of 'not feeling needed', either because local populations were not deemed 'poor enough' to require foreign assistance or because the programmes were not equipped to deliver humanitarian support. Most people felt useless and often somewhat deceived. As one volunteer aptly put it:

> They made it sound as if you weren't there, Ghana would fall apart, as if your presence was sought for. They painted a picture that's not in any way correct. ... I don't think I've helped anyone while I was here. Only I benefited. I changed but I don't think I initiated any change. After I leave I'd have made a difference to myself but not to anyone else.

Surprisingly, however, these discontents did nothing to diminish the allure of volunteer tourism. Volunteers quickly found alternative ways to pass the time. They traveled independently, befriended locals and explored the local culture. At home, they continued to enjoy the support and admiration of friends, family and colleagues. Not surprisingly, the industry has been enjoying rising enrolment figures. This is not just the effect of clever marketing. It indicates that, while volunteer tourism takes place in the Global South, its effects are valorized in terms of the governmental rationalities and socio-economic conditions of advanced neoliberal societies. Volunteer tourism may not be able to redress the material and ecological ailments of the global poor, but in exposing young adults to the adventure and authenticity they believe they are missing from modern capitalist life, it continues to be an attractive experience, especially because the dispositions and competencies acquired on such a trip are convertible into social and economic capital. Although this book does not track the actual benefits volunteers gain from this practice (whether they are admitted to better universities or find jobs as a result of having volunteered abroad), I maintain that by experimenting with 'alternative' modes of being, that is, by living and working in places that are considered to lie 'outside' modernity, young adults learn how to operate in multicultural settings and global spaces, assert a credible professional identity, embody desirable cultural values and norms, and live more fully in the global moment. In other words, volunteer tourism combines entrepreneurship and enjoyment to help white middle-class individuals manage and expand the 'field of possibilities' of their political subjectivity (Foucault 2001: 341).

Volunteer tourism is certainly not the only strategy of this sort. The blurring of economic and ethical values is characteristic of late capitalism, and can be found in many places, from communicative modes of production to 'lifestyle'-based consumption patterns, flexible management styles, creative cities, social networks and fluid family structures. For Foucault this would not have been a surprise. A neoliberal society that takes the market as its guiding principle was never destined to lead to standardization, mass consumption and spectacle, as the Left (from the Frankfurt School to the Situationists) once feared. Rather, it would be a society oriented 'towards the multiplicity and differentiation of enterprises' (Foucault 2008: 149), a society that would revitalize, not stifle, the spiritual, emotional and communal foundations of modern existence. Autonomist Marxists agree: networked organization structures along with flexible forms of production introduced in post-Fordist capitalism have radically multiplied the possibilities for individual autonomy and enjoyment. But they have also created a set of ethico-political confusions to suggest that market economy can save the environment, put an end to poverty, inject meaning in our lives *and* generate profit at the same time. This is clearly a farce, which now, in light of growing income inequalities and global food insecurity, might be closer to a tragedy (Zizek 2009: 34). The fantasy of 'caring' capitalism or 'humane' neoliberalism is little more than a clever smokescreen. It attaches itself to our dreams for a more just world and meaningful existence in essentially precarious and exploitative economic arrangements, and places what are potentially radical, affective and intellectual predispositions in the service of accumulation.

To make sense of these ethico-political confusions, this chapter traces the genealogical roots of current socio-economic and cultural transformations, and positions volunteer tourism as a symptom of these. The argument is structured in four parts. The first part introduces Foucault's interpretation of neoliberalism. It takes a long historical view of the liberal rationality of government, and tries to offer a more sophisticated understanding of the term that blurs the state/market, individual/society, power/agency dichotomies that humanist theories (both liberal and Marxist) are so comfortably anchored it. According to Foucault neoliberalism extends the entrepreneurial form across the entire social field without violating the rights and freedoms of the populace. To

30 *The self as enterprise*

show how this is possible the second section turns to the question of biopolitics. Here, I expand on Foucault's discussion of the concept to argue that biopower, far from being limited to transgressive and violent moments, also contains a benevolent intent, namely, to make life live by aligning it with the principles of market rationality. In the third section, we see that this project could not have garnered support without neoliberalism's skillful incorporation of dissident language and bohemian values. The emphasis on personal freedom and choice has made capital accumulation more tolerable, even more pleasurable for some individuals. It has also widened the scope of neoliberal subjectivity far beyond the injunctions of market rationality to include intellect, affect and sociality. For some this is an indication that we have entered a more 'humane' form of government or 'caring' mode of capitalism. But as I demonstrate in the final section, through the example of volunteer tourism, the contrary is the case. Neoliberal governmentality extends the principle of competition to the realm of political subjectivity. Only those individuals who are able to live up to the expectations of capital stand to benefit from the present condition. Volunteer tourists are on the fortunate end of this struggle, which is precisely why we should scrutinize the admirable and pleasurable effects of this practice more closely.

A short story of neoliberalism

David Harvey's *A Brief History of Neoliberalism* (2005) offers what is perhaps the most succinct story to date of 'where neoliberalization came from and how it proliferated so comprehensively on the world stage' (ibid.: 4). In 1944, Harvey begins, a new institutional framework was devised to avoid the beggar-thy-neighbor strategies and economic crises that had led to the Second World War. The Bretton Woods system, backed by US gold reserves and military might, was supposed to free the flow of goods and capital through a series of trade agreements and price stabilization mechanisms. On the domestic front, a deal was struck between capital and labour, in which liberal democratic governments would pursue full employment, economic growth and public welfare in exchange for labour discipline and rising productivity. Key to the success of this so-called Fordist compromise was the dramatic surge in industrial productivity achieved through assembly line production methods and scientific management principles first developed in Ford manufacturing plants. For the next couple of decades, what in retrospect has been called the Golden Age of capitalism, the Western world would experience unprecedented rates of growth thanks largely to the imperial benevolence of the US. The latter was willing to run deficits with other countries and absorb excess exports as well as deploy its military might to protect this fortress of wealth. But in the early 1970s this Fordist model of production experienced a deep crisis of profitability induced mainly by the rising cost of the welfare state, the saturation of consumer markets, rising global competition and shop floor disaffection (Dyer-Whiteford 1999: 106). The toxic mix of slow economic growth, high unemployment and

The self as enterprise 31

rising prices known as 'stagflation', which haunted the American economy and its protégés for most of the following decade, cleared the way for the ascent of neoliberal economic policies.

If in the years immediately after the Second World War neoliberals were a scattered minority within American policy circles, by the mid-1970s, neoliberal economists like Nobel Prize winner Friedrich van Hayek and Chicago school of economics founder Milton Friedman gained considerable ground from their Keynesian rivals. At first their influence was limited to the backdoors of politics: think tanks, research institutes, business schools and media outlets. But with the election of Margaret Thatcher in 1979 and Ronald Reagan in 1980 their vision of free-market capitalism would become the new orthodoxy. In the decades that followed, supply-side economics (the idea that lower taxes and weaker regulation would stimulate growth and create jobs) together with monetarism (the theory that the economically prudent thing for governments to do is to control the supply of money in the economy, not full employment and social security), would come to dictate the limits of political imagination the entire world over.

But, as Harvey explains, there was nothing obvious or inevitable about the triumph of neoliberalism. Policy makers in the 1970s did not have a clear, cohesive solution to stagflation. Reagan or Thatcher did not come into office carrying a neoliberal blueprint. There was a great deal of experimentation, tension and hesitance in what might be accurately described as a 'stumbling' towards neoliberalization (Harvey 2005: 13). What ultimately secured the victory of neoliberalism over other Keynesian or more heterodox alternatives was, in Harvey's view, neoliberalism's promise to restore class power. Supply-side economics and monetarism may not have been able to reinstate pre-1970s levels of growth, but they were successful in concentrating economic power in the hands of the few (ibid.: 19). There is growing consensus that the Fordist crisis of profitability was never solved – only moved to other economic sectors (e.g. finance capital) and geographic sites (e.g. the Global South). The transfer of wealth that followed was essentially a political strategy to tame the mounting antagonism of workers, students and minorities at the time. Gradually, fiscal discipline, spending cutbacks, labour deregulation, financialization and occasional police brutality and military intervention dissolved the class composition and social institutions that had sustained the Fordist compromise. Similar strategies were extended across the developing world under the oversight of the IMF and the World Bank to undermine any indigenous forms of solidarity and self-sufficiency that might interfere with the continuous search for new sites of capital accumulation.

But while Harvey's book presents us with a detailed historical overview of how neoliberalism gained vertiginous global currency, 'the actual process by which it became hegemonic, to the point of becoming common sense, is not examined' (Read 2009a: 25). Harvey is too concerned with the historical and institutional processes that enabled the ascendancy of neoliberalism as an economic doctrine to realize that this is not simply 'a transformation … *of* ideology',

32   *The self as enterprise*

but rather a whole new type of power with profound implications for how we understand the role of the state, government, economic value and human nature. To study neoliberalism is not just to study a political programme, a set of policies and agreements; it is to launch a critique of traditional concepts of power, ideology and identity (Brown 2003: 25–26). For an idea of what this line of inquiry might look like we turn to Foucault's later writings on neoliberal governmentality.

Foucault's thinking on neoliberalism is impressive not only because it preceded the reforms of the Reagan–Thatcher Right, but because it gives us a new theory of social control that bypasses the old dichotomies between state and society, control and autonomy, public and private, which both liberal and Marxist thinking draw upon. In *The Birth of Biopolitics* (2008), Foucault's most comprehensive engagement with the problem of neoliberalism, he dismisses three common misreadings of the term. Neoliberalism, he argues, is not a continuation of classic liberal economics, the commodification of all social relations or an ideological cover-up for the recent wave of free-market reforms. In other words, neoliberalism is not Adam Smith revisited (classical liberalism with a vengeance), Marx reloaded (a generalized market society) or even Solzhenitsyn on a global scale (a sovereign conspiracy). In all three cases, neoliberalism is made out to be 'nothing at all, or anyway, nothing but always the same thing, and always the same thing but worse' (Foucault 2008: 130). Instead, Foucault argues, neoliberalism is something entirely new: it is a philosophy of government that 'assumes the market as the test and means of intelligibility, as the truth and the measure of society' (Lazzarato cited in Weidner 2009: 405). The enduring mantra of Foucault's last lecture series is not that the 'effects of the economy are extended across all of society, rather it is an economic *perspective*, that of the market, that becomes coextensive with all of society' (Read 2009a: 32, emphasis added).

At first sight, this definition is not so different from that presented by David Harvey, who describes neoliberalism as 'a theory of political economic practices that proposes that human well-being can best be advanced by liberating individual entrepreneurial freedoms and skills within an institutional framework characterized by strong private property rights, free markets, and free trade' (2005: 2). Both readings accept that neoliberalism extends market rationality across the entire social field into the deepest crevices of individuality. Where they part ways, however, is Foucault's long historical view, which locates the origins of neoliberalism within a larger transformation of Western political thought about what counts as effective government, social order and rational conduct. As we shall see, this split will come to define the debate between the Marxist and Foucauldian interpretation of neoliberalism.

Beginning with the eighteenth century, Foucault explains, the concern of sovereign power changed to 'redirect the energies of government from the control of territorial sovereignty to the *management* of populations and things' (Nelson 2009: 104, original emphasis). The ambition was less to 'insur[e] the obedience of citizen-subjects and the security of a territory [than to effect] the *correct disposition, administration and distribution of things,'* populations and subjectivities (ibid.: 105, original emphasis). During that period, population growth and complex socio-economic networks were making it increasingly difficult for centralized power to know and manage the conduct of the entire populace. The liberal solution was to have central government delegate some of its original responsibilities to non-state agencies of power (mainly hospitals, prisons, schools, and workplaces) but also across communities and even households. Rather than merely obey the law, the social body should internalize and reproduce the injunctions of government voluntarily and spontaneously. Sovereign power had to learn how to operate 'at a distance' by 'affect[ing] the way in which individuals *conduct themselves'* while still leaving them their rights and freedoms (Burchell 1996: 20, original emphasis). Governmentality, as Foucault called this new philosophy of rule, marked a shift in Western politics from the imposition of order through sovereign power to the construction of order in the hearts and minds of citizens themselves. While the medieval *raison d'état* logic of the state was concerned with the order, stability and peacefulness of the territorial unit, the liberal theory of the state takes the population as the object and target of government, and political economy as the principle in the name of which government should be organized and assessed (Foucault 2007: 91–106).

At the same time, governmentality also marked a transition from political to economic liberalism. Broadly speaking, political liberalism is consumed with the origins and legitimacy of power, whereas economic liberalism takes the existence of government as given and is more preoccupied with procedural and administrative considerations (Scott 2009). While political liberals like Kant, Hobbes and Rousseau were more concerned with establishing the legitimacy of power by setting up a correspondence between law and popular will, 'through a notion of rights, which are given as anterior and external to sovereignty', economic liberals like Hume, Smith, Ricardo, and James and Stuart Mill were more interested in the internal limitation of sovereign power, which they found 'in the evidence constituted by the naturalness of economic processes' (Terranova 2009: 237). 'Because utilitarian and economic liberalism attach no special importance to the question of power's origin (unlike the revolutionary or natural-rights tradition), they effectively dispense with the need for juridical foundations' (Behrent 2009: 562), allowing them to devote more attention to the ways in which power can be mobilized (and limited) for the 'betterment of the population' (Nelson 2009: 109).

This does not mean that the two are entirely divorced: the political principles of liberalism (individual rights, rule of law and liberty of expression) are essential for a functional market economy organized around private property, competition and entrepreneurship. Still, the shift in emphasis from political to economic liberalism constitutes a radical redefinition of the modern art of government. Effective government would no longer be measured on the basis of the juridical legitimacy of power but in terms of its ability to improve the livelihood and longevity of its population. The market becomes an ideal measuring rod

34 *The self as enterprise*

for this task. Because it is seen as a natural meeting ground for people's interests and passions it is considered useful both for limiting sovereign power and for testing its ability to govern (Terranova 2009: 245).

Although the eighteenth-century origins of governmentality far predate post-Second World War neoliberalism, this philosophy of rule should be viewed as an indispensable condition of possibility for what was to emerge in the latter half of the twentieth century. Seen against the historical background of governmentality, it becomes clear that neoliberalism is not simply a set of economic policies aimed at reducing government power for the benefit of political and managerial elites, but a larger rationality 'which produces subjects, forms of citizenship and behavior, and a new organization of the social' (Brown 2003: 2). Neoliberalism is essentially 'a constructivist project [that] takes as its task the development, dissemination, and institutionalization of [economic] rationality' (ibid.: 9).

Neoliberalism borrows two things from classical liberalism: its unabashed confidence in political economy and its concern with managing the conduct of the population. But it also introduces a fundamental modification. Instead of the naturalistic logic of exchange at the heart of classical political economy, the guiding principle for neoliberalism becomes competition:

> According to Foucault ... the market is not defined by the human instinct to exchange ... by market we must always understand competition and inequality, rather than equality of exchange. Here, the subjects are not merchants but entrepreneurs. The market is therefore the market of enterprises and of their differential and non-egalitarian logic.
>
> (Lazzarato cited in Weidner 2009: 405)

This modification changes the entire relation between state, market and people. In classical liberalism the state was expected to keep out of market affairs to allow individuals to pursue their appetites through the natural exchange of goods and services. If the state intervened it was only to supervise the smooth functioning of economic transactions or settle occasional disputes. For twentieth-century neoliberals, especially the German Ordoliberal school of the 1930s and 1940s, which Foucault credits with the invention of the doctrine, this laissez-faire logic suffers from 'naïve naturalism' (Foucault 2008: 120). It is what caused the economic disasters of the Weimar Republic and ultimately cleared the way for Nazi rule. Contrary to classical liberals who viewed the market as a 'primitive' given, neoliberals of both the German and American variety are fully cognizant of its fragility and artificiality. The distinction between nature and culture, between a 'free' market and an 'artificial' government no longer holds. Both are social constructions that must be harmonized through political intervention. The spirit of competition, in particular, is seen as a carefully orchestrated process that needs anchoring in appropriate types of policy and sociality. The task of government, then, becomes the advancement of social and moral orders conducive to competition and entrepreneurial conduct (Foucault 2008: 131).

Government, in this context, also referred to by the neologism of governmentality, is not limited to the state and its apparatuses of power. Because liberal rule is a mode of power meant to affect the way in which individuals conduct themselves without violating their autonomy, government also extends across non-state areas like work practices, consumption patterns, education curricula, health and reproduction policies, financial mechanisms, urban planning schemes, transportation and communication modes, aesthetic conventions, personal and sexual conduct and so much more. This is not to say that the state is no longer relevant in liberal governmentality. On the contrary! Communities, households and individuals have to continue the work of the state at their own expense (because the state performs them too poorly or at too high a cost). So the logic of the state extends through the entire social field. Meanwhile, the state does not wither away – it remains the central ally of capital. This is true both for developmentalist countries like China or Singapore where the state assumes a proactive role in lubricating market transactions and neoliberal champions like the United States or Britain where capital is aided through a well-orchestrated 'retreat' of certain social and regulatory capacities of the state. The means might be different, but the result the same: neoliberal government is not about pushing the state out of the equation but about shifting its focus and priorities to govern the population more efficiently according to market rules (Isin 2000: 154–55).

This idea that neoliberalism actually requires government to 'accompany the market economy from start to finish' (Foucault 2008: 121) might come as a surprise given that both in Europe and the United States neoliberalism emerged as a reaction to the strong state demanded by the Fordist compromise (Foucault 2008: 79, 216). It reveals the great disconnect that exists between the grammar of neoliberalism, which requires the state to uphold legally sanctioned conventions regarding private property, labour power, credit and money, and neoliberal dogma that tries to fully do away with the state. The neoliberal ideal of an ungoverned market society is unviable and unattainable (Peck 2010b: 7). Any historical analysis of neoliberal policy making can attest to this. In its initial phase, neoliberalism was busy 'rolling-back' (privatizing, deregulating, downsizing) the institutions and protections of the post-war welfare state, regarded as fetters of capitalist accumulation. This policy approach, however, generated successive waves of instability and vulnerability in terms of rising unemployment, poverty and social discontent. To mitigate the social costs of neoliberalization, new 'market-conforming' institutions, regulations and discursive strategies had to be introduced. The general discourse gradually shifted 'from dogmatic deregulation to market-friendly reregulation, from structural adjustment to good governance, from budget cuts to regulation-by-audit, from welfare retrenchment to active social policy, from privatization to public-private partnerships, [and] from greed-is-good to markets-with-morals' (Peck 2010a: 106). The 'roll-out' phase of neoliberalism, also known as the 'Third Way' introduced by social democrats like Bill Clinton, Tony Blair and Gerhard Schröder during the 1990s, was all about managing 'the costs and contradictions of

36   *The self as enterprise*

earlier waves of neoliberalization' (ibid.) without actually doing anything to reign in the hegemony of market principles over social life.

This periodization also illustrates the crucial difference between the type of state intervention required by Keynesianism and that tolerated by neoliberalism. In the former case the state intervenes in the market to ensure full employment, price stability and a certain measure of wealth redistribution. In the latter situation the state intervenes *in society* to create the necessary conditions for competitive markets and entrepreneurial conduct, and align social and ethical life with economic criteria and expectations (Foucault 2008: 117–20). Government is not supposed to correct the destructive effects of the market, but must 'universalize the entrepreneurial form' across the social field (Lemke 2001: 195). But how is this to happen? How is government supposed to make entrepreneurship coterminous with social life without violating the fantasy of a self-regulating free market economy? As the next section reveals, successful government cannot 'dupe' or 'whip' us into obedience, it must enlarge our capacities and freedoms, appeal to our demand for order and justice, and enlist our aspirations for self-determination and self-realization. In short, for change to be effective, it must be *affective* (Mazzarella 2009: 299).

Governmentality and its tools

At the heart of the neoliberal rationality of government lies a great paradox: on the one hand, neoliberalism tries to limit the power of government, while, on the other hand, government has to intervene in the life of the population to extend market-friendly cultural norms and social orderings (Senellart 2008: 330). How is government to affect the conduct of its population without directly manipulating the lives of its subjects? How is it to align individual behaviour with market principles without abusing its sovereign power? For free-market champions, from Friedrich von Hayek to the Tea Party, the answer seems to be simple. In the words of Ronald Reagan, neoliberalism should 'take government off the backs of the [people], and turn [them] loose again to do those things that [they] can do so well'. But this turns out to be a populist trick. It leads people to believe that sovereign power is just about taxing and regulating economic conduct, when, in fact, neoliberal theory requires government to play a far more proactive and subtle role in bringing about the conditions for market capitalism. To realize this without violating the individual freedom and autonomy needed for entrepreneurial conduct, neoliberal government has to resort to biopolitics.

Contrary to what the title of his 1978–79 lecture series *The Birth of Biopolitics* suggests, Foucault devoted almost no attention to biopolitics in his second to last course at the *Collège de France*. In the first lecture Foucault explains that the concept cannot be attacked until we have understand 'the condition of intelligibility of biopolitics' (Senellart 2008: 328), the 'general regime of governmental reason' in which it exists, which is liberalism (ibid.: 21–22). He then goes on to explore the complex origins of twentieth-century neoliberalism

The self as enterprise 37

never to return to 'the politics of life' (Senellart 2008: 328). Although he discusses the strategies and programmes designed to integrate biological life (health, productivity, life expectancy, health, reproduction and race) into the sphere of politics elsewhere (Foucault 2007). Foucault has relatively little to say about 'how individual beings are made [and make themselves into] subjects' of liberalism (Foucault 2001: 326). He later apologizes for this detour. A few clues, especially regarding the *homo oeconomicus* model of action, can be found in *The Birth of Biopolitics*, but, for the most part, the problem of political subjectivity in neoliberalism is left up to the imagination of his epigones.

One of these epigones is Giogio Agamben (1998), who famously defined biopolitics as the moment when sovereign power abuses liberal democratic politics to reduce life to a worthless category. This so-called 'state of exception', Agamben argues, has been generalized to the point where denigrating life has become the original activity of modern institutions (ibid.: 6) and, indeed, a political inevitability inscribed in the structure of liberal democratic politics (Neal 2008: 45). Coming from the discipline of international relations, where this version of biopolitics has featured prominently in relation to post-9/11 politics, in particular the War on Terror, exceptional incarceration and interrogation tactics, and the rise of digital and biometric surveillance and security strategies (Dillon and Reid 2001, 2009; Shapiro, Edkins and Pin-Fat 2004; Dauphinee and Masters 2007), my understanding of biopolitics has, for a long time, been monopolized by this catastrophic reading. But if you read Foucault carefully, as some people in IR have began to do (Larner and Walters 2004; Walters and Haahr 2005; Langley 2008; Lisle 2010; Kiersey 2009; Weidner 2009; Moore 2010), you notice an important difference between governmental programmes that 'protect life and [those that] authorize a holocaust' (Agamben 1998: 3).

Biopolitics does not manifest itself exclusively in the absence of the law or citizen protections (Neal 2008). It is also instrumental in producing a healthy and productive workforce, creating a society that can thrive with only limited government intervention, and disseminating the rights and freedoms necessary for individuals to give their lives an entrepreneurial shape. In fact, biopolitics has a benevolent intent. In its individualizing orientation, biopolitics provides individuals with the necessary skills and resources to govern themselves freely in light of economic principles and axioms. In its totalizing form, it tries to bridge the distance between economic rationality and social welfare by mobilizing market principles to satisfy certain normative aspirations for social cohesion, order and dignity. This is not to deny the excesses of biopolitics, the fact that optimizing the human body and the body politic as a whole often involves incarcerating the poor, deporting the undocumented, torturing the suspect, segregating the sick and subjecting everyone else to profitability calculations. Biopolitics makes it clear that the promise of life can be realized only at the point in which it is subsumed to the principles of competition and accumulation.

Still, if we turn our attention from the spectacular events of international politics to the 'trivial' elements of everyday life (work, consumption, education,

38   *The self as enterprise*

social reproduction, architecture, art, leisure and sexuality), we recognize that biopower is not only concerned with managing births and deaths but also with organizing the space *between* birth and death. In its mundane form, bio-politics is more concerned with reproducing life than disallowing it (Foucault 1976: 138). As Mitchell Dean explains, if biopower

> is concerned with matters of life and death, with birth and propagation, with health and illness, both physical and mental and with the processes that sustain or retard the optimization of the life of a population[, it] must then also concern the social, cultural, environmental, economic and geographic conditions under which humans live, procreate, become ill, maintain health or become healthy and die. From this perspective, bio-politics is concerned with the family, with housing, living and working conditions, with what we call 'lifestyle', with public health issues, patterns of migration, levels of economic growth and standards of living. It is concerned with the bio-sphere in which humans dwell.
>
> (Dean cited in Selby 2007: 333)

According to Foucault, the roots of this liberal ambition to 'exert a positive influence upon life' (cited in Kiersey and Weidner 2009: 345–5) can already be found in the Christian pastoral. The pastoral narrative, Foucault explains, introduces a code of ethics derived from Judeo-Christian principles of love and care for the living, entirely different from that of the ancient world (Prozorov 2007: 54). Just as with biopolitics, the ideological function of the pastoral is both totalizing and individualizing: it wants, on the one hand, to optimize the life of the entire flock through sacrifice and salvation and, on the other hand, care for each individual in part through confession and exploration of the soul. In its secularized variant, instead of saving people or preparing them for the afterlife, the pastoral logic of power or what now becomes 'benevolent' biopolitics is supposed to optimize the life of the population through improved health, security and standard of living. It also seeks to incite individuals to know and monitor themselves through statistical, therapeutic and biotechno-logical means. Shepherding responsibilities are divided (often unequally) between various state institutions (police, welfare organizations, schools, prisons, cha-rities) and responsible, self-reliant and entrepreneurial individuals (Foucault 2001: 334–35). Ironically, this take on 'benevolent' biopower shows that 'the paradigmatic subject of biopolitics is not, *pace* Agamben, the *homo sacer* of the concentration camp but rather the Swedish middle-class social democrat, the object of universal care' (Prozorov 2007: 66).

Economic liberalism, despite being accused of ignoring questions of rights and justice to devote more attention to pecuniary affairs, has not remained oblivious to these normative concerns. Contrary to the common Marxist idea that capitalism is the only social formation completely devoid of a moral logic of its own and, therefore, entirely dependent upon external persuasion mechanisms and normative principles (Boltanski and Chiapello 2005), economic liberalism posits *the market as a normative good in itself.* From its very beginning, economic liberalism has used Judeo-Christian principles to legitimate economic drives, which until the eighteenth century were discredited as vulgar passions prone to avarice and greed. In *The Passions and the Interests* (1977), Albert Hirschman explains that, for liberalism to become a dominant ideology, it had to demonstrate the beneficial impact of economic drives. Enlightenment figures like Locke, Smith and Hume were convinced that, if practiced in moderation, acquisitive drives could have various restorative effects (improve collective welfare, promote industriousness and bring about a more predictable and constant human environment), while also keeping in check other far more destructive passions, like aggressiveness and promiscuity.

We find similar claims being made by contemporary supporters of neoliberalism, who believe that a free-market economy will allow individuals greater freedom to satisfy their interests, explore their talents, and reach their full potential in complete harmony with the larger welfare of society. Individuals, households, communities and even entire nations should be governed according to the principles of political economy so as to maximize their longevity, productivity and general happiness. In a world where human action is prone to error and corruption, the best model for organizing human affairs is the market because it is on this natural meeting ground that people can pursue and resolve their appetites in a fair, rational and mutually satisfactory way.

But how is government supposed to align the conduct of the population with market principles without directly manipulating the lives of its subjects? Neoliberalism, just like classic liberal economics, remains distrustful of government intervention. Following the devastation of the interwar period, however, neoliberal theory has to accept that government needs to at least intervene *in society* to produce 'the condition[s] of possibility for a market economy' (Foucault 2008: 160). Once it becomes clear that there is no natural correspondence between economy and society, neoliberalism takes it upon itself to make the social conform to the economic by aligning individual conduct with economic axioms. The market comes to acquire a pedagogical function for how individuals are to remake and conduct themselves. It becomes 'a kind of technology of the self' (Kiersey 2011: 35) that teaches individuals how to conduct themselves like rational and calculating economic men. With many of the post-war social protections gone, citizen-subjects must assume responsibility for their own well-being, prosperity and security 'within a variety of micro-moral domains or "communities" – families, workplaces, schools, leisure associations, neighbourhoods' (Rose 1996: 57) so as to withstand the inevitable volatilities of living in a market society (sudden layoffs, spending cuts, market crashes).

Different from classical political economy, however, the neoliberal *homo oeconomicus* turns from an ahistorical being found in nature into a socially programmed animal, from a partner of exchange to an entrepreneur of himself (Foucault 2008: 226). This 'artificially created form of behavior' (Lemke 2001:

40   *The self as enterprise*

201) is produced through various biopolitical tactics encouraging individuals to *independently* and *spontaneously* assess the costs and benefits of their choices, assume responsibility for their actions, and apply economic criteria to every aspect of their lives, from their profession to their private property, physical appearance, personal relations and private lives (Foucault 2008: 241). '[W]here the Christian pastoral took the conveyance into heaven as its goal, today's capitalism actively seeks out the deep capacities of human capital, especially the capacities of subjectivization, in order to generate surplus capital from them' (Kiersey 2011: 38). The pastoral goal of biopolitics, then, is to endow individuals with the necessary resources and strategies to anchor themselves in the realm of the economic.

For many people this story of neoliberalism brings to mind a capitalist dystopia: a world governed by market principles, where every human relation and social ideal is subordinated to a consumerist logic. Popular culture is littered with stories that confirm this fear: books like Bret Easton Ellis' *American Psycho*, Chuck Palahniuk's *Fight Club*, Frédéric Beigbeder's *99 Francs*, Michel Houellebecq's *Platform*, Victor Pelevin's *Babylon*, Gary Shteyngart's *The Russian Debutante's Handbook*, Don DeLillo's *Cosmopolis*, and films like *The Matrix*, *Wall Street* and its recent sequel *Money Never Sleeps* are a constant reminder of how desolate and dehumanized life has become in a world governed by hypercapitalist drives. We find a similar discontent in post-war critical theory, which bemoans the rise of a political subject so sedated by the material and technological comforts of middle-class existence that it loses any individual freedom or political force. What Adorno's *Authoritarian Personality*, Marcuse's *One-Dimensional Man*, William Whyte's *Organization Man*, C. Wright Mill's *White Collar*, Sartre's portrait of the 'serialized man' and Cornelius Castoriadis' takedown of bureaucratic productivism have in common is a biting critique of the alienating and repressive effects of modern capitalist existence, and its social constellation of tedious men in grey flannel suits (Holmes 2002: 4). To some extent Foucauldian scholarship on neoliberal governmentality has continued this tradition.

The advantage of the Foucauldian account of neoliberalism is that it grants subjectivity a constitutive role in historical processes. Foucauldians are well aware that disciplinary control starts at the level of the most intimate and private aspects of our lives. The subjective condition is 'where the social link is forged' (Madra and Ceren Özselcuk 2010: 482), the place where political attachments are formed, power relations are subscribed to or shaken off, and political action acquires meaning. This represents an important corrective to both classic liberalism and orthodox Marxist analyses, which treat capitalism like a naturalistic machine with an inherent logic and intrinsic contradictions. Nevertheless, there is a worrying tendency that Foucauldian scholarship on neoliberal governmentality (Rose 1991; Rose and Miller 1990, 1992; Barry, Osborne and Rose 1996; Lemke 2001, 2007; Brown 2003) has a tendency 'to deduce the actual state of subjectivity under neoliberalism from the homo oeconomicus' model and, as such, use subjectivity simply to reproduce the

The self as enterprise 41

outcome of a story we know all too well (Madra and Özselcuk 2010: 484). I am not convinced that economic schemata (cost–benefit calculations, efficiency assessments, key performance indicators, and competition) provide an exhaustive explanation for entrepreneurial conduct. This would imply that neoliberalism produces nothing but a series of Patrick Bateman-like figures obsessed with evaluating their bank accounts, credentials, looks and body count to the exclusion of all social, moral and affective considerations. Or that we live in a society numbed by goods and products. Or that market rationality is limited to instrumental action and bureaucratic organization styles. Such a world would quickly become intolerable.

What Foucauldians have been slow to notice is that a lot of the criticisms advanced against the callous, dispassionate and hyperindividualistic ethos of neoliberalism have already been resolved by the advent of so-called 'caring capitalism'. Today's flexible capitalism, with its de-centred bureaucratic structures, self-directed work styles, good governance and microfinance programmes, public–private partnerships, creative cities and so on, is *already* an answer to our collective dissatisfaction with a system governed purely by economic rationality. Capitalism has, for some people at least (the kinds of people this book is concerned with), become far more pleasurable and gratifying than this story suggests. There is much more room for emotions (Illouz 2007; Fortier 2010), enjoyment (Holmes 2002; Boltanski and Chiapello 2005) and community values (Rose 2000) in entrepreneurial conduct than the *homo oeconomicus* story of subjectivization allows. Many Foucauldian analyses, however, have failed to take seriously enough the power of neoliberal ideology to put forth *credible* affective structures and the ability of individuals to derive *genuine* pleasure from them.

This is not necessarily a problem that Foucault himself holds the blame for. In *The Birth of Biopolitics*, Foucault is clear that, since competition has replaced the logic of exchange as the guiding principle of the market, what neoliberalism needs is not a society numbed by goods and products, but a social body that is invigorated, inspired even by the dynamics of enterprise (Foucault 2008: 147). Neoliberal government dispenses with the negative, repressive, coercive connotations of government in favour of a type of social regulation that incites and seduces individuals to be proactive, innovative and even risk taking. For the enterprise form to become a 'universally generalized social model' it needed a 'society for the market and a society against the market', a society that would abide by economic principles and a society that would use these to achieve social order and personal meaning (ibid.: 242). Even Ordoliberals recognized that the 'cold' mechanisms of competition had to be embedded in a set of 'warm' moral and cultural values that could compensate for the otherwise mechanistic and alienating consequences of economic rationality. If the task of neoliberalism is to turn enterprise into 'a general style of thought, analysis, and imagination' (ibid.: 219) nothing could have been more suited to that end than the incorporation of the democratic distemper of the 1960s into the new spirit of capitalism.

42 *The self as enterprise*

Discipline and distemper

After two decades of unprecedented economic growth and relative political stability, at least in the advanced industrial economies, the 1960s and 1970s experienced a period of revolt staged by students and workers dissatisfied with the hierarchical, undemocratic and stultifying effects of industrial capitalism. Weber's worst fears of a modern world disenchanted with the effects of bureaucratic rationalism had come true. Alienating jobs, sclerotic institutions and rigid social structures were locking people in tedious, conformist forms of life, from which only consumerism or, even worse, violence and civic disobedience could offer relief. The situation was even worse for racial, gendered and sexual minorities, not to mention developing populations excluded both from the blue-collar blues and white-collar woes. Race riots, student revolts and wildcat strikes stretching from Berkeley to Belgrade, together with the anti-imperialist critique voiced by developing nations at the Bandung Conference indicated that the Fordist compromise, which traded worker discipline for middle-class comforts for only a small minority of the world's population, needed to be urgently rethought.

But rethinking quickly gave way to restructuring. For neoliberal reformers, student and worker revolts only confirmed what the crisis of profitability in the 1970s was already hinting at – that Fordism had to be let go. The changes that followed did more to widen the gap between rich and poor than satisfy the demands of a generation in revolt. The globalization of trade and production led to deindustrialization and labour casualization in the Global North, and structural adjustment programmes in the South. At the same time, the rise of information technology introduced greater labour surveillance and speedup, and unleashed the powers of finance capital. Together these changes would have people work more hours for less money than ever before since the Great Depression. If we consider that the slogan of the Italian autonomist movement of the 1970s was 'lavorare meno, lavorare tutti' (all working less) one can only conclude that neoliberalism was capital's way to 'take people's desire for less work, for forms of flexible labour and arrangements ... to impose increasingly uncertain conditions' (Shukaitis 2007).

None of these reforms would have been possible, though, had there not also been a carrot to go along with this heavy stick. Neoliberalism proved especially adept at incorporating the 'democratic distemper' (Holmes 2002) of the 1968 student movement to make capitalism tolerable and necessary again. The student movement never managed to reconcile what Boltanski and Chiapello (2005) refer to as the social and the artistic critique of capital, the call for social justice and the demand for greater freedom and personal choice chewing away at the heart of the Left. In blaming big government (but also mass consumerism) for the conformism of modern existence, the New Left alienated working-class people, who very much relied on the state in their confrontation with capital. New Left critique also rendered itself vulnerable to cooptation by management and marketing gurus who used their appeal to

The self as enterprise   43

freedom and personal choice to craft a more flexible and diversified economy (Harvey 2005: 42–43). When Reagan promised to take government 'off the backs of the people' he was presenting deregulation, privatization and de-unionization as democratic concessions to this popular discontent. Jobs would be casual but rewarding and self-directed, consumption would be ready-to-assemble but diversified, citizens would lack adequate protection but they would be autonomous, lifestyles would be transient but mobile and meaningful. But this was nothing but a great bait-and-switch strategy, a betrayal of the original demands of the 1960s revolt with no other ambition than to rid people of the safety nets and social ties that would enable them to collectively resist the onslaught of overwork, precarity and private indebtedness in the future. The ambition was to replace the 'rigidities' of the old system with disciplinary mechanisms (overwork, debt peonage, surveillance, militarization of public spaces) that would prevent a 'crisis of governability', like that of the 1960s, from ever happening again (Gorz 1999: 10–11).

But there were also those who saw flexible capitalism as an opportunity to pursue their creative talents and self-expressive drives. A perfect example of this logic is Richard Florida, urban policy consultant and free-market guru *extraordinaire*. Popular with urban planners, public policy makers and start-up entrepreneurs, Florida has no qualms about extolling the virtues of the new economy. In his bestselling book *The Rise of the Creative Class* (2002) he explains that we have entered a new economic phase, where the main driving forces of production are no longer technological (land, resources, manpower) but human: '[a]ccess to talented and creative people is to modern business what access to coal and iron was to steelmaking' (ibid.: 6). According to Florida's spurious calculations some 30 per cent of the US workforce now belongs to the so-called creative class, including artists, designers, architects, performers and writers, but also highly skilled professionals in science, education, health care, law, business and finance. Although smaller than the service economy, the creative class – by virtue of its high-earning status – has become 'the norm-setting class of our time' (ibid.: 9). It changes the way we work, where we live and how we socialize. Every aspect of our daily lives is being reorganized to accommodate creativity. Nations and cities who want to stay afloat in this sink-or-swim economy, Florida argues in his second book *Who's Your City* (2008), must attract creatives by offering them an exhilarating cultural climate to pursue and develop their talents. Florida envisions a world where creativity will eventually trickle down to all members of society, including the cheap unskilled workforce now servicing the creative class (Peck 2005, Ravensbergen 2008). Given the right place to live, everyone should be able to unlock their creative potential. This is utopia *within* capitalism: if we rework capital to account for dignity, autonomy and innovation, it can give expression to the highest human ambitions (Szeman and Cazdyn 2011: 99).

At the opposite end of the political spectrum, Slavoj Zizek has no patience for the new elites, who believe 'that we can have the global capitalist cake, i.e., thrive as profitable entrepreneurs, and eat it, too, i.e., endorse the anti-capitalist

44 *The self as enterprise*

causes of social responsibility and ecological concerns' (2008b: 16). These so-called 'liberal communists' are the people from 'Porto Davos' who hope to earn money as an unintentional, almost accidental side-effect of doing good works, the environmental pragmatists who understand that going green is the new gold, and 'philantrepreneurs' like George Soros and Bill Gates who use their fortunes to appease the capitalist crises they themselves perpetuated and benefited from (ibid.: 23). Whether we are talking about frugal consumers, social entrepreneurs or creative workers, what Zizek takes issue with here is not simply the hypocritical nature of these acts, but the ethico-political confusion they engender. Dressing up business as usual in a new moral cloth makes it increasingly difficult to question the conditions that make the oxymoron of 'capitalism with morals' necessary in the first place.

Despite their differences, both Florida and Zizek make it clear that the shift in production is accompanied by a transformation at the level of political subjectivity. In post-Fordist capital, where organization styles are more horizontal and inclusive, work is rewarding and immaterial, production happens just in time and consumption is ready to assemble. Elements that were once external, if not inimical, to the market economy (creativity, cooperation, self-expression, multicultural tolerance and social responsibility) suddenly become key to the entrepreneurial spirit (Holmes 2002). Today's 'new entrepreneur' has to complement economic rationality with emotive dispositions and social competencies that were once merely ornamental to capitalism. Social networking skills and sophisticated cultural tastes have become prerequisites for professional advancement, material security and other more cultural forms of privilege.

Where free marketeers and radical Marxists differ, however, is about how this shift in subjectivity occurred. For Florida it was a smooth transformation. The creative economy is not 'being imposed on us from above' (2002: 134), but expresses a popular desire for more fulfilling work and life arrangements. According to Florida's questionable historic account, which mentions nothing of the effects of economic globalization, and manages to reduce vast empirical data to an 'elabourate market profile of an upscale consumer' (Ross 2003: 124), the 1960s' revolt produced a 'big morph' between the countercultural demand for individual liberties and personal self-actualization and bourgeois values such as thrift, hard work and entrepreneurship. There was no cooptation or corruption to speak of because it was never the goal of the student protests 'to fundamentally transform the world of work and economics' (ibid.: 203). They were much more concerned with the critique of alienation, conformism and consumer culture than with problems of injustice and redistribution. As a result, it was easy to use bohemian values to reform capitalism from within rather than overthrow it completely. When millions lost their jobs during the economic restructuring of the 1980s and 1990s, they did not take to the streets, but rather saw this as an opportunity to 'take control of their own lives' and pursue more rewarding and satisfying career paths (ibid.: 112). For Florida, this is further confirmation of the fact that so great is our desire for creative self-expression that '[w]e simply accept … things [as they] are and go about our busy lives' (ibid.: 115).

Marxists, on the other hand, attribute this change in subjectivity to cooptation. Neoliberalism, with all its government spending cuts, job losses, wage reductions, income disparities and sharp division of labour enforced through undemocratic police tactics, would not have been accepted so readily had it not incorporated the dissident language of the 1960s along with the cultural tastes and styles of bohemia (Frank and Weiland 2002). Boltanski and Chiapello have famously argued that capitalism is the only mode of social organization completely devoid of a moral logic of its own. This makes capitalism completely dependent upon already-existing persuasion mechanisms and normative principles to justify the 'accumulation of capital by formally peaceful means' (Boltanski and Chiapello 2005: 4). Critique is the motor of change within capitalism: when capitalism is found to fall short of certain normative ideals, critique jumps in to realign the logic with dominant principles of social order and justice. Critique helps capitalism incorporate 'some of the values in whose name it was criticized' (ibid.: 28). This is what makes it often difficult to draw a clear line between cultural paradigms designed to promote capitalism and those intended to critique it. Often the same registers are involved in both justifying and condemning capitalism.

Tiziana Terranova complicates this theory of cooptation, contending that 'late capitalism does not appropriate anything: it nurtures, exploits, and exhausts its labour force and its cultural and affective production' (2000: 51). Rather than capital extending its tentacles into authentic culture, it is more useful to think of cooptation as an immanent process where capital organizes already existing forms of life, cooperation and language towards economically profitable results. 'Incorporation is not about capital descending on authentic culture but a more immanent process of channeling collective labour (even as cultural labour) into monetary flows and its structuration within capitalist business practices' (ibid.: 38–39). This keeps with the autonomist Marxist idea of capital being a parasitical add-on, which places our spontaneous dispositions towards communication, friendship and creativity in the service of relentless production and consumption (Hardt and Negri 2009).

These subtleties have not been entirely lost on Foucauldian scholarship on neoliberal governmentality. Especially with the advent of 'Third Way' neoliberalism in the 1990s, Foucauldians have started noticing that the current mode of government relies on a much more intimate relation between market rationality and moral action than their original interpretation of the entrepreneurial self assumed.

Probably no one has done more than sociologist Eva Illouz to dispel the myth that capitalism is a lifeless rational formation with no use for emotions. Charting the influence of Freudian psychoanalysis on industrial relations, management theory, self-help literature, gender identities and interpersonal relations, Illouz (1997, 2003, 2007) contradicts the Weberian vision that modern capitalism stands in the way of maintaining intimate relations and a meaningful existence. Capitalism, she argues, mobilizes psychology and the culture of therapy to manage social affairs in market-friendly ways. Far from being entirely

46 *The self as enterprise*

rational and calculated, the economy is a primary site for symbolic production and cultural meaning. In what she dubs 'emotional capitalism', 'affect is made an essential aspect of economic behaviour' (Illouz 2007: 5). 'Emotional life [becomes] imbued with the metaphors and rationality of economics; conversely, economic behaviour [is] consistently shaped by the sphere of emotions and sentiments' (Illouz 2007: 60).

This is not to say that emotions are co-opted and added onto economic rationality. Instead, emotions become integral to economic rationality – they become a type of reason. 'Every age in the history of philosophy has its own preoccupations and [its own] mode of handling problems' (Illouz 2007: 6). Ours happens to be the 'emotionalization of economic conduct': knowing how to form and maintain social relations, communicate effectively with people of various backgrounds, take initiative, mediate conflicts and sensitive situations and control 'bad' emotions, all become essential parts of professional identity and competence (ibid.). What Illouz's work demonstrates is that there is less of a difference between emotion and reason than there is between emotions conducive to entrepreneurial action (compassion, courage, confidence) and those detrimental to it (anger, anxiety, boredom, lust and depression). While the latter must be 'treated', the rest can be used to realign entrepreneurial conduct with principles of social order, intimacy and autonomy (Boltanski and Chiapello 2005).

Focusing on ethics rather than emotion, Nikolas Rose reaches similar conclusions in his discussion of 'ethopolitics' and 'government through community'. After successive rounds of privatization, spending cuts and austerity budgets have eroded the ability of public institutions and communal associations to adequately care for their constituents, 'ethopolitics' (Rose 2000) emerges as a strategy of rule that treats individuals as ethical creatures responsible for their own well-being and that of their relevant communities. (David Cameron's Big Society initiative, which uses volunteerism, co-ops and social entrepreneurship to 'empower' communities to provide for their own security and prosperity without state support is a case in point.) 'Ethopolitics' kills three birds with one stone: it lends the current regime of accumulation (and dispossession) a human face that makes it more tolerable; it downloads state power to the community level in the hopes of unburdening state structures and disciplining the body politic; and it transforms citizenship from a rights-based entitlement into a merit-based asset. Similar functions are being served by 'government through community' (Rose 2004: 136), which encourages individuals to bind themselves to their relevant communities in order to realize their full status as citizens in congruence with these. With their emphasis on individual autonomy and associational life, 'ethopolitics' and 'government through community' may seem like emancipatory alternatives to government from above. But, upon closer inspection, these governmental strategies function to 'inscribe the norms of self-control more deeply into the soul of each citizen' by passing down the classic obligations of the state onto the shoulders of private individuals (Rose 2000: 1409). As Rose aptly puts it: '[p]olitics is to be returned to society itself,

The self as enterprise   47

but no longer in a social form: in the form of individual morality, organizational responsibility, and ethical community' (ibid.: 1400).

In effect, the incorporation of previous modes of dissent, be they rooted in the romantic distemper of the 1960s and 1970s, the emotional language of psychotherapy or radical aspirations of dignity, autonomy and self-governance, has been instrumental in producing a capitalist economy that is in many ways more diversified and rewarding than the rationalist story of neoliberal government would allow. It has also produced a new form of subjectivity. Every mode of government 'presupposes and reproduces particular forms of sociality and subjectivity' (Read 2003: 135). What is distinctive about neoliberalism is that it theorizes a model of government that shapes individuals – their property, health, profession, morality, household – without violating the 'formally autonomous' character of political subjectivity (McNay 2009: 61). The individual does not have to renounce its desires or submit passively to the dictums of consumerism and standardization, but is invited to innovate and expand the limits of what is possible under neoliberalism. The new spirit of enterprise is less a matter of conforming to a prescribed model of action than an injunction to improve one's life through economic diversification, aesthetic proliferation and responsible *jouissance* (ibid.: 62). More even, the good neoliberal subject is supposed to extend some of her entrepreneurial gifts to the community at large. With government spending and social programmes in the red, social solidarity becomes a matter of individual responsibility and even performance. We are still dealing with a calculating, risk-assessing, responsible subject, except that this time around these dispositions are not limited to the economic terrain. The 'ethopolitical' subject must align self-interest with collective interest to defer the crisis of the welfare state and the economy at large (Lessernich 2008).

For some people this might seem like reason for celebration. Gone are the rapacious factory bosses. Over are the days of rigid bureaucratic structures. A more equitable and meaningful world can begin. But what seems like a more 'humane' form of capitalism is, in fact, the dawn of an economically and politically uncertain future. In a governmental regime that sets up the individual as an entrepreneur of himself who constantly relates to others as competitors (McNay 2009: 63), political subjectivity becomes 'conditional on conduct' (Rose 2000: 1408) – an unequal privilege, bestowed only upon those who can live up to the demands of capital (Ong 2005: 698).

Subject-as-capital

So far this chapter has shifted back and forth between the Marxist and the Foucauldian interpretation of neoliberalism. Whereas someone like David Harvey locates the origins of neoliberalism with political and economic elites' wilful seizure of working class wealth and power, Foucault's anti-humanism and anti-normative definition of power make this interpretation look simplistic and even conspiratorial. The idea that subjects are not given a priori

48 *The self as enterprise*

but constructed with the help of power, which both subjugates and empowers people to position themselves within a matrix of possible social meanings, prevents a clean separation between the perpetuators and the victims of neo-liberalism, between bankers and homeowners. This complication undermines the possibility of collective outrage and action against a clearly defined group of power holders. Marxism is not entirely oblivious to the role of subjectivity in historical processes. Marx famously described capitalism as a system of class relations, not a static inanimate structure. Beginning with the original phase of primitive accumulation in sixteenth-century Britain, the goal of capitalism has always been to produce a proletarian class *identity* as separate from the bourgeoisie (Tronti 1966). Class divisions are not only a matter of economics but are also perpetuated through education, cultural tastes and everyday practices of identification. But still, their assumption of a fundamental antagonism between workers and owners is not easily reconciled with the much more differentiated account of subjectivity offered by Foucault.

This split has grave political ramifications. Whereas the Marxist story offers the possibility for political action against dispossession and exploitation, Foucauldian thought illustrates how capitalism functions to commodify and absorb resistance. What Marxism offers in terms of utopian fervour it fails to deliver on the theoretical front, whereas what intellectual sophistication Foucault brings to the table is handicapped by his reluctance to propose any convincing strategy of opposition.

An important way out of this impasse is offered by Italian autonomist thought (Cleaver 1979; Negri 1989; Virno and Hardt 1996; Hardt and Negri 2000, 2004, 2009; Virno 2004; Lotringer and Marazzi 2007; Marazzi 2008, 2010; Fumagalli and Mezzadra 2010), which injects Marxism with a much-needed dose of Continental theory. Autonomist Marxism demonstrates that the success of neoliberalism is not secured in spite of individual autonomy or at the expense of the social fabric that holds us together, but rather with our active participation. In 'cognitive capitalism', where production is less about turning raw materials into consumer goods than about producing producers congruent with the spirit of accumulation, work evolves from a limited action done in the service of capital to an activity that spreads over the entire social field. This collapses labour and leisure, prosperity and sociality, philanthropy and entrepreneurship into a so-called 'social factory' (Hardt 1996). Although similar to Foucault's understanding of neoliberal governmentality, the effects of 'biopolitical production' or 'bioeconomy' are far more insidious. Whereas neoliberal governmentality tries to make the 'economic perspective ... coextensive with all of society' (Read 2009a: 32), 'biopolitical production' recognizes the limits of economic rationality and makes the 'raw material of human relations' (The Invisible Committee 2009: 18), meaning all the things we usually think of as autonomous or alternative to capital, central to value production. In other words, 'cognitive capitalism' places our propensity towards communication, creativity and community at the heart of economic production, and makes capital immanent to our social being. For autonomists this is not

The self as enterprise 49

reason for despair. Because the subjectivities and creative energies of workers remain anterior to and autonomous from capitalist command, they trust in the power of workers to appreciate the parasitical nature of capital and seek liberation from its acts of enclosure.

Through some advanced theoretical acrobatics, which are far too complex to explore here in full detail, autonomists combine the classic Marxist (antagonistic) and the Foucauldian/Continental (immanent) view of power into a powerful new hypothesis. They accept that subjectivity is central for the social reproduction of capital. For capitalism to work we must wake up every morning to sell our labour power, buy commodities, invest on the stock exchange as if it were our second nature. But they continue to insist that capital perverts our possibilities for leading a more fulfilling and just existence. For them neoliberalism is not an attack launched by capitalists against workers, as Harvey tells us. It is also not the case that we are all neoliberals now, as Foucault declares. Rather, the autonomist mantra holds that we are all *victims* of neoliberalism. All of us work to reproduce the spirit of capitalism regardless of our employment status and material profit, bankers and homeowners alike. The question is only how to channel the energy of our collective labour out of capitalist value structures and into autonomous structures of valorization. As can be imagined, this position has generated considerable hostility amongst fellow Marxists, who accuse autonomists of having given up on the explanatory primacy of relations of production, objective class interest and the utopia of communism in favor of an analysis that is too vague to mobilize political action (McGee 1997: 203; see also Caffentzis 1999, 2005; Zizek 2001; Brennan 2005; Robbins 2010). For our present purposes, however, what is important to take away from the autonomist school is their compelling understanding of the subject-as-capital.

Perhaps one of the greatest merits of autonomia is to have made labour, something that both classic political economy and scientific Marx neglected, the subject of historical transformation. Workers are given ontological primacy not only as a factor of production or the source of value, but as the force behind capital innovation and, ultimately, the basis of human progress (Cleaver 1979: 65). What is more, work escapes the confines of the factory to seep into the larger social field where it comes to have a direct bearing upon the formation of subjectivity and social reality. Contrary to Foucault's fluid neoliberal subject, whose relation to capital remains vague despite being cast as thoroughly entrepreneurial, autonomists are not shy about framing subjectivity as a type of capital. For them, the worker-subject is 'not simply ... something which must be produced but something which is in fact productive in a very broad sense' (Kiersey 2011: 36). The neoliberal subject is first and foremost a worker.

Volunteer tourism is a perfect example of how this intricate game of cooptation and valorization works. But it is also a fitting cautionary tale about the dangers of late capitalism. Situated at the intersection between the de-responsibilized post-Fordist state and the re-responsibilized entrepreneurial self, volunteerism is well poised to capture the great Foucauldian lesson on neoliberal government:

50 *The self as enterprise*

under neoliberalism, the task of government is not to correct market imbalances through Fordist interventions like deficit spending, tax increases or job creation but rather to make sure the social field contains the necessary values, tastes and attitudes for flexible accumulation to operate smoothly. Volunteering is one such form of intervention. It is a carefully designed technology of government that can be mobilized to perform various functions, including governing communities without direct government intervention (and spending); investing individuals with the social and emotional competencies necessary for producing value in communicative capitalism; and producing flexible citizens that combine economic rationality with moral responsibility. While volunteers may very well seek to enhance their education and employability by doing charitable work, this should not automatically peg them as hypocrites or victims of 'liberal guilt'. Very often volunteering will seize upon people's genuine emotional attachment to community and sociality to fill the void left by a shrinking welfare state or a crippled developing economy, not to mention get individuals to organize their lives in an enterprising fashion. This is why volunteerism is best understood as a mode of rule at the intersection between neoliberal state practices and global flows of capital.

At this point one might interject that, while volunteer tourism may be an apt illustration of how neoliberalism has reached a hegemonic status by making itself coterminous with other less market-oriented fields, the practice only speaks to the subjective condition of a narrow minority of the world's population. Not coincidentally, this is something both Foucauldian governmentality studies and the autonomist school have been accused of: exaggerating the global scope of conditions that apply only to liberal, post-industrial societies.

In recent years, there has been quite an animated debate in international relations around whether neoliberal government describes a global reality (Selby 2007; Joseph 2009, 2010a, 2010b; Chandler 2009, 2010). The concern is that scaling up Foucault's concept of governmentality from the national to the international realm, in the form of global governmentality, might overstate the success of liberalism and obscure the persistence of geopolitical differences and hierarchies. A global liberal project is impeded both by the inherently unequal and competitive nature of world politics, and rising levels of political apathy, which make liberal democracy, even on a domestic level, increasingly difficult. But this is where critics err. When Foucauldians talk of global liberalism or global governmentality they do not refer to political liberalism, with its emphasis on natural rights, representative politics and juridical conceptions of legitimacy. This is, indeed, a political form specific to the Western experience. What makes the world go round, Foucauldians argue, is a different type of liberalism – one inspired by the principles of economic liberalism. This is a form of liberalism that, although not global in reach, harbours a universal ambition (Vrasti 2011).

This does not mean that neoliberalism is ubiquitous. To quote Kiersey: 'global neoliberal government ... does not, and cannot, work on a truly global population' (Kiersey 2009: 385). For now, at least, the liberal ideal seems to describe

The self as enterprise 51

best the condition of advanced industrial nations or select urban conglomerations and high-value production sites across the globe. At the same time, however, this does not undercut the hegemony of the liberal programme, which is global not in actuality, but as a *tendency*. Global governmentality manifests its force not through the actual number of populations or states it controls, but by acting as a standard of reference against which all forms of life (individual, communal, political) can be assessed according to modern conceptions of civilization and order. From that perspective, market rule delineates the political possibilities of every nation on earth.

A similar criticism has been raised against autonomist Marxists who, sceptics argue, extrapolate their conclusions about the global dominance of immaterial value production from the experiences of post-industrial workers in advanced capitalist economies (Henwood 2003; Brennan 2005; Neilson and Rossiter 2005, 2008; Wright 2005; Federici 2004; Shukaitis 2007). The proposition that the present form of capitalism extracts 'profits without production' (Henwood 2003: 27) is a 'matter of faith rather than anything resembling an analysis of the record' (Brennan 2005: 344). For it to be true we would have to ignore the slave-like conditions characteristic of 'guest-worker systems, uncapitalized agriculture, and the archipelagos of maquiladoras at the heart of globalization's gulag' (ibid.: 338). This pegs autonomist Marxism as a type of bourgeois theory. It seems to appeal mostly to left-leaning elites who can afford to ignore the sharp global division of labour (and its racial, gendered and environmental ramifications), and who are reluctant to make the necessary commitments to the state, party politics and class-based interests for organizing substantial change.

Michael Hardt and Antonio Negri, who are the usual targets of this attack, are quite sympathetic to these charges. In *Multitude* (2004), the second volume of their trilogy, they are careful to specify that, although agriculture and industry remain the dominant sectors of the economy, the hegemony of immaterial production makes itself felt in 'qualitative terms and has imposed a tendency on other forms of labour and society itself' (ibid.: 109). Immaterial labour is now in the same position as industrial labour was 150 years ago. Just as all fields of action in the nineteenth century had to conform to the logics of industrial production, so all of life today has to become informationalized, intelligent, communicative and affective. In fact, the value of immaterial production is so high that, in spite if its numeric inferiority, it is responsible for the deproletarianization of the traditional working class, which has been demoted from the 'salt of the earth' to the 'scum of the earth'. As Richard Florida already intuited, the creative class has become the 'the norm-setting class of our time' (2002: 9) reconfiguring economic relations, social institutions and living spaces to their advantage, and to the exclusion of everyone else.

Still, we must be careful not to overstate the historical novelty and geographical reach of these transformations or they can become misleading and vacuous. We do not inhabit a smooth and homogenous global space (Larner and Williams 2004: 5). Neoliberal practices and technologies remain 'much

52 *The self as enterprise*

more unevenly distributed' (Selby 2007: 339) than vast terms such as global governmentality or cognitive capitalism suggest. Neoliberalism is not a global reality, but a quite selective and stratified 'field of possibilities' (Foucault 2001: 343), which nonetheless harbors a distinct universal ambition. If certain bodies or places are excluded that doesn't mean that they exist 'outside' the neo-liberal project. It only means that they must work harder (by acting in a responsible, self-reliant fashion) to become worthy of the benefits of neoliberal government (Rose 2000: 1397–98). Some will succeed, others will fail, and many more will be somewhere in between.

Foucault argues that subjection, 'the work of turning human beings into subjects' (Dean 1994: 297) is an inescapable fact of modern power. What he fails to mention, however, is that, just like in the famous *Animal Farm* phrase 'we are all equal, but some of are more equal', some of us end up with more fortunate subject positions than others. Those individuals who possess the skill, talent and entrepreneurial spirit to respond to the demands of capital will enjoy greater access to job markets, housing options, residence permits and cultural goods around the world. Similarly, those states that can abide by the dictums of good governance, fiscal responsibility and foreign security will receive better credit ratings, lending agreements and international support. Those who fail to conform will become second-order citizens, confined to slums and ghettos, doomed to perform low-skilled and tedious jobs, or perpetually developing states, stuck in a tight spot between foreign intervention and humanitarian assistance.

> On the one hand, there are those for whom subjectivity, capital, and satiat-ing pleasures and rights are being forever promised. This occurs [...] at the expense of compliance with, or perhaps distraction from, the larger structural underpinnings of social relations and processes. On the other hand, there are the (non)subjects for whom the same promise has not been issued, the abject(s) whose lives and deaths are completely nonspectacular within the dominant imaginations.
>
> (Agathangelou *et al.* 2008: 137)

So far, volunteer tourists have found themselves on the fortunate end of this exchange. While abroad, volunteers demonstrate a desire for social change, an ability to operate in distant and diverse settings, and an interest in experiment-ing with one's self and the world around it. All of these are necessary skills for tackling the professional, informational and cultural challenges of network capitalism. What better way to demonstrate these aptitudes than working for change in a foreign country without modern amenities? Possessing emotional and cultural competencies, along with a genuine wish to 'make a difference' through self-sacrificial acts of charity and compassion, helps volunteers acquire much sought-after social capital. According to Pierre Bourdieu (1984) this is the sum of all real and potential resources an individual possesses to perform on and improve his or her condition on the market. An increase in social

The self as enterprise   53

capital allows volunteers to become mobile and desirable, employable and experienced, comfortable and confident, esteemed and assertive. They are allowed to inhabit and extend into space as they like: gain admission to graduate programmes, obtain more favourable employment, join relief teams to remote locations and conflict zones, and swiftly cross racial, professional and spatial divides. Meanwhile subaltern bodies are made to feel at odds with themselves (Ahmed 2006: 133). This is especially true for the voluntour*ed*, whose lack of material opportunities and ecological, pedagogical and medical expertise renders them vulnerable to foreign inspection.

It does not matter that volunteer tourists are only a small elite of white, liberal-educated mobile Westerners. The neoliberal self is a hegemonic condition not because of its world-wide application, but because it represents a standard of truth against which the entire social field can be assessed. Volunteers cannot be held directly responsible for this inequity. Although one can take issue with the moral justifications for volunteering in the Global South or the day-to-day operations of volunteer projects, on the whole volunteer tourism is only a symptom of wider economic and political transformations. For instance, when volunteers are accused of being careerist opportunists, what is forgotten is that the labour market has been casualized to such an extent that university graduates are now forced to resort to such 'creative' methods to maximize their chances of employment. The labour market is no longer a meritocratic race based exclusively on skill and expertise. It probably never was. But in the present mode of production, where the value of labour is measured in terms of the inner qualities of the person doing the work, immaterial skills like those cultivated during a volunteering trip have become essential to social mobility (Foucault 2008: 226). This has also clear political implications. With work no longer functioning as a 'collective identificatory framework' and 'social coagulant' that ensures equal membership in a political community (Muehlebach 2011: 64), citizenship becomes a bundle of material goods and status symbols distributed selectively according to merit and market value (Ong 2007b). Quite problematically, extending the principle of competition and the measure of value to the realm of political subjectivity deprives democratic politics of its most essential requirement: equal subjects of rights.

The criteria for becoming a sovereign subject who can participate fully in social interaction, an 'upstanding citizen' as it were, may have become more diversified and exploratory, as the example of volunteer tourism vividly shows, but they are also increasingly competitive and ambiguous. Against what someone like Richard Florida suggests, importing bohemian principles into neoliberalism has not made government more humane or capitalism more equitable. On the contrary, it inaugurated a more competitive and hierarchical struggle for subjectivity. While some individuals can organize their lives in accordance with (exceedingly demanding) criteria for entrepreneurship, others are *de-subjectified* – they are excluded at the same time that they become the object of suspicion, compassion or intervention (Neal 2008: 51). As political rights and economic security are made increasingly dependent upon loose

54 *The self as enterprise*

moral, emotional and aesthetic criteria, a new 'graduated' hierarchy takes shape between individuals who can afford to do fun jobs, combine lifelong learning with leisure, engage in ethical consumption and aesthetic politics, and those who are not creative and mobile enough to keep up with the race for innovation. For the former group, the options of where to live, shop, study, work out or go on holidays are becoming only wider. For the latter these choices are thin and constraining (Bauman 1998). In addition to the classic division between haves and have-nots (educated/uneducated, skilled/unskilled labour, office/factory work), neoliberalism draws an equally sharp line between privileged subjects 1and those destined to remain suspect or, worse even, abject. As Agamben predicted, biopolitics makes this division mutable and profoundly arbitrary. Anyone can end up on either side of the line at any time.

Conclusion

It would be easy to conclude from the story presented here, particularly when viewed through the lens of volunteer tourism, that neoliberalism has given us a profoundly depoliticized public that is 'aware of what it wants and unaware of what is being done to it' (Foucault 2007: 105). Yet, against this somewhat defeatist reading, we must keep in mind that the entrepreneurial subject exists only in 'the gerundive – it is not to be found, only to be produced'. It is not an empirical reality, but an ideal to be produced through constructive discipline and mobilizing injunctions (Bröckling 2007: 47). The neoliberal subject 'does not describe an empirically observed entity, but a mode in which subjects are addressed, and the direction in which they are changed and expected to change' (ibid.). As such, subjectivity remains an open battlefield. While incorporation and valorization remain a constant threat, the entire struggle between power and subjectivity is premised on the possibility of resistance. The next chapters examine how volunteers negotiate this tension with various degrees of success.

In closing, let me say a final word on the ambition of this book. It has never been my intention to advise people on whether they should join a volunteering programme or not. This needs to remain a personal choice, while being fully aware that not even the 'personal' is safe from power. What this book hopes to achieve by approaching the topic of volunteer tourism from the perspective of neoliberal subjectivity is to encourage a more rigorous examination of our most intimate normative desires and emotional investments, what Foucault called a 'critical ontology of the self' (1997c: 32). The irony of thinking that we can maximize our freedom (and that of others) by making our private and intimate selves the focus of ethical and aesthetic practices is that often such efforts are perfectly aligned with the disciplinary injunctions of neoliberalism. I would hope that this chapter has demonstrated that the autonomous, self-governing subject is 'not the opposite of, or limit to, neoliberal governance, rather it lies at the heart of its disciplinary control' (McNay 2009: 62). We live in dangerous times. Working to make the self into an ethical being and working to enhance the entrepreneurial potentials of the self have become closely intertwined. The distinction between Foucault's 'care of the self' (Foucault 1997a, 1997b) and the discourse of self-work is often blurry. As self-government crosses over into self-care, economic profitability into ethical responsibility, and entrepreneurship into emotion, there is no longer an 'outside' to power. There are no more registers of feeling and action that cannot be used to further the spirit of capitalism. It is not that we have acquiesced to neoliberalism; rather we have become emotionally attached to it. The case of volunteer tourism should bring us closer to confronting this danger.

3 Multicultural sensibilities in Guatemala

Proving the ethical merit of volunteer tourism is always easier than showing that the formula is complicit with colonial and capitalist forms of rule. In distancing itself from the ecological destruction, economic exploitation and commercial orientation of modern mass tourism, volunteer tourism appears to be advancing a critique of the tedium and estrangement of modern industrial society that strikes a chord with many people in the West. Add to that the fact that volunteer tourism also seems to suggest that 'another world is possible', a world of cultural exchange governed by transnational responsibility and charitable ambitions, and you have a commodity beyond moral reproach. What this chapter sets out to demonstrate, however, is the opposite, namely that volunteer tourism is a politically suspect practice that does more to consolidate than to challenge Orientalist sensibilities and the consumerist spirit of capitalism.

Volunteering in Guatemala failed to elicit the care and compassion I had originally expected from a grassroots philanthropic enterprise (the first section). Volunteers could understand neither the purpose of their work projects nor the problems they were supposed to address (the second section). But this did not cause the experience to lose its legitimacy or be regarded as a failure. The affective response volunteering produced instead drew upon a romantic longing for authentic meaning and spiritual renewal, deeply lodged in the consciousness of affluent Western consumers (the third section) and produced a multicultural appreciation for the 'poor-but-happy' lifestyle of developing populations (the fourth section). If the town of San Andres was not 'poor enough' for volunteers to demonstrate their humanitarian sensibilities, it at least was small and simple enough to allow tourists to 'fall in love' with the local people and culture. As was to be expected, though, this sentimental education had nefarious consequences.

This chapter intersperses stories and events from 'the field' with an analysis of the romantic spirit of capitalism and a critique of multiculturalism to show that, despite their anti-modernist pretensions and democratic ambitions, these emotional regimes do nothing to unsettle the status quo. As critical thinkers from Edward Said to Slavoj Zizek have already pointed out, idealizing and sympathizing with the Other is never a safe bet against colonial and capitalist violences. Rather, these emotional styles subsume difference to the consumptive logic of capitalism and serve only to validate the moral superiority of white middle-class subjects. Despite their pretense to launch a critique of capitalist modernity, these seemingly benevolent sentiments work to preclude political reflection and prevent a collective model for social justice that can transcend cultural particulars. They depoliticize the material and historical roots of difference and, as a result, end up denying local people's claims to development, progress and equality in the name of cultural preservation. The logic of multiculturalism, in particular, comes short of its cosmopolitan ambitions revealing itself as a tool for managing diversity according to the needs of global capital accumulation. The conclusion is that without a political pedagogy to introduce volunteers to the socio-economic conditions that banish places like San Andres to the frontiers of modernity, volunteer tourism cannot fulfill its transformatory promise. It gets reduced to a commodity designed to enhance the cultural competencies and symbolic value of sophisticated Western consumers.

What this story proves is that capitalism incorporates values and dispositions supposed to be inimical or external to market relations, leaving nothing 'outside' of its reach. Whether we are talking of volunteers' compassionate desire to do good or their romantic fascination with cultural diversity and natural beauty, neoliberal capital reduces these potentially critical impulses to personal branding techniques. Even so-called moments of rupture are vulnerable to this process of reincorporation. This is especially true in a mode of production where, to put it simply, surplus value is extracted not from working with the hands, but from codes, images and social relations produced with the brain, the subject becomes the true bearer of capital, with the self having to be constantly curated and displayed, and its strategic assets produced and demonstrated. As already discussed in the previous chapter, this introduces a sharp distinction between normative and abject bodies, between those subjects able to garner status according to the fickle needs of capital and those forced to settle for backbreaking jobs and static lives. The distinction is not based on skills or merit, but is 'conditional on conduct' (Rose 2000: 1408), conditional on values, habits and consumer tastes. There are not many other better ways to demonstrate one's social status than joining an overseas volunteering trip. The market is saturated with flexible, individually tailored consumer goods that customers can use both for self-expression and political contestation, but few are as well-positioned to attest to the magnanimity, worldliness and adaptability of the buyer as volunteer tourism is.

Volunteer Peten, Guatemala

San Andres is a rural community of 15,000 and growing located at the heart of Guatemala's northern province of Peten. The *Lonely Planet* guide to Guatemala describes Peten as a 'vast, sparsely-populated and jungle covered' (2007a) region ideal for trekking through the rainforest (preferably on the way to one of the ancient Mayan temples located in the north), spotting toucans, iguanas,

58   *Multicultural sensibilities in Guatemala*

howler monkeys and jaguars, or for taking a dip in one of its many deep-blue lakes. Chances are, however, that Peten is more famous today for its dire poverty, rampant deforestation, and the decapitation of 27 people related to drug trafficking, incidentally on a ranch near San Andres. Among the working poor and foreign resource extraction companies the region is best known for its mahogany and timber riches hidden deep in the rainforest.

According to the latest government estimates, over the past four decades Peten's population jumped from 25,207 to an estimated 614,000 (Schwartz 1990: 11). Every year thousands of Guatemalans from the western and southern regions of the country flock to places like San Andres in search of work and a better living standard. They are usually landless and land-poor peasants relocated by decades of civil war, a dismal land tenure system and the colonizing activities of development agencies that administer government land concessions (Sundberg 1998: 394). Initially, migrants were drawn by the colonization activities of the Empresa Nacional de Fomento y Desarrollo de Peten (FYDEP, the National Development Agency for Peten), a military-led government institution given 'extensive and in practice exclusive authority' in Peten, ostensibly to promote economic development in the region. The agency sold land parcels, established infrastructure to promote social and economic development and regulated the forestry industry (Schwartz 1990: 252–53). In 1986 FYDEP was dismantled and quickly replaced with privately owned cattle and farming ranches, foreign resource extraction companies and transnational NGOs, which today make up the region's main sources of employment (Sundberg 1998: 394). Still, despite relatively abundant employment in agriculture and small-scale cattle ranching, in saw mills, small stores (*tiendas*) and the service industry, San Andreseños continue to live on $4 a day without plumbing, clean water, a proper garbage disposal system, safe transport and textbooks, not to mention 'luxuries' like job security, social benefits, sports and recreation facilities and freedom of movement (for work or leisure).

The dramatic rise in population does not come without its problems. The 14,000 square miles of Peten have lost over half of their tropical vegetation as a cumulative result of commercial logging, cattle ranching, agriculture, oil exploitation, corruption, drug trade, violent crime and the enduring strong arm of the military (Mahler 1993: 263). Peten is losing its forest at a rate of 100,000 acres per year. The fact that almost half of the province's surface has been placed under the protection of the Reserva de Biosphera Maya (the Mayan Biosphere Reserve) created in 1990 has not helped stall this trend. The stated mission of the Reserve is to reconcile environmental ambitions with the economic needs of a population whose livelihood depends upon natural resource extraction (ibid.: 388). In reality, however, the government – together with the Consejo National de Areas Protegidas (CONAP) charged with administering the Reserve – lacks both the political will and the economic muscle to protect such a massive and fertile stretch of land in the face of rising unemployment and absent land reforms. State- and private-funded conservation projects in Guatemala prefer to blame environmental degradation on the local population and their behavioural faults (their 'lack of education' and 'ignorance'), rather than acknowledge the government's systematic failure to address land reform, tackle corruption and introduce environmental legislation. A serious discussion on the larger tension that exists between conservationist ideals and the economic needs of people living in fragile natural habitats is painfully absent (Sundberg 1998).

Still, San Andreseños find it difficult to leave the region. A vicious cycle of low education levels, precarious employment, low income standards, few savings opportunities and sparse social provisions ties families to the working place of their employed (preponderantly male) members. Although a few people manage to find seasonal jobs in construction or tourism across the border in Belize and sometimes the United States, immigration is an option only for the very few. Not even the young dare to imagine a different future. A chronic lack of qualified teaching staff and school supplies makes even higher education in the capital or elsewhere a distant and unaffordable dream for most people in San Andres. Yet when compared to neighbouring towns, like Carmelita, which suffers from an even more dismal economic situation or, like San Benito, which is riddled with violent gang and drug-related crime, San Andres no longer seems like a such a bad place to settle down.

The dozens of tourists who arrive in town every month would certainly agree with this assessment. Fed up with the overcrowded 'gringo trail' that runs from Mexico to Panama, young Westerners choose San Andres for its accessible volunteering programs and language courses, but also for its small size, off-the-beaten-track location, lush natural surroundings, affordable prices and pristine culture. Most of them are looking to escape the conformism of backpacker tourism and 'travel with a purpose' to a more 'authentic' locale. They want to 'help and see how local people live' or just simply 'have something to do' on vacation. While some cited personal reasons for volunteering, like taking a break from the hectic yet tedious routine at home, others had more professional ambitions or explicitly political goals like doing research on volunteer tourism or 'develop[ing] a social consciousness'. Without exception, all volunteers had been lured by the promise of an out-of-the-ordinary experience. They wanted to travel to a smaller, slower and quieter place, a place where people are warm and hospitable and where tradition has not yet been corrupted by modernity. San Andres, with its picturesque lakeside location, surrounded by natural reservations, church bells, Sunday soccer games, with people who know their neighbours by name and a lifestyle that seems to have been unfolding according to the same cyclical rhythm since time immemorial seemed like the perfect candidate to satiate this 'search for "experience" and for their "origin" through the rural, the primitive, the childlike, the unpolluted, the pure and the original' (Bruner cited in Badone 2004: 183). The fact that San Andres also hosted an exceptionally affordable, not-for-profit organization like Volunteer Peter only made this romantic fantasy more alluring.

Founded in 2003 by former Peace Corps volunteer Matthew (Mateo) Peters, Volunteer Peten (VP) covers a breadth of issues pertinent to the region from

60 *Multicultural sensibilities in Guatemala*

'environmental education, general education, reforestation, forest management, medicinal plants and working with the public library and public schools' to a variety of more personalized projects designed to suit the individual needs and abilities of volunteers. Its stated mission is 'to aid development in Guatemala by training international volunteers to participate in, design and implement sustainable projects' (http: //www.volunteerpeten.org/Volunteering.htm). Although in less than a decade the organization built three schools, a library, a conservation park and a School of Natural History (its most ambitious project to date is a three-year professional degree that provides students with hands-on experience and technical expertise in wildlife management, forest management, agro-forestry, agriculture, environmental law and administration), Volunteer Peten has miraculously succeeded in retaining a certain aura of transparency and virtuous localism. Funded exclusively by volunteers and a few additional funds from Mateo's family and friends, with no head or branch offices in other countries, a small staff on the ground and extremely affordable pricing, Volunteer Peten is not only the opposite of mass tourism but also an exception to the heavily corporatized volunteer tourism industry. It is the epitome of grassroots development work.

For a modest fee of $350/month Volunteer Peten allows volunteers to acquire a sense of what it means, for a while at least, to feel 'independent and self-sufficient' in a foreign situation. It provides volunteers with everything they need to feel at home from the moment they set foot in San Andres: a home, a substitute family, three meals a day, an occupation and a circle of friends. In other words, VP distills the overwhelming foreignness of living in the Global South to a manageable routine. Thanks to Mateo, who has spent a decade in San Andres, learning the language, the bureaucratic ins and outs, the social norms that govern the place and virtually everyone's name, volunteers can enjoy an intimate, almost family-like experience.

Depending on the time of year, Volunteer Peten will receive anywhere between two and 40 volunteers per week. During the months I spent in San Andres, August–September 2008, summer vacation was just coming to an end and the enrollment numbers were dwindling. Our group consisted mostly of students, many of whom were getting ready to go back to school, and a few gap year travelers, all from Western countries.

The work routine was fairly straightforward, for those who could keep up: in the mornings we would walk out to the conservation park just outside San Andres where we dug ditches, made compost and built trails for what was supposed to become a one-square kilometer replica of pristine jungle vegetation. Needless to say, the work was physically extenuating and slow to progress. Those who still had the energy could come back out after lunch to teach English to what most people described as apathetic students. Most of us, however, exhausted from the morning shift, would take the afternoon off. When I did not use the time to catch up on my field notes and interviews, I would join the others at the lake or the market in the nearby Flores. Then, in the evenings, we would often reconvene at the library to help local children with their homework or play a round of basketball.

Multicultural sensibilities in Guatemala   61

Few were the days when we worked all three shifts. It was more common for us to take an entire day off or even a week to travel through Guatemala or Belize than to follow Mateo's trying work schedule. The times when we did work, though, it was always in Mateo's shadow (although not under his direct supervision). It was his vision and social network that animated the organization. We felt 'at home' in San Andres because Mateo had made this distant place *available* for their intervention. He had outfitted the community with schools, a public library and a conservation park as well as provided a source of income for families selected to host volunteers. This had earned him a reputation of trust and credibility, which we were invited to take advantage of. Left to our own devices (most of us did not speak Spanish), we would quickly lose momentum and direction. Mateo was the only one to actually work an eight-hour day every day. Plus, on the weekends he would screen movies and organize dance parties or live soccer transmissions at the cultural centre in town. In his time off, he took care of the paperwork, accounting and fundraising, wrote newsletters, updated the website, selected host families and maintained regular email contact with volunteers.

Not surprisingly, in our eyes Mateo was a hero, albeit an indecipherable one. He never bothered to share with us his vision of development for San Andres or even give us clear directions on our work projects, not to mention supervise our daily activities or monitor our whereabouts. His leadership style was decentralized to the point of inchoate. So we had no clear way of knowing either what his political beliefs were, or what our role in the organization was. But his hectic work schedule, tireless dedication, and almost obsessive enthusiasm for the wellbeing of San Andreseños were enough to vouch for his credibility. Volunteers were particularly impressed with the readiness with which he had traded in the comforts of American living for a modest, sometimes arduous existence in rural Guatemala. They considered this the utmost sign of selflessness and magnanimity.

One volunteer described Volunteer Peten as a 'dude operation', referring to Mateo's aloof demeanor as well as his inspiring presence. A paradoxical mixture but perhaps not such a surprising one when we think that many utopian communities were built under the charismatic yet nontransparent leadership of visionaries like Robert Owen.

For Mateo, however, there was nothing mysterious or curious about his way of life. He speaks of his decision to move to San Andres and his work there with the matter of factness of a man completely disenchanted with the goods industrial modernity has to offer:

> I can't imagine ever having a job and a pay check. I've done these kinds of jobs at home and they all just want to get through the day and get to the weekend. It seems ridiculous to work only for the time that you spend outside your work, for the weekends and evenings, hobbies and vacations. What a waste of time! I just can't function in that kind of an environment. This is my hobby. It doesn't feel like work to me. I can live here with very little to no money. Whereas at home I couldn't function. I used to get very

62 *Multicultural sensibilities in Guatemala*

depressed. If other volunteers don't want to put in the same effort as me, that doesn't affect me. Everyone's different. This is not a job and it is not for everybody.

Like an obsessively passionate Fitzcarraldo, Mateo is neither interested in making a profit off volunteer tourism nor in bringing the light of Western civilization to San Andres. What animates him rather is the ambition to create the conditions for greater self-sufficiency, ecological sustainability and perhaps even happiness in San Andres and also in his own life. For Mateo, then, relocating to San Andres was not a matter of renunciation or self-sacrifice. On the contrary, choosing a life of frugality and social development in rural Guatemala was a way of extricating himself from the arbitrary and conformist rule of modern society in the name of greater personal autonomy and self-governance. Interestingly, this is precisely what volunteer tourism is supposed to provide, at least for a brief period of time, in a prepackaged, predigested form. But just like Fitzcarraldo was derided by his countrymen and misunderstood by the Amazon natives for his perplexing motives and ambitions, Mateo's vision of utopia was considered by many to be admirable but too vague and lofty to ever generate concrete results. Mateo's lifestyle defied the rules and norms by which we usually organize work (discipline and authority), measure value (utility and profitability) and assign merit (expertise and prestige). Judged by these standards, Mateo's Sisyphean efforts seemed to go nowhere and benefit no one. While this incongruence says something about the limits of Western rationality, it is also indicative of the undemocratic organization structure and ineffective leadership style at Volunteer Peten. These problems would eventually cause volunteers to loose interest in their work projects and opt for more enjoyable but no less problematic relations with the local community.

Design destinations

With his loose organizational style and detached disposition Mateo had trouble sustaining the initial commitment and enthusiasm of volunteers for the entire duration of their two to three months stay. Without an effective organizational structure in place to explain the importance and merit of their efforts, volunteers quickly grew bored with their work. Also without a clear pedagogical message about the political function of aid and development work, volunteers had difficulty recognizing San Andres as a poverty-stricken place in need of foreign assistance.

'The park is not a real project', was the refrain, 'it's Mateo's baby'. Because the park already employed a full-time personnel, however small, the tasks we were assigned seemed trivial and pointless. While the staff were in charge of landscaping and larger construction, we were clearing weeds, planting trees and building trails – menial tasks that required little skill beyond patience and physical endurance. For instance, I spent an entire week carrying sacks of saw dust from one part of the park to another to build a couple hundred meters of park trail. One day I took Paula, a geography student from Poland, along with me. She had come to San Andres to work with another environmentally minded volunteering organization named the Eco-Escuela but found it to be a 'waste of time'. If at first she was thrilled about the idea of working in the park, especially when she got the chance to plant her first banana tree, as soon as we got to working on the trail she became angry with its slow progress and the primitive technology we were using.

The fact that the community showed very little interest in the project only made matters worse. During the time I was there no one came to enjoy the natural wonders we were so arduously recreating. No one even inquired about the progress of the park. 'What's the point of building trails nobody will walk on?' Alice once asked me, later on adding that she felt the reforestation project was just a way to attract funding from volunteers. Although she accepted that the park was necessary for VP to remain solvent (pay bills and salaries), she thought it was the organization's responsibility to give volunteers something meaningful to do, a purposeful existence, during their stay. 'We are paying a nice chunk of money while we're here and it would be nice to feel useful. It is no coincidence that as soon as the construction project [that had gone on during the summer] was done, everybody left'. Kirsten raised similar concerns: 'I have yet to find out what good the park is doing'. But although the park did not seem to cater to local needs, in theory, everyone agreed that conserving the natural resources of an area so violently stricken with deforestation was imperative. They just did not want to do it themselves.

Teaching English in schools was seen as equally futile. After years of attending Mateo's language classes, most students had not progressed beyond a few introductory phrases. The general conclusion was that 'Mateo could forget about it' because, as Kristen already noted during her first week, San Andreseños did not seem to place any 'cultural' value on education:

> I am disheartened at the schools, seeing that adolescents don't want to learn English. I had the presumption they wanted to learn English. I have been trying to teach [my host family] a few words in English and show them where Australia was on the map. But they couldn't care less. They don't even reward children's performance in school or reprimand the lack thereof. There is generally a gross indifference towards education, which I can't understand because I learn just for the fun. I came all this way just to learn about their culture.

Others, like Joanna, justified the futility of teaching English on more 'objective' grounds, like the fact that young people in San Andres did not seem to have any interest in ever leaving the community and, therefore, could not have any use for English:

> The people here have lived in these places for thousands of years and will continue to do so. It is amazing how rooted and traditional these people

64 *Multicultural sensibilities in Guatemala*

are. No one wants to move or immigrate. All they want is to get married and build a house. They don't want to learn English and explore the world.

In time, the flexible, almost chaotic organizational structure and lack of communication left volunteers confused and frustrated about the purpose of their work and the quality of volunteering programs in general. If there ever was a larger vision behind Volunteer Peten it seemed to be 'in Mateo's head', as Rebecca complained, and was rarely shared with volunteers. Kristen, who had an ample record of volunteering in her native Australia, found it surprising that, at Volunteer Peten,

> there is no obligation for time, energy or participation. There is not enough communication between Mateo and the volunteers. He has a vision, but we don't know what it is. I've just received the newsletter in my email the other day and I learned more about the organization than from the team leader. In the places that I've volunteered before, we used to get together at the start of the day or the week to discuss the direction, the goals of the organization.

Although she found Mateo to be an 'inspirational presence' she complained about the 'lack of creative energy between Mateo and the volunteers.'

> Volunteering is not as hard work as I expected. It's actually very easy and I often feel like I'm not giving enough. Also, the fact that we are not paid, that this is not an obligation, makes you ask yourself: are you happy with what you're doing? Or are you happy with giving only a little of your time? There's also the option of having no motivation, of doing nothing. You don't have to be continually moving. Maybe, we are culturally lazy. Maybe not lazy, but the volunteers I've been working with haven't got any experience with physical jobs.

Slacking was most difficult for newcomers, who were easily plagued by guilt whenever they did not complete the tasks Mateo had loosely entrusted them with. But they were quickly put at ease by more veteran volunteers, who normalized idleness with their stories of travel and after-work fun or by complaining about Mateo's poor organizational skills and pointing out the ineffectiveness of his various projects. Gradually, as the respectful awe the group initially shared for Mateo and his programs turned into comical curiosity, the charitable ambitions volunteers originally had for joining the trip gave way to frustrations – frustrations about having wasted their time and money for a cause they could not identify with or understand the purpose of.

While it may seem like overseas volunteering is just a covert form of leisure for the affluent, volunteers expect this experience to break out of the dull and conformist sea-sand-and-sex formula of mass tourism, and revolve around 'something bigger than just a couple of weeks of sitting on a beach'. Besides

Multicultural sensibilities in Guatemala   65

relaxation and travel, volunteers want to be placed in situations they have never experienced before, test their endurance limits, do something outside their normal comfort zone, and demolish the cultural barriers that separate them from others. Because they expend their labour power for free (and actually pay money to do so), volunteers want their work to break with the tedious, low-skill jobs they have to perform at home to put themselves through school and pay back student loans. The blurring of work and leisure time that comes with higher productivity requirements and precarious economic conditions does not bother volunteers as long as the work programs are deemed socially relevant and gratifying. On top of that, destinations should not be too familiar or too affluent, they should not be inundated with modern cultural and semiotic goods. On the other hand, the needs of local people should be evident and urgent.

Measured against these hopes, which are not surprising given the emphasis placed in the brochure discourse on 'making a difference' and 'having a unique experience', San Andres could be regarded as a 'failed' volunteer tourism destination. Volunteers found their work to be menial and pointless and San Andres not 'poor enough' to require foreign assistance. It would be unfair, however, to place the entire blame for this on Mateo. Volunteer destinations are carefully designed sites of intervention, the urgency and credibility of which depends on a host of other social, cultural and inter-subjective factors. As Mateo explains, attractive destinations 'cannot be found out there', but have to strike the right balance between, on the one hand, places that are destitute enough to convince volunteers about the usefulness and urgency of their work and, on the other, places that are safe and affluent enough to host, feed and entertain volunteers.

> Sure, there are places which are far worse than San Andres, where people live in extreme poverty, but you can't go there. What would you do there? Where would you stay? What would you eat? And can't do anything there, but go and stare at the poverty.

San Andres seemed to fare well on the second count, but less so on the first. Volunteers agreed that, compared to the neighboring communities of San Benito, La Libertad or Carmelita, not to mention Guatemala City, San Andres was 'pretty well-off'. All of the people in San Andres had three meals a day, a roof over their heads and a job that paid regular salaries. Some of the families even had indoor plumbing (thanks to revenues earned by hosting volunteers). And the crime rate was low. To quote Kristen:

> [A]lthough most volunteers think of San Andres as unsafe and destitute, because that's what most websites and guidebooks report about Guatemala, I learned that locals have more than they need. They have enough water and food for their children, common spirit, shelter, sun, some education, recreational facilities, a soccer field and basketball court. They even have TVs and electronic products, not that I rate poverty based on

66 *Multicultural sensibilities in Guatemala*

these, but I'm surprised. They are over the poverty line. There are no starving people in the streets; it's reasonably clean; not overpopulated; there is general well-being. Life doesn't seem to be a struggle, just very mundane. But people here seem happy with the mundane.

Although most San Andreseños had poor access to basic utilities, lacked recreational possibilities, retired late and had little social mobility (not to mention geographical mobility), volunteers considered these to be luxuries not necessary for a decent standard of living. Poverty is elsewhere, not in this 'urban centre in the midst of a rural world', Zack argued. 'If you want to see poverty, go to Carmelita or Santa Elena, where people really live in dirt'. While none of us could imagine spending the rest of our lives in San Andres, which is why we thought Mateo was being heroic for choosing to do precisely that, San Andreseños were considered fortunate enough to have their basic needs covered. This came as a surprise to me, not only because studies indicate that Peten is one of the most poverty-stricken regions of a country where, according to the World Bank, 51 per cent of the population lives beyond the poverty line, but also because, judging by the brochure discourse, I had assumed volunteers were motivated by feelings of care and compassion for the global poor. Instead, what I would discover is that volunteers' love for cultural difference and commitment to protecting cultural diversity from the homogenizing force of modernization far superseded their desire to 'make a difference' in the world.

'Of course [people in San Andres] are poor,' Mateo interjected.

There is no electricity, no water, women have to get up at four in the morning to grind maize, people have to make sacrifices to send their children to school. ... Here people make $4 a day. Does that mean they are not poor? You can have a house, electricity, water, food, basic things, but you can't have any purchasing power, you can't travel anywhere, you can't have a bank account, you can't save any money or plan for the future. In Guatemala 60 per cent of the people are poor. They just make it day by day.

Poverty in San Andres may not have assumed the disturbing form volunteers had grown accustomed to through *Save the Children* ads and other photogenic/pornographic displays of poverty, but this does not mean that the place is not steeped in material need and economic uncertainty. Poverty includes a variety of dimensions beyond food and shelter, from community participation, to use of modern technology, access to economic and social security provisions and opportunities for self-advancement and improvement (Chrisinger *et al.* 2009). The problem with most of these dimensions of poverty is that they are not visible to the naked eye. They must be conjured through aesthetic, often pornographic conventions of destituteness, disease and the dissolution of the normal order of things (Hutnyk 2004; Nyers 2005). In the same way that poverty is a social construct, our response to poverty is also a trained emotional style. Whether we feel compassion or disgust at the sight of a poorly fed, poorly clothed person, these are not spontaneous emotions but socially learned behaviours (Berlant 2004: 7). San Andreseños with their regular eating habits, literate children, cell phones and colour TVs with foreign cable could not solicit compassion, which is why volunteers often complained of feeling useless.

Had Mateo assumed a more proactive role in helping volunteers understand the multi-dimensional structure of need in San Andres and its relation to wider patterns of domination and exploitation, the programme would have had radically different results: a deeper understanding of local conditions, more politically anchored and socially relevant work, and more substantial work partnerships with the local community. Yet Mateo had a more naturalistic view of volunteering. His hope was that, simply by participating in the work projects and staying with local families, simply by experiencing life in San Andres first hand, volunteers would come to understand the intricacies of local everyday life: they would get to see what locals have to do to get by, cook meals, send their children to school and so on. But this learning-by-doing strategy produced meager results. Although Volunteer Peten allowed tourists to participate in a world they usually only get to see from a distance, from tour busses or the pages of *National Geographic*, it lacked the political pedagogy necessary to turn this purely observational encounter into a more substantial engagement.

Mateo did not see this as a missed opportunity. On the contrary, Mateo was intent on keeping Volunteer Peten a strictly grassroots organization 'separate from politics', and away from the highly professional and disconnected field of aid and development work. Talking about his days working in the development sector, Mateo recalls his dissatisfaction with the field's bureaucratic rigidities:

> You get [on the field] and they take you to a fancy downtown office, with a computer, where they make you feel important. On the first day there is a presentation, on the second day there's a seminar and on the third one – a conference. There are meet and greets, luncheons, occasional field trips in armored vehicles and workshops, but no contacts with the local community. Even if you want to, it's hard to get involved because most of the time is spent at the headquarters, rather than in the field.

There is some truth to this story. Different from the 1960s and 1970s, when a certain focus on self-restraint, sacrifice and frugality encouraged aid workers to form collabourative and informal relations with the local population, today's heightened security and litigation risks have produced a 'fortified aid compound'. Safety protocols, gated barracks, barbed wire and armored vehicles cut off aid workers from the communities they are supposed to serve (Duffield 2009). To counteract this, the 'grassroots' has emerged as a virtuous location, a pre-political, morally pure terrain, ideal for philanthropic intervention. The 'grassroots' is supposed to be a small and innocent locale that can allow for bottom-up democratic government without the oversight of centralized bureaucracies

68 *Multicultural sensibilities in Guatemala*

and out-of-touch leaders. It is meant to conjure a spontaneous and intimate community able to break with the alienating, conformist effects of state-sponsored mass utopias. Volunteer Peten fits nicely with this description. Its small size and affordable pricing make sure that volunteers are as close as possible to the 'root' of the problem, and that their encounter with suffering and destitution remains unspoiled by political scuffles, stuffy technocrats and ideological demagogies.

Underneath this virtuous localism, however, lies a larger suspicion of politics in the form of bureaucratic, centralized rule. This scepticism has gained notoriety on both sides of the ideological divide. It echoes the wider attack launched against the state from the Right as well as the fascination for networked and small-scale forms of organization discovered by the New Left. Although they are motivated by radically different understandings of freedom (the Right would like to free capital from all institutional barriers, while the Left would like to free our democratic impulses from the discipline of police and state power), both camps suggest that the ossified remnants of centralized government be replaced with more organic, communitarian forms of organization. The voluntary sector has happily jumped on this bandwagon. Growing increasingly impatient with government-sponsored aid, it has favoured more flexible and dynamic forms of 'corporate giving' and private donations from higher education institutions, religious organizations and wealthy benefactors (Hudson Institute 2010). The assumption here is that aid is better governed by market principles and privatized sensoriums than through politics, which in recent years has become shorthand for corruption, nepotism and sclerotic bureaucratism. But this position ignores the fact that a retreat from centralized political organization only clears the way for a neoliberal attack on social regulations and institutional protections. It also betrays a deep ignorance of what politics is and how it functions.

No matter how small or transparent an organization is, it can never be apolitical because politics, at its most basic, is the process of organizing life collectively. Not even the 'grassroots' is exempt from this. The grassroots is nothing more than development speak for what Nikolas Rose coined 'government through community' (2004). The smallest social unit is chosen as the appropriate scale of government for its supposedly pre-political character to conceal the real political machinations that have cut the local loose from government aid, and made it dependent upon private responsibility and philanthropy. Volunteer tourism might seem removed from politics in its emphasis on grassroots activism and disdain for hierarchy and technocracy, but by bringing local communities together with transnational actors to address issues of poverty and inequality it is a political activity through and through. To claim otherwise and hide the power relations at work in voluntourism behind the mantle of spontaneous benevolence deprives volunteers of any possibility to meaningfully insert themselves in the local community, causing them to feel disoriented and frustrated. Most importantly, perhaps, this retreat from politics demotes volunteer tourism from the transformative force it claims to be to a commodity tailored to the sophisticated tastes of post-Fordist consumers.

Consuming a 'small place'

Once volunteers had given up on their 'useless' work projects, they were free to fill their time with more pleasurable, leisurely pursuits: they learned to cook traditional dishes, played on the local basketball and soccer teams, shopped for souvenirs and learned local crafts. They immersed themselves in the local culture, grateful that it had retained some of the traditional structures of meaning the West had sacrificed on the altar of modernization. Almost without exception, all volunteers 'loved' San Andres for its tranquility, traditional values and natural beauty. Although the municipality of San Andres stretches over some 55 rural communities and numbers a population of 20,000 people (Mateo tells me the actual size is closer to 107 villages and 40,000 people), it could still entertain volunteers' fantasies of romantic localism and sentimental cravings for adventure and authenticity. If San Andres was not 'poor enough' to allow volunteers to demonstrate their compassion, at least it was slow, quaint and remote enough to let volunteers develop a cultural sensibility of the romantic sort. Set on the shores of the turquoise lake Peten Itza, surrounded by green pastures, Mayan ruins and occasional patches of jungle vegetation, San Andres seemed like a perfect candidate for what Jamaica Kincaid calls in her eponymous book a 'small place' (1988), a place *imagined* to lie outside the bounds of modernity, where tradition is still intact, culture still authentic and people still friendly.

Joanna describes San Andres as a 'small, traditional, peaceful and relaxing' place. Similarly, for Alice, life in San Andres is 'pleasant, beautiful and nice'. When she leaves she will miss everything 'except the food'. In the three months that she has spent there she 'fell in love with San Andres' and its 'cute' and 'adorable' inhabitants. But San Andres is not just a place to vacation in. Many volunteers also have come to consider it their home. Being able to 'live in the community', stay with a host family, learn about the local culture and maybe even *be* local for a while is a great source of consolation for volunteers frustrated with the unrewarding placements they signed up for. Kristen, who is on a round-the-world trip, explains that she has no interest in moving all the time: 'I would rather live with a family in an affordable place than switch hotels every night. I don't want to just be a spectator, traveling all the time. I want to live in a community'. San Andres has lived up to all her expectations:

> I feel like I live in the most beautiful place on earth. I can watch the lake from my house, swim, work in the jungle with plants and trees. I am surrounded by good people. It is not too Westernized although it's creeping in. People help one another. It's not so individualized yet. Just the natural surroundings. I am happy to be here and not somewhere else.

Mateo was not disappointed that volunteers seemed to be more interested in the romantic delights of this rural lifestyle than in doing volunteer work:

70 *Multicultural sensibilities in Guatemala*

It doesn't depress me if volunteers do not put all their efforts into the projects. I invite them to come along. But if they don't, it doesn't affect me, one way or the other. This is not a job and it is not for everybody. Some are more attracted to the small town than to the work. Everyone's different. Even people who come here just to relax and have a good time, make a big difference. Most people in the US and Canada never travel or make an effort to come to Guatemala or get out of Antigua, away from the tourist track. Coming here will change their way of looking at the world, forever.

During the early days of Volunteer Peten

volunteers used to live out in the park, ten at a time and just talk in English about their travels [and] their favourite beers. I said, that's it, you got to stay with a family, you have to interact with locals at least once a day. You can't just come here to make friends. We were in the middle of building a house [at the park] and I realized this is not what I want, this subculture.

Consequently, since 2005 volunteers have been staying with local families, which Mateo handpicks depending on their living conditions (for instance, cement floors are a must; indoor plumbing is not). This helped increase the pull of the organization because the final frontier, for most volunteers, is to live like the natives do: abandon all modern amenities (not internet and cell phones, but hot water, high-speed internet, modern transportation and Western cooking) and become an integral part of the local community. They want to 'see how locals live', eat home-cooked meals and find a home away from home.

But I was not convinced that Volunteer Peten's transition to home stays had engendered the intimate encounters and transformative experiences Mateo had hoped for. While closer contact with San Andreseños caused volunteers to 'fall in love' with the local culture and people, it also taught them that Guatemalans led content, self-sufficient lives threatened only by imminent modernization. Personally, I could not understand what exactly was so 'fascinating' or 'adorable' about the meager nutrition, poor sanitary conditions and the gargantuan ecological challenges we were surrounded by. In my journal I would often complain about the tedium of rural life: 'There is no movie theatre, no newspaper stand and no decent radio station. Only the incredibly slow internet café and the twenty-or-so books I brought with me make the time go by.' I could not understand the fascination my fellow volunteers shared for traditional forms of living or, to put it in broader terms, the reason why romantic idealizations of smallness and simplicity had become so pervasive in late modern culture. Did this romantic critique of modern industrial society contain any critical potential to be reckoned with or was it just a cultural narrative supposed to move ethically conscious products and help affluent consumers feel better about themselves?

Multicultural sensibilities in Guatemala   71

Volunteer tourism is by no means unique or exceptional in its romantic orientation, in its belief that modern values of individualism, materialism and rationality have emptied the world of its original meaning, abandoning us to the eternal wrath of anomie and alienation. This narrative of rupture and loss shapes the entire temporal self-constitution of modernity. We find it both in Weber's story of instrumental rationality, which supposedly empties the world of meaning just as it makes it knowable and calculable and in Marx's theory of alienation, where industrial modernity 'melts all that is solid into thin air' at the same time that it ushers in a more advanced stage of history. Over a century later this narrative is still with us. It informs our vision of the good life and contains our utopian horizon. The longing for a more innocent and authentic life, unspoiled by the ills of industrial modernity, is everywhere from cultural products to consumption patterns, aesthetic practices, urban design, public policies and artistic styles. It is conceived both in terms of time, as a return to a simpler past and mapped onto space, as an escape to more underdeveloped pastures. Unfortunately, however, this romantic nostalgia for 'simpler times' and 'smaller places' is yet to produce a substantial critique of modernity.

In his groundbreaking study on *The Romantic Ethic and the Spirit of Modern Consumerism* (1987), Colin Campbell shows that romantic values and dispositions have always, since their rise to prominence during the Industrial Revolution, been instrumental in refurbishing capital accumulation, specifically its consumerist spirit. It is not the case that romantic beliefs have been co-opted by consumer society, as critical theory à la the Frankfurt School suggests. The romantic cult of hedonism and aestheticism played a crucial role in launching the consumer culture needed to fuel industrial capitalism. Its critique of the mechanistic and materialistic West and its fascination for 'primitive' people, authentic culture and unspoiled nature, helped widen people's tastes for new and non-essential consumer goods and provided a steady influx of stimulating cultural products. Early romantics were not unaware of their function in modern capitalism and tried to extricate themselves from this unholy alliance by opposing commodity culture and materialism and insisting that pleasure seeking be used only as a 'means to moral and spiritual renewal':

> Far from endorsing consumerism, the first Romantics initiated that form of mass culture critique so characteristic of modern intellectuals, in which the unrestrained pursuit of profit and personal gain is seen as the primary factor which acts to prevent people from experiencing that spiritual enlightenment which is their birthright.
>
> (Campbell 1987: 207)

But this elitist attitude mixed with the romantic 'cult of the self' had the opposite effect. It created even more possibilities for individuals to consume imaginatively and use commodities to express their unique individuality and authentic selves. Whether through luxury goods imported from the colonies,

72 *Multicultural sensibilities in Guatemala*

collector items, ethical consumption, vintage and second-hand products, or other DIY schemes, the 'self-centred legacies of Romanticism have continued to renew the spirit of consumerism' for the past two hundred years (Boden and Williams 2002: 496).

The field of tourism brings this problem into sharp focus. Mass tourism began as a romantic quest for redemptive meaning. Thomas Cook, the pioneer of affordable tourism, for instance, wanted to ennoble his customers through spiritual pilgrimages packaged as consumer goods (Lisle 2010). This ambition continued throughout the twentieth century when, in response to the increasing automation and routinization of our work and residential practices, the holiday acquired mythical proportions. Vacations became time–space capsules where everything was permitted, where the virtue, order and temperance modern society demanded from us dissipated into excess, but also into useful pleasures and meaningful hedonism. But as tourism became increasingly more affordable and commercial in the post-war period, these mythical connotations would lose ground. Package tourists, the complaint goes, travelled in herd-like formation reminiscent of the standardized jobs and pre-fabricated houses they had at home, and often arrived too late at their destination to find any authenticity left. Amidst this wasteland of meaning alternative tourism rose to prominence in the 1980s and 1990s hoping to succeed where modern mass tourism had failed.

Alternative or responsible tourism is an umbrella term describing a variety of low-impact varieties of travel, such as eco-tourism, heritage tourism and volunteer tourism. Volunteer tourism is one of the most attractive options in this category. Mixing travel and work, hedonism and purpose, charity and self-growth, volunteer tourism seems well-poised to solve the pervasive problem of modern alienation and loss. At a time when the dissolution of wage labour and Fordist social bonds is depriving many people of a sense of social utility and civic purpose, volunteer tourism's emphasis on useful, charitable work helps young people assert their identity in a world of fragmenting meanings and semiotic confusion. Voluntary labour, especially for students precariously included in the labour market, becomes an apt substitute for types of sociality and citizenship that can no longer be obtained from traditional modes of production (Muehlebach 2010). On top of this, overseas volunteering also promises an unmediated encounter with pristine cultural objects modelled after romantic ideals of personal liberation and self-expression.

The temporary 'escape from mainstream modern capitalist society' (Pupavac 2010a: 92) being staged here for white middle-class people essentially takes Brian Latour's phrase 'we have never been modern' and replaces it with 'we are finished with being modern': we want to broaden our cultural horizons, authentically engage with local people, regain a long-lost proximity to nature and recover a space of moral simplicity. This is not to say that volunteer tourism is the polar opposite (different, better, nobler) of mass tourism. The moralization and purification of mass tourism does not automatically make it into a virtuous transnational relation. Despite critiquing modern industrial

Multicultural sensibilities in Guatemala 73

life and idealizing the traditional other, alternative tourism remains complicit both with capitalist consumer culture and Oriental fantasies of difference.

This complicity might become clearer if we consider the socio-political context in which volunteer tourism rose to prominence. Overseas volunteering is the most recent addition to a long lineage of Romantic ideas about non-Western peoples and cultures that can be traced back to the rise of nineteenth-century philanthropy and the British abolitionist movement (Rai 2002) reaching all the way to the popular revolts of the 1960s and 1970s when romantic aspirations made a comeback in various areas of social life (Boltanski and Chiapello 2005). In the development world, for instance, we see a shift in thinking from state-run welfare programmes over to 'romantic counter-cultural development myths' (Pupavac 2010b: 708) inspired by an 'inverse relation between material prosperity and the good life' (ibid.: 702). Disappointed with the meager results and Eurocentric bias of state-run pro-growth measures, in the 1970s the development sector started embracing a 'small is beautiful' approach that celebrated the simplicity, humility and even poverty of developing populations as a fragile cultural repository threatened by modernization. We find parallel developments in the aid world where the post-Washington Consensus of the 1990s replaces the draconian economism of structural adjustment plans with a more benign emphasis on good governance and human rights, as well as in foreign policy circles where the imperialist logic of the Cold War gives way to humanitarianism and the Responsibility to Protect. The examples could continue because after the 1960s' revolts we find everywhere a romantic discontent with the grinding banality of consumer culture and the stultifying effects of productivist capital practically everywhere. The solution, most clearly expressed in transnational practices like aid, development and tourism would be to embrace a simpler, smaller lifestyle modelled after cultures not yet touched by industrial modernity.

While it is true that post-development, good governance and humanitarianism bring much-needed corrections to earlier neocolonial relations with the Global South, they also function to depoliticize the push for material redistribution coming from developing nations at the exact same time that neoliberal austerity measures, the rush for fossil fuels and massive land grabs are making this goal increasingly elusive. There is something to the claim that industrial-based strategies of growth have run their course. Technology seems to have made the dream of a global proletariat redundant and the ecological limits of growth make it seem undesirable. But this does not mean that abundance, security and dignity are no longer universal goals worth pursuing. Faced with environmental destruction, widespread famine and state-sanctioned poverty, these values are more urgent than ever. Unfortunately, they cannot be accomplished simply through cultural preservation and environmental conservation. Romantic aspirations such as these are better suited at invigorating the spirit of consumerism with a new impetus for ethical consumption than at making substantial strides against the onslaught of industrial modernity.

74　*Multicultural sensibilities in Guatemala*

Volunteer tourism expresses what may be in fact a legitimate discontent with modernity, particularly regarding the global reach and homogenizing effects of its individualistic, materialist and mechanistic ethos. But, as we have seen in the case of Volunteer Peten, the formula lacks the tools needed to translate this dissatisfaction into meaningful action. Unable (or untrained) to recognize the material wants, economic insecurity and ecological destruction prevalent in Peten, volunteers chose to romanticize the pastoral Other because it allowed them to pursue their fantasies of magnanimity and worldliness undisturbed by ethical doubts. This caused them to ignore the 'boarder inequalities that characterize the world we live in' (Butcher 2003: 99) and become complicit with the consumerist spirit of capitalism. Concealing the material and historical relations governing life in the Global South reduces a place like San Andres to a hollow but quaint cultural product that functions as a 'supply point' of desire for Western tourists (Ahmed 2006: 115). Instead of precarity and discontentment, volunteers see only cultural riches, natural beauty, warmth and hospitality, resources the ordered and mechanistic West is claimed to have lost in the process of modernization and which volunteers are now in a position to recover by cultivating their sympathy, tolerance and recognition for local people and culture. Without a political pedagogy to meaningfully insert volunteers into the local landscape, the formula is reduced to a glossy commodity tailored to enlightened tastes and affluent pockets. It may be a more flexible and perhaps ethically conscious form of travel than resort tourism, but a capitalist consumer good determined by fickle fashions and tastes nonetheless (Pupavac 2010b: 695).

This is illustrative of the larger pseudo-political relevance the field of consumption has acquired in recent years. With production no longer a satisfactory medium for political contestation, consumption has come to occupy the place of work in post-Fordism, 'the cognitive and moral focus of life, the integrative bond of the society' (Bauman cited in Butcher 2003: 104). What binds us together is the global commodity market (what we buy in one country has repercussions the entire world over), not politics, transnational relations, community ties and the environment. These things either appear to be out of reach to the individual or they have been historically discredited. Since many of the traditional political channels and social bonds, like parties, churches and unions, have lost their clout, ethical consumption emerges also as the preferred mode of political action. We vote with our wallets because consumer politics has a clean record: 'it involves no allegiance to grand schemes, no association with apparently failed political projects' (ibid.: 106). It frees us from the stifling bonds of class and nationhood to indulge in the joys of personal self-experimentation *guilt-free*. The mark-up we pay for ethical products, be they Starbucks coffee or volunteer tourism, is our entry price to a better world or, in the case of volunteer tourism, to a more worldly subjectivity.

Ethical consumption practices, then, should be understood as an emblem of the seemingly post-ideological yet profoundly neoliberal age we find ourselves in, where retreat from politics is rampant (Fukuyama 1992). Faced with the failure of mass utopian projects, both on the liberal democratic and the socialist front, the exodus from politics today is greater than ever. The depoliticizing force of volunteer tourism is at its most visible here. No matter how rewarding or 'realistic' consumer politics may be, in reality the only ones standing to make a profit out of it are affluent consumers and their corporate patrons. Consumer politics can only ever be a highly unequal exchange because, after all, the market is the last thing we have in common.

The fate of volunteer tourism, however, does not need to be set in stone. Neoliberalism's ideological stronghold is always disputed on an uncertain battleground between power and resistance, activation and disciplining, incorporation and withdrawal. In theory, there is hope for moments of rupture in the normal sequence of events. For instance, volunteers' deep-rooted distaste for the individualizing and alienating consequences of capitalist modernity, and their boredom with the institutional strictures of volunteer tourism, could have counted as moments of this sort except that they took a romantic guise that precluded such rupture. Romanticism, this uneasy shadow of modernity, has always been intended as a 'reactionary discourse to the disenchantments of the external world through modernity' (Boden and Williams 2002: 496) and an attempt to re-enchant the world through the individual pursuit of meaning. But its impact continues to disappoint. Because the romantic critique addresses only the subjective, experiential effects of modernity divorced from their socio-economic foundation, it has difficulty moving beyond the level of aesthetic politics. Instead of pushing for more inclusive forms of participation and wealth redistribution, the romantic critique retreats into the past and the personal. This is true for nineteenth-century bohemians, hippie communes of the 1960s, cyber-utopias of the 1970s, all the way to contemporary lifestyle activists like volunteer tourists.

Multicultural sensibilities in Guatemala

Equipped with a romantic vision of pre-modern bliss, volunteers in San Andres quickly developed multicultural sensibilities that would allow them to finally overcome their boredom and frustrations, and feel at home in the world. They moved beyond simply enjoying life amidst what appeared to be a 'small place' that belonged to a 'simpler time' and began acting as the stewards of an endangered cultural habitat that needed protection from the onslaught of Western material goods and consumer tastes. The proximity between romantic dispositions and multicultural emotions suggests that a great deal of the ideological force behind the logic of multiculturalism derives from older romantic aspirations for authentic meaning and personal liberation. The idea that life on the frontier of modernity is better equipped at providing these goods compels us to protect minorities and celebrate cultural diversity as if they held the key to whatever it is the ordered and mechanistic West has lost. This is, of course, a profoundly Western narrative that essentializes and idealizes the non-liberal other solely for the benefit of the West. It is also a very old narrative that

76 *Multicultural sensibilities in Guatemala*

dates back to Judeo-Christian narratives of rupture from Eden, to liberal theories of the state of nature, and all the way to contemporary back-to-the-land lifestyle experiments.

Unfortunately, this was not my experience in the field. I had trouble sharing the enthusiasm of my fellow volunteers and could not see anything enchanting or worthwhile about preserving life on the poverty line. At the same time, Continental theory had taught me that linear notions of progress and development could not be the answer. So I remained stuck between my almost instinctual aversion to romanticism and my liberal arts education, with no prospect for ever inhabiting the mobile, magnanimous subjectivity other travellers seemed to find so much comfort in. There would be no personal growth and no self-discovery for me, beyond the discovery that I was perhaps too impatient and cynical a person to appreciate the small wonders of 'pre-modern' life and 'simple' people. Luckily, there is by now an abundance of critiques of multiculturalism to appease my angst.

Critical theory of the late twentieth century has spilled a lot of ink over the vagaries of staging an ethical encounter with difference, specifically over how to engage difference without reducing it to 'a projection of ourselves or of our ideals' (Todorov 1992: 168). For a short time, multiculturalism seemed to be the preferred answer, which is why around the 1980s it established itself as the dominant model for justice in liberal democracies and the limit of our utopian horizon (Brown 2006: 2). Its ambition was to de-centre the liberal (white, heterosexual, Judeo-Christian) subject as the standard of reference for what counts as normal, rational and virtuous and prepare the way for a more inclusive multicultural and multiracial democracy. Very quickly though post-structuralist and postcolonial scholars (Goldberg 1993, 1994; Chow 1993; Agathangelou *et al.* 2008) started pointing out that behind multiculturalism's insistence on tolerance and anti-discrimination lies the same sovereign subject as before. Not only does multiculturalism work with a limited, arguably incorrect understanding of what culture is (often reducing culture to essentialized terms and claims of authenticity), it also forces subaltern subjects to embrace liberal notions of individuality, morality and citizenship if they are to be tolerated (gay couples, for instance, have to embrace heteronormative values of matrimony to enjoy equal rights). For most of critical theory multiculturalism is an embarrassment because it remains 'so intimately bound up in many parts of the world with those practices and discourses which manage (often in the sense of police and control) "diversity"' (Gunew 2001: 85). In its current formulation, feminist and postcolonial scholars argue, multiculturalism is a liberal strategy of government to handle claims of identity and recognition without having to rethink their fundamental commitment to European Enlightenment values or unsettle the authority of the nation state as the exclusive guarantor of rights.

Marxist critics have taken this argument a step further (Zizek 1997, 1999, 2008a; Brown 2006; Michaels 2006, 2008; Fraser 2000; Fraser *et al.* 2008). They insist that the problem with multiculturalism is not necessarily its Eurocentric bias, but the skill with which it reduces the material and historical origins of difference to benign aesthetic categories ready for private consumption and lifestyle experimentation. The real trouble with multiculturalism, they argue, is not just the universalization of liberal subjectivity. To reduce the discussion to this cultural/ideological level suggests that, were multiculturalism to rid itself of its ethnocentric roots, it might very well serve as a model for cosmopolitan justice. According to Marxists this is illusory. What is universalized here is not just Eurocentric liberalism but capitalist rule in general, which thanks to multiculturalism can now function in conjunction with any cultural values (e.g., capitalism with Asian values) despite the persistence of material inequalities and historical injustices across the globe (Zizek 2008a). Multiculturalism, Marxists are clear on this, will never be a suitable launching pad for human emancipation and social justice, because its purpose is to contain and depoliticize the antagonisms that would allow a collective struggle of such scope to ever emerge.

The Left has not always been hostile to multiculturalism. The New Left, for instance, disenchanted with the authoritarian undertones of Stalinism and the reformist politics of Western social democratic regimes and their working class constituencies, turned to racial and gendered minorities at home and Third World liberation struggles abroad for revolutionary inspiration. They criticized the importance the Old Left had placed on class, as the master category of politics and subjectivity, and demanded that gender, race and sexuality be recognized as equally important, intersecting sources of domination and exploitation. Class, they argued, was no longer a foundational identity category, but 'one amongst a diversity of semiotically constructed identities', none of which can be granted precedence over the other (Dyer-Witheford 1999: 13). The New Left never called this multiculturalism. Theirs was a broader aspiration for revolutionary struggle across difference and from below. Over the next decades, however, multiculturalism would slowly emerge as an institutionally embedded and legally sanctioned response to this demand. Multiculturalism would be adapted to already-existing structures of power, and its radical dimension rapidly diluted into an insipid celebration of identity politics and cultural diversity, divorced from material conditions and reduced to food, fashion and festivals. It is only in its watered-down version that multiculturalism became one of the most forceful visions for global justice and democracy to date. Marxists have not been shy about expressing their profound scepticism with multiculturalism. They accuse it of staging a retreat from politics into the personal and the cultural, and even blame it for fragmenting and aestheticizing the Left, which indeed was quick to divide the spirit of multiculturalism into profitable yet reified fields of study: women's studies, queer studies, race studies, postcolonial studies, whiteness studies and so on.

Marxist critics raise three specific discontents with multiculturalism: (1) it obscures the material roots of cross-cultural and cross-racial antagonisms; (2) it reifies culture into an exotic victim of modernity that needs protection even at the cost of material dispossession; (3) and it bestows excessive value and

78 *Multicultural sensibilities in Guatemala*

social capital upon those individuals conversant in its emotional styles. As we shall see, each of these are surfaces in volunteer tourism.

The culturalization of politics

If 'real cultural differences always take on meaning within contexts of sharp social and economic inequality' (Ferguson 2006: 19), with multiculturalism 'political differences, differences conditioned by political inequality, economic exploitation and so on, are naturalized and neutralized into cultural differences' (Zizek 2008a: 660). Therefore, it was easier for volunteers in Guatemala 'to see culture rather than people' (Butcher 2003: 94). They loved the culture but could not see the impoverished conditions of the people.

The only way life in San Andres could be celebrated for its exotic properties was if volunteers treated the distinctiveness of the place as a given, beyond historical investigation and political questioning. For San Andres to live up to volunteers' dreams of tranquility, tradition and slowness, its geography, history, economy and politics had to be obfuscated. While it is true that San Andres is a village buried amidst Mayan ruins, jungle vegetation and the turquoise Peten Itza lake, where almost everyone knows everyone, family is the most important social institution and life follows a quiet rhythm punctuated by Sunday soccer matches, traditional celebrations and church services – this is not a complete picture. San Andres is also a place where plastic garbage is burned every day at 6pm to make fire, the illiteracy rate is one of the highest in Central America, the land tenure system determines entire family structures, the yearly food intake is made up of roughly six staples, sewage pipelines flow into the turquoise lake and the frustration of locals is manifested through mocking, cheating or seducing tourists. Western fantasies of loss and redemption glorify 'small places' like San Andres as repositories of traditional values and natural beauty, but they fail to mention that 'small places' are also suffocated by boredom, lack and political stagnation.

This romantic portrayal of San Andres is not only factually incomplete, it also strips the 'small place' of its political and material troubles. To think that the people of San Andres are static is to ignore Peten's recent population increase and the economic reasons for it. To think the San Andreseños are traditional people is to ignore how much of what volunteers celebrate as 'local knowledge' (medicinal plants, natural resources management, animal treatment) is in fact an improvised substitute for missing funds and more advanced tools. To think they are tranquil is to dismiss the 'muscular tension' (Fanon 1961), the prowess, anger, envy and sarcasm most locals share for *gringos*. Volunteers 'fell in love' with San Andres because they thought it contained all the virtues and qualities modernity has lost, namely, tradition, community, tranquillity, hospitality, honesty and natural beauty. The point is not that San Andres is none of the above, but that in reducing San Andres and its inhabitants to these romantic attributes, their distinctiveness becomes yet another consumer commodity for tourists to adorn themselves with. This is more than just a sign of benign ignorance or naiveté on the part of tourists. It is also a refined colonial stance, in which the inhumane treatment and violent exploitation of local populations is replaced with humanist reverence and enlightened relativism *vis-à-vis* local skin color, living conditions and ways of life. Albeit more benign, the latter stance is no less problematic. Edward Said (1979) has pointed out that Orientalism is not limited to denigrating the other as a barbarian counterpart to the civilized West, but can also idealize the subaltern to launch a self-critique of the West. While the second stance may seem more desirable, it does nothing to address the political injustices and material deprivations at the root of cultural and identity differences, only to promote a politics of recognition-without-redistribution that leaves the present structure of power intact.

The 'trouble with diversity', Walter Benn Michaels (2006) explains in his eponymous book, is that it has helped take the poor, this troublesome reminder of the historic failure of liberal capitalism, out of the equation and replace them with a smorgasbord of self-contained identities and cultures. The masses have always been viewed with suspicion for their antagonistic proclivities but they have learned to use this stigma to their advantage, playing on elite fears of revolt to achieve substantive gains in rights and wealth. Today multiculturalism stands in the way of any such common struggle. It divides the mass of working-class people into innocuous cultural and identity categories. These are made tolerable through aesthetic consumption practices and privatized emotions and rendered docile through policy 'solutions' like affirmative action, gender mainstreaming, awareness and recognition. The culturalization of politics we find at the basis of multiculturalism shatters the original antagonism between capital and labour into a million little *cultural* antagonisms that divide labour along racial, gendered and cultural lines.

The reification of culture

A second problem with multiculturalism deals with its tendency to reify culture and identity as natural containers of meaning and, in so doing, act as capitalism's preferred 'style of rule' (Rai 2002). All too often multiculturalism hollows out culture of its social, collective dimension to treat it as a static, bounded thing of the past, always on the verge of disappearance and in need of protection.

Fascinated with the timeless qualities of local culture and people, volunteers began acting as gatekeepers of modernity, trying to protect this uncorrupted paradise from external influences. Zack, for instance, was afraid that, as more people moved to San Andres, 'which no one knows where they come from or what their business is, they risk destroying what is beautiful about San Andres'. What is beautiful about San Andres, according to Zack, 'is the sincerity that results from a small town world, from not having a life of incredible excess'. Whereas in the United States, where he is from, people are afflicted by stress, overwork and an excessively materialistic culture, life in San Andres

80 *Multicultural sensibilities in Guatemala*

is simpler, slower and more anchored in community values. But 'things were changing,' as Zack noted. 'There are tons of people who come from the outside and soon San Andres will become an urban centre like Santa Elena'. The least volunteers could do to preserve the 'not-too-Westernized' charm of San Andres was to avoid the so-called 'demonstration effect' (Butcher 2003: 104). They could make sure locals were not exposed to Western consumer goods and tastes that could open especially young people's appetite for urban life or foreign lands and stir inter-generational conflict. There were also environmental reasons for this. The concern was that as more commodities entered San Andres, the lake and its surroundings would become increasingly polluted because, to put it in Rebecca's terms, these 'young consumers' had not yet learned the basics of environmental protection. Having fixed culture in a romantic past, having actually mistaken culture to be a synonym for the past, every instance of change or progress posed a threat to the integrity of this unspoiled gem. And since locals could not be trusted to possess the creative subjectivity needed to adapt their culture to new material conditions, social change had to be avoided at all cost.

The accusation Johannes Fabian (1983) launched against fellow anthropologists for fixing 'primitive' cultures in the past, denying them a coeval, contemporary place in history also applies to volunteer tourism. Underlying anthropological forms of knowledge and representation is a problematic 'chronopolitics' that portrays the other as both backward in time and timeless: '[t]he Other is both a prisoner of time (frozen in a certain stage of history) and an escapee (outside the time grid, timeless, outside history)' (Anand 2007: 31). While, historically, the exclusion of non-European peoples from the present has been used to justify foreign intervention and colonial rule, today a more popular usage of chronopolitics is to celebrate the backward, timeless other as a source of wisdom. This 'gerontification' of the other sets up places like San Andres as appropriate sources of spiritual regeneration for bored and alienated Western consumers (Anand 2007: 31). Acting as amateur anthropologists eager to learn about the local culture and minimize their impact upon the host society (Butcher 2003: 86), volunteers were able to ignore the coevalness (contemporary presence) of San Andreseños and charge themselves with the responsibility to actively prevent it. The violence of multicultural appreciation, then, does not lie in Westerners trying to impose modernist principles of progress and development on local populations through thinly veiled imperialist schemes, but in masking the material injustice that makes 'tradition' so appealing to the Western eye.

There is a gross double standard at work here. While white middle-class individuals may possess the necessary means to demonstrate their allegiance to anti-modernist values and dispositions through sophisticated consumer tastes, a great majority of the world's population has no desire to resist the material and semiotic richness identified with the West. Many of the working poor living in the Global South, but also in the inner cities, deindustrialized towns and rural hinterland of advanced capitalist nations continue to aspire to the status

Multicultural sensibilities in Guatemala 81

markers new elites can afford to dismiss as naive or tasteless. Speaking of Africa, James Ferguson argues that 'most Africans can hardly feel that they are being forced to take on the goods and forms of a homogenizing global culture when those goods and forms are, in fact, largely unavailable to them' (2006: 21). If anything, globalization has made Africans more aware of the material and cultural gap separating them from the West, encouraging them to devise ingenious ways of mimicking the goods and manners Westerners like to deplore as materialist evils. Similarly, in reference to the 'Orient', Nevzat Soguk (1993) claims that there are more people who wish to adopt Western modes of dress, speech, education, professional conduct and government than those trying to 'provincialize Europe' (Chakrabarty 2000). The poor-but-resistant subject, which postcolonial theory is so eager to celebrate and volunteers are eager to preserve, is a romantic fantasy conjured by academia and popular culture. It is the new noble savage divorced from the material realities as well as the subjective fantasies of most people across the developing world (Soguk 1993: 368–69). This is not to say that easier access to consumer goods is the road to emancipation. Certainly the frustration working-class people feel when they recognize the corruption and hypocrisy of elite looters could be better used for demanding a more equitable distribution of wealth than for raiding electronics and sporting goods stores. But it is hard to imagine how this indignation might be given political expression when the claims of the poor are being systematically dismissed in the name of preserving the 'legality' of the present order or the authenticity of 'poor-but-happy' lifestyles.

Confronted with the constant danger of racist, xenophobic and fundamentalist acts of exclusion and terror, multiculturalism might seem like the closest thing we have to a vision of cosmopolitan justice. And there is certainly something to be said about the ideals of tolerance and recognition having helped marginalized individuals and groups organize substantial claims around employment, equal rights and political inclusion. But we should also keep in mind the fact multiculturalism is a modern solution to a problem capital itself has created a long time ago. In her seminal book on the transition from feudalism to capitalism, Sylvia Federici explains that the enclosure of common land in the sixteenth and seventeenth century 'was not simply an accumulation of land and concentration of exploitable workers and capital. It was also an *accumulation of differences and divisions* within the working class, whereby hierarchies built upon gender, as well as "race" and age, became constitutive of class rule and the formation of the modern proletariat' (Federici 2004: 63–64, original emphasis). To remove women from peasant relations of mutual help and self-reliance, female bodies had to be subjected to the rule of celibacy, domesticity and morality and enslaved to procreation and unpaid social reproduction. Similarly, racialized bodies had to be constructed as inferior to justify the continued exploitation of free labour and resources from the colonies for cheap domestic consumption. Capitalism then emerged as an ordering process that cut through the communal associations of self-help and self-sufficiency of the feudal age to produce cultural, racial and religious differences adequate

82 *Multicultural sensibilities in Guatemala*

for the extraction of surplus value (Walker 2011). But if these tensions and hierarchies were productive for merchant or industrial capitalism, in an age of global accumulation they have to be resolved or at least reconfigured to allow for the unfettered mobility of capital and labour across borders.

This shows that although socially constructed, difference remains firmly anchored in material reality. Even if race, gender and sexuality are the cumulative result of cultural representations, bodily performances and ritualized habits, as continental theorists from Foucault (1976) to Judith Butler (1990) have shown, divisions and hierarchies within the labouring masses bear concrete political implications for the freedom and opportunities of every individual. They assign people their 'proper' place within the capitalist social structure. As Sara Ahmed aptly observed, the question is not so much what a body is, but what a body can do: how it can move into space, what kinds of rights and privileges it can enjoy, what modes of being and action are open to it and which remain closed off (2006: 130). Therefore, we need to be weary of attitudes and sentiments that treat culture as the sum of distinct worldviews, beliefs and customs yet ignore the power relations that organize cultures in conjunction with gender, race, sexuality and religiosity. Multiculturalism does precisely this. It erases the distance (the historical tension) between individuals, and reduces all sources of tension (racial, gendered, sexual) to harmless subcategories of a worldwide cultural smorgasboard. When this relational space is gone, politics is erased as well. Difference becomes yet another commodity for bourgeois consumers to adorn themselves with.

Multiculturalism as social capital

Without an appeal to material redistribution and social justice, volunteer tourism can benefit only Western consumers who can afford to engage in 'responsible' tourism to bolster their social capital and demonstrate their cosmopolitan sensibilities (Butcher 2007). What exactly these benefits entail and how they manifest themselves remains somewhat mysterious, in the sense that they defy the Fordist notions of value and utility we have grown used to for organizing our education, careers and social institutions.

Paula was appropriately baffled by the inexplicable professional value of volunteer tourism. Volunteering is far more valuable than other jobs available to students, even though the work requires neither skill nor results, only discretionary funds:

> It is unfair that, at a job interview, it matters more if you have volunteered in [the Global South] than if you have been serving tables at a restaurant at home. Waitressing is much harder and it shows you need the money. Volunteering only shows your parents are rich.

Originally from Poland, Paula had invested all her savings in pursuing a geography degree in Britain and then some to volunteer in Guatemala for

Multicultural sensibilities in Guatemala 83

extracurricular credit. Like me, she failed to share in the multicultural enthusiasm of the rest of our group (something which had her stand out as 'intense') and felt like a perpetually maladapted outsider. She could see neither the professional opportunities not the personal riches volunteering in San Andres promised. All she could see was a desolate place she felt unable to do anything about.

The merits of volunteer tourism are both diffuse and durable. While overseas volunteering does not always result in future professional and material returns, I maintain that the affective competencies volunteers develop abroad effect a long-lasting transformation in political subjectivity. If we understand subjectivity to be the sum of experiences and practices through which individuals become aware of themselves and their possibilities for action in the world, volunteer tourism certainly makes a difference in how these young adults understand their potentials and opportunities. As amateur anthropologists ready to go native, volunteers show themselves capable to assume a flexible subjectivity that can live fully in the global moment, bypassing the difficulties and constraints that govern the lives of racialized and impoverished bodies (Ahmed 2006). Whereas San Andreseños are more or less 'fixed' by their income, race and citizenship status, volunteers are free to move at their heart's desire (and are baffled when local people do not share their interest in foreign cultures and languages). Their Western passports, disposable income and white complexion allow them not just the freedom to travel someplace else, they also posses the flexibility to *be* someone else for a while (Ahmed 2006). Volunteerism has the advantage of producing a *kulturlos* subject, a subject that can be at home in any culture, unencumbered by sovereign or cultural boundaries, a universal capitalist subject that can transcend and even be critical of his Western heritage (Zizek 2008a).

This hierarchical subjectivization mirrors the logic of multiculturalism, which is predicated upon an unequal gaze. There is an inevitable epistemological and ethical distance between the observer and the observed, between the liberal cosmopolitan subject able to travel the world, appreciate other cultures, and enjoy unspoiled natural vistas and the authentic (read static), traditional (read ignorant) other the former needs to assert his superiority (Zizek 1999: 216). As a result, multiculturalism cannot be practiced from the margins. Those who stand to benefit the most from its sympathetic gaze are usually the benefactors. They get to occupy a deterritorialized position, 'the empty point of universality', as Zizek (1999: 216) calls it, from which to survey, inventory and respect other cultures. This is not just a problem with multiculturalism, but also the historic function of romantic emotional styles, the historic purpose of which has been to distinguish their possessors from less sophisticated consumers and less virtuous citizens.

To establish itself as a class with rights and powers of its own, the bourgeoisie had to distance itself both from the aristocracy and lower rank people. In the nineteenth century, for instance, the British middle classes used philanthropy towards the poor and the colonized to carve out a stable place for themselves in modern society, with conducts, tastes and emotions different

84 *Multicultural sensibilities in Guatemala*

from those of the noblesse. They found that fighting for the end of slavery in the colonies helped their cause, whereas acting in solidarity with the domestic working classes did not, which is why they shied away from extending their magnanimity at home (Rai 2002: 18–20). Similarly, today's middle class engages in transnational charitable acts, like volunteer tourism, to demonstrate they possess the competencies and dispositions needed to enter the ranks of the new cognitively adept and globally mobile workforce.

The hope behind volunteer tourism is that gains in political subjectivity will translate into more tangible material benefits in the form of career advancement, ethical consumption and material wealth (Illouz 2007: 66–67). After all, in an age of global accumulation, where the workforce is ethnically and racially diverse, multiculturalism is good for business. Culturally adept workers are deemed to be more mobile, productive and ahead of the creative curve. In choosing a place that is seemingly so far off the map of modernity, volunteers adorn themselves with the moral virtues and cultural competencies (versatility, open-mindedness, tolerance, creativity) expected from a globally mobile workforce. As discussed, however, the price for this is social justice. If cultural diversity has become integral to the mission statement of any respectable corporation and a core pillar of business school curricula, it is because multiculturalism has turned out to be a great management tool for taming antagonisms of a more material nature. Anti-discrimination and affirmative action legislation help resolve labour shortages, smoothen worker disputes, tackle the population crisis in Western countries, resolve issues of integration and ease the pressure exerted upon welfare structures. Poverty, however, is the only problem that cannot be resolved with politically benign promises of cultural recognition and respect. Including the dimension of poverty would imply rethinking the entire current mode of economic organization (Michaels 2006).

Conclusion

The above narrative follows a certain chronological progression. It begins with volunteer tourists' hope to recover some sense of personal meaning through socially relevant work and out-of-the-ordinary cultural experiences. Disappointed with the ineffectuality of their volunteering programmes and discouraged by the backbreaking nature of their work, however, volunteers in San Andres turned their backs to charity and aid work for more leisurely pursuits. The multicultural appreciation they developed in the process allowed them to believe that the cultural and natural riches San Andreseños had at their disposal made up for whatever material wants the local population might have. This false dichotomy between authentic meaning and material progress, where the former is under constant attack from the latter, derives from an older romantic critique of modernity, which has seeped into the logic of multiculturalism, but also in aid and development circles, foreign policy, academic knowledge and popular culture to conceal the political nature of the contradictions capitalist modernity throws in our face.

Multicultural sensibilities in Guatemala 85

While it is true that capitalism has hollowed the world of meaning and people of their dignity, we cannot reject progress and development out of hand, particularly not when the economic and ecological crises we face today make social change imperative. We might be disappointed with direct political solutions (socialist programmes, mass utopias, the welfare state, armed struggles). We might also recognize the fallen potential of 'counter-cultural' movements. But that does not mean that we can withdraw from politics, defined as the collective negotiation of social life, into the cultural, the personal or the past. Such retro-utopia would be devastating (Buden 2011). It would mean abandoning citizenship and political life as 'domain[s] in which conflict can be productively articulated and addressed' (Brown cited in Zizek 2008a: 660) for tolerance, philanthropy and other such 'postpolitical ersatz' (ibid.). Romantic retro-utopia dilutes the deliberative disposition that could build transformative coalitions across distinct modes of being, and it undermines the possibility for social solidarity and collective action that transcend difference.

If capitalism functions on a *kulturlos*, universal basis, then resistance must also cultivate a universal form based on common experiences of dispossession and suffering. 'Every historical epoch [needs] to find its own specific way to accomplish the breakthrough to universality' (Zizek 2008a: 674). Ours should begin by turning the tables on multiculturalism and politicizing culture: instead of tolerating or celebrating our differences, we must identify some common struggle to help us overcome the plethora of cultural antagonisms dividing us now. We must overcome the postpolitics ushered in by multiculturalism (but also consumerism, possessive individualism and violent forms of community and attachment) to identify universal political demands to be addressed in solidarity. To do otherwise would be to remain complicit with the status quo: to deny the importance of material redistribution for the sake of some reified notion of cultural diversity is irresponsible, while to reject the creative agency of people to adapt their cultural and natural repositories to changing social needs is patronizing. Just because modern society, as it was conceived by industrial capital, has exhausted its capacity for meaning, does not mean that we have no more use for sociality: there is still room (and need) for altruism and love. However, if these are not rooted in collective experiences, but in individual possibilities to stage one's existence with an eye to profit maximization it is difficult to imagine how this might produce something other than more of the same (Buden 2011).

4 Entrepreneurial education in Ghana

It is a misnomer to refer to volunteer tourism as 'taking time off' from other, more pressing responsibilities that might await one at home. What motivates young people to travel halfway around the world, expose themselves to radically foreign and often painfully confusing cultural environments and bear the high cost of volunteering programmes is the hope that they will gather professional experience or, at least, have the opportunity to experiment with various professional identities and ways of life. Once 'in the field', however, volunteers are often *forced* to take a vacation (travel, read, hang out in expat bars) because they lack the necessary skills or institutional framework to perform a meaningful social function abroad. In principle, volunteer tourism is not supposed to be about middle-class youths escaping the pressures and responsibilities of modern life. On the contrary, it is about getting as much done as possible, expanding your human capital, gathering professional assets, acquiring new knowledge, even while on *vacation*. It is a reflection of the neoliberal injunction to organize all temporalities of life according to calculations of future gain. Sara, a first-year political science student from Australia who 'took a year off' school to travel, explains:

> I didn't want it to be just one year of traveling. If you're going to take so much time off, then you should get something out of it, something tangible, something that's not so selfish, something emotionally and morally rewarding. And on an entirely superficial but legitimate note, it looks great on my CV because I want to go into international relations, maybe work for an NGO. And I know this is a far cry, but anything helps.

Seeing volunteer tourism as another form of 'continuing education' or 'lifelong learning' is not the same as saying that volunteers are self-interested individuals who perform charitable acts only to boost their résumés. This chapter plans to unpack this behaviourist assumption to address the more complex socio-economic conditions and governmental rationalities responsible for valorizing overseas volunteering. The exigencies of neoliberal capital, I argue, force individuals to treat all of social existence, even leisure time, as work or an investment in one's future ability to work. This is especially true for students and graduates whose only insurance policy against cheap and contingent labour is an 'entrepreneurial education' that goes beyond professional expertise, academic credentials and the classroom experience. Paying $2,500/month to volunteer in Ghana may seem absurd or overpriced, but it is a small price to pay for an educational experience that could help students transition from the reserve army of labour to the professional middle class and beyond. In a flexible and highly competitive economic climate, like the one we currently find ourselves in, the 'gap year' is no longer an obscure form of travel reserved for 'hippies' and hedonists but an institutionally accepted and commercially successful asset (Simpson 2005: 448).

The promise of volunteer tourism is to produce a 'professional, self-governing, careerist persona' (Simpson 2005: 447). Whether a certain programme actually manages to 'make a difference' or endow students with much-desired work experience is secondary. What matters is that, by having lived for a few months in a radically different cultural setting, without local language skills, modern amenities or the comfort of loved ones, students and graduates develop sought-after cognitive and communicative skills. This rite of passage helps young adults embody the responsible, resourceful and self-enterprising subject needed to navigate the contingencies of neoliberal capital. Even if volunteering has few charitable contributions and little concrete professional value, from a governmental perspective, the formula remains an effective strategy for teaching young adults how to operate in multicultural settings and globalized sites to better consolidate their entrepreneurial future. The reason why this contradiction can be ignored is because the merits of overseas volunteering are mainly assessed *at home*, in the imagination of friends, family, guidance councilors, admission officers and employers, most of which associate volunteer tourism with heroism and self-sacrifice and Africa with danger and chaos. Other than in modern mass tourism, where the dangerous and mysterious non-West serves as a playground for bourgeois fantasies, in volunteer tourism the adventurous and destitute Global South becomes a classroom where young adults learn how to 'mediate between diverse traditions and communities on a global scale' (Ong 2006: 141). By volunteering abroad young adults can literally earn a 'world-class' degree that will set them apart from others in the race and leave those at home in awe.

The argument proceeds in five parts. I begin by describing Projects Abroad, the organization I travelled with to Ghana and the town of Ho, where I lived for two months. I then lay out the theoretical framework of the chapter, arguing that volunteer tourism is an educational strategy designed to enhance the employability and economic vitality of young adults in an increasingly competitive and precarious economic climate. In the third section I return to the ethnographic field to review volunteers' various sources of dissatisfaction with their work programmes. Although, just like in Guatemala, volunteering in Ghana did not cultivate any concrete professional skills, the experience was still ripe with opportunities for self-growth. The fourth section discusses these opportunities, in particular the racial tensions between volunteers and their

88 *Entrepreneurial education in Ghana*

hosts. The Ghanaian habit of making white bodies visible and cognizant of their privilege and particularity caused volunteers a great deal of anger and anxiety, but ultimately proved to be an important vehicle for learning all sorts of cultural and interpersonal competencies required in a multicultural society and multinational economy. As the final section shows, there is no better place for acquiring these skills than Africa, a continent that the West imagines to be the flipside of modernity yet still bears strange similarities with the contingency, chaos and cultural diversity characteristic of global capital.

Projects Abroad, Ghana

After having volunteered in Guatemala with a small and relatively affordable grassroots organization, I wanted, for my second field trip, to join an organization from the other end of the spectrum. I was curious to know whether a more reputable and costly programme (approx. $2,500/month excluding flights) would attract a different demographic and present new encounters of mobility. I chose Projects Abroad, a full-blown 'charity factory' headquartered in the UK, but counting 162 staff members, 166 volunteering projects spread over 20 countries (Projects Abroad 2008a: 47). The first thing that struck me about Projects Abroad, even before I arrived in Ghana, was its professionalism. Different from Volunteer Peten, which was an ad-hoc aid organization run by kind-hearted amateurs, everything about Projects Abroad, from our email correspondence to my arrival in Ghana and all the way to the satisfaction survey at the end of my trip, corresponded to the highest standards in customer service. Compared to my experience with Volunteer Peten, where email contact was sporadic and onsite supervision virtually nonexistent, at Projects Abroad I was made to feel like a valued customer at all times. Both the UK and the Toronto office I was in contact with were diligent in helping me sign up for the trip, sending me information brochures about Ghana and my future host family and assisting me with visa applications and vaccinations. This culture of chaperoning only continued with greater zeal upon my arrival in Ghana.

At the airport in Accra I was welcomed by Charles, our regional coordinator. He drove me to the Projects Abroad 'compound', where new arrivals could spend the night before they dispersed to their placements all over the country. The next morning Charles and I fetched a tro-tro (minibus) ride to Ho, three hours east of Accra. He introduced me to my host family and gave me a tour of the town's main landmarks, including the internet café, the grocery store and the local hangout spot. The following day he accompanied me to the school I was going to volunteer at, introducing me to the staff and making sure I felt comfortable in my new role. For three days, Charles was my personal guide to Ghana. He provides this service for every volunteer, which during the summer can be as many as 20 new arrivals per month, *without pay.* As a recent political science graduate from the University of Accra, Charles is required by law to do one year of unpaid civic service. But he also does not receive health insurance from Projects Abroad, despite having repeatedly

Entrepreneurial education in Ghana 89

asked for it given how frequently he has to travel to Accra under quite perilous traffic conditions.

Preserving this culture of service excellence takes up so many of Projects Abroad's resources, that there is little left for volunteering projects and local staff. Beyond the introductory tour, there are weekly meet-and-greets, monthly parties, farewell get-togethers, an exit survey and a complimentary tee-shirt at the end. On site, Charles is available around the clock to help volunteers obtain a cell phone, do their banking, organize weekend trips, handle food allergies and attend to their medical issues. His job is not to coordinate or supervise our work (although this did occasionally happen), but attend to volunteers' leisurely, culinary and emotional needs. For larger questions and concerns, regarding work placements for instance, volunteers can get in touch with the expat staff working in the Accra office. This attention might seem exaggerated but it helps explain the organization's record-high enrolment rates. With its corporate service and trustworthy appearance Projects Abroad does an excellent job in appeasing the anxieties surrounding travel to Africa. Both travellers and their parents can rest assured that, in exchange for a hefty price, volunteers will enjoy a safe and useful experience.

In exchange for these services, volunteers were asked to respect certain rules of conduct to preserve the local authority and credibility of the organization. The *Ghana Handbook*, which we were given upon arrival, discourages drunkenness, absenteeism, serious rowdiness and flirting (Projects Abroad 2008a: 42). Any of these can result in disciplinary behaviour, including the risk of being sent home. A 'good' volunteer is expected to '[b]ring the energy and enthusiasm that sustains this ongoing volunteer movement. You may be there for a relatively short time, but your efforts and skills are part of a wider, ongoing network that ensures the projects' success' (ibid.: 45). If overwhelmed with unfamiliar customs, languages, sights and smells, volunteers are encouraged to throw themselves headfirst into 'culture shock'. On the other hand, they are warned to wear proper attire and refrain from smoking if they want to be taken seriously in local society. But these sacrifices are well worth it because 'you have the unique chance of living and working entirely immersed within a very different culture, an experience that you will carry with you always and one which brings us one step closer to a worldwide community of true multi-cultural understanding' (ibid.: 45). Strangely enough, *The Handbook* contains no information about the kind of work Projects Abroad does in Ghana. The brochure has nothing to say about the projects run by the organization or the general impact and value volunteering has on the local community. The company website, where Ghana is described as a vibrant, colourful and exciting 'introduction to Africa' (Projects Abroad 2008b) offers equally little information. It remains a mystery what exactly is so problematic about the country that requires the urgent intervention of white vacationing youths.

Ghana is the most popular destination of Projects Abroad. It accounts for 40 per cent of its revenues. Each of the organization's five sites – Accra, Akuapem Hills, Cape Coast, Kumasi and Ho – receives five to 15 volunteers

90 *Entrepreneurial education in Ghana*

a month. But the enrolment figures can swell up to 25 volunteers per month during the high season in June–August. The reasons for Ghana's popularity are manifold. The country accommodates all types of placements, from teaching to healthcare, construction, sports, journalism and law. The only programs not represented are archaeology and conservation, which is ironic given that Ghana is home to one of the most aggressive forestry industries. Also, Ghana represents the best of both worlds: it is exotic enough to count as part of 'black' or 'real' Africa and, at the same time, white enough to still act as a 'safe learning environment' for volunteers eager to gather work- and school-related experience. Like most other Projects Abroad destinations (Ethiopia, Tanzania, South Africa, Cambodia, Nepal, Sri Lanka, Costa Rica, Peru and Bolivia), Ghana strikes a perfect balance between economic need and political security. Although it has a low GDP, a relatively high illiteracy rate and a preponderantly agricultural economy, it can boast a stable democracy and safe travel conditions. Certainly, we can think of countries with even higher poverty levels and more rampant mortality rates than Ghana, countries where humanitarian aid is more urgently needed. But places such as these are either politically unstable, like Sierra Leone, or closed off to foreigners, like Burma, or both.

I chose Ho, a mid-sized town of approximately 60,000 people in the South-Eastern Volta region, on the border with Togo, because of its high enrollment rate. Ho also numbers an impressive number of NGOs, charities and grassroots third-sector initiatives that attract an ever-rotating population of volunteers, missionaries, exchange students and artists. The networks and trajectories of these itinerant figures create a maze that is almost impossible to keep track of. Generally, the main pub, ironically enough called the White House, was a good tracking device for the new, the old and the passing through. Most visitors stay for at least three months (to justify the exorbitant plane ticket), teaching elementary school, helping out in the health sector, coaching soccer, building infrastructure, or working in orphanages. Others stay for a year to attend school or run medical programs. Still others remain for an indeterminate period of time managing Christian missions, working in agriculture, or helping out with arts and crafts.

Although I zig-zagged across the country several times, hanging out with other volunteers, expats, missionaries and the local comprador elite, sometimes running into the same people in different towns and resorts, I did not meet a single tourist during my stay in Ghana. The independent backpacker, hopping from one hostel to another in search for the next expat whiskey bar, is a trope from a different continent. If Central America has the 'gringo trail' and Southeast Asia the 'banana-pancake trail', Ghana has more ambiguous forms of travel. I did meet the occasional roughneck who toured the world in a safari jeep or on a dirt bike, but everyone else had a secondary motive for being in Africa: they worked, volunteered or did research. Depending on the length of their stay and the type of the work they did, everyone eventually worked out a unique compromise between stillness and movement, boredom and productivity, work and leisure, holiday and residential experiences. For us, Projects

Abroad volunteers, time in Ho was divided in two: we would work in the local hospitals, schools or daycare centres during the week and travel on the weekends. Without anyone to supervise our work, initiate group projects, or assess our progress, the longer we stayed in Ho, the more we travelled and the less we volunteered. Ho was what we considered home ('home sweet Ho' was our refrain), it was where our host families lived, where we had our local bars and food joints and where we knew street vendors by name. But it was also the place where a Sunday afternoon could turn into a suffocating nightmare. When this happened travelling became a much-needed break from our small-town routine and a well-deserved reward for our otherwise tedious work.

There were many similarities between my experience in Ghana and volunteering in Guatemala. Although I picked a far more expensive program in the hope of finding a different demographic group, volunteers were still middle-class high school and college graduates from Western countries. And while the website and staff at Projects Abroad promised a greater degree of professionalism, their programmes were equally disorganized and ineffective, causing volunteers to be disappointed with their work and frustrated about the money they had spent. Also, just like in Guatemala, Ghana did not live up to the pornographic images of misery we had been trained to expect in Africa. Local people were not crippled, malnourished or on their deathbed and there was generally very little interest in having us intervene in local affairs.

Yet different from Guatemala, volunteers did not abandon their work projects entirely to seek refuge in some romantic fantasy of traditional culture. Instead, Projects Abroad volunteers proceeded to find alternative ways to capitalize on their experience abroad by turning even the leisurely aspects of their trip into competencies valued at home. Perhaps this difference can be attributed to the exorbitant pricing of the programme: spending $5,000, without airfare and spending money, on a three-month trip to Ghana might motivate volunteers to use their time wisely and productively. A more pertinent explanation, though, one that does not hinge on volunteers' willed intentions, could be the fact that the coalition of sympathy volunteers had forged with locals in Guatemala was impossible to replicate in Ghana. In the latter case, racial tensions complicated volunteers' multicultural sensibilities, pushing them to adopt a more judicious and intrepid approach to cultural difference with clear pedagogical implications and potential market value.

Volunteers are already workers

In early 2011 Verso published a book provocatively entitled *Intern Nation: How to Learn Nothing and Earn Little in the Brave New Economy*. Drawing on the experience of hundreds of university students and graduates, it offered a devastating critique of the 'internship boom' in America, receiving a great deal of attention from journalists and bloggers on both sides of the Atlantic. Author Ross Perlin argues that, although often unpaid, unregulated and pedagogically worthless, internships have become de rigeur in advanced capitalist economies

92 Entrepreneurial education in Ghana

where university degrees are no longer a secure or sufficient guarantee for decent employment. Far from being an inevitable side effect of economic globalization, the exploitation of interns happens with the blessing of universities, employers and government regulators, all of whom stand to benefit from the abundance of cheap (free) labour and eager (desperate) workers.

Nothing in this book, however, except maybe the daunting details about the everyday life of interns, is news. A number of books have already helped expose the myth of a 'new economy' where information technology and higher education would spur steady economic growth and provide decent and meaningful jobs for all (Andresky 2001; Henwood 2003; Ross 2003, 2009; Huws 2003; Ehrenreich 2005). What drives the 'weightless economy' or the 'knowledge economy', championed in the 1990s by Wall Street, Silicon Valley, Bill Clinton and Allan Greenspan, is not the Internet Revolution and the cognitive skills that go with it, but more unglamorous things such as the outsourcing of dangerous and difficult labour, the rise in non-standard and informal types of employment, overwork, speedup and surveillance and the reluctance of owners to share their profits with workers (Henwood 2003: 25). Seen from this perspective, talk of a 'new economy' is little more than a rhetorical ploy that 'appeals to utopian impulses in these largely anti-utopian times' (ibid.: 37). It is a mobilizing discourse designed to produce entrepreneurial subjects willing to accept hard work for meager pay as an inevitable fact of life.

But there was also another reason why Perlin's book attracted so much attention. Published two years after the global financial meltdown, at a time when student loans became the single largest source of US debt ($1 trillion) causing fears of an 'education bubble' (Harris 2011), *Intern Nation* resonated with wider questions about the value of higher education and the quality of its institutions, which a dizzying number of recent publications has been dedicated to (see Brooks 2011 and Grafton 2011). Although not a book directly about the corporatization of higher education, *Intern Nation* recognizes that the reason why students and graduates are prepared to work for little or no money, without health insurance, sick days and legal protection is because the only way for overeducated, underemployed graduates to secure rewarding and well-rewarded jobs is to complement their in-class education with internships, study abroad programs, foreign language skills and, why not, volunteer tourism experiences. For students and parents, who have already taken out tens of thousands of dollars in student loans, paying for an internship or a volunteering trip to Ghana seems like just another investment towards a potentially lucrative future. Obviously, these options are only open to those who can afford them.

But there is a troubling paradox at work here: why, if we are told that we live in a 'knowledge economy' or 'information economy' that thrives on highly educated, mobile and sophisticated human resources, are university graduates, who are groomed for this production model since kindergarten, not able to find jobs? Is it because university degrees have lost their market value? Or maybe because higher education does not endow students with relevant job

Entrepreneurial education in Ghana 93

skills? There are supporters for both sides. Some argue that the price of university education is vastly inflated (speculative even) compared to what students are promised to earn after graduation. Therefore students would do well to carefully assess the economic worth of their degree (archaeology is bad, engineering is good) and post-secondary education, in general, before deciding to take out a hefty student loan. Others dismiss higher education altogether, arguing that a lot of the cognitive and communicative skills liberal arts degrees teach can now be learned on the job. In a controversial move, startup entrepreneur Peter Thiel has even suggested that students would be better off abandoning the life of the mind altogether and using the money spent on pursuing a degree to start their own businesses. Besides their utter logical and moral bankruptcy, neither of these lines of reason takes into account the larger transformation of capital dating back to the crisis of Fordism in the late 1960s. As such, they fail to provide adequate explanations for the changing organization of production and work in post-industrial economies or for the corporatization of higher education.

During the late 1960s and early 1970s the Fordist model of production had to be let go. The old balance between mass production and mass consumption precariously supported through incremental wage increases, social legislation and welfare provisions became untenable because of the integration of global markets and production (Lipietz 1992: 12). In its stead would emerge a new regime of accumulation based on networked and decentralized organization structures, flexible production modes, differentiated consumption and minimal government intervention. The transition was anything but smooth and automatic. Wages and social provisions had to be cut, austerity programs implemented, jobs rendered redundant or casual, work schedules sped up and the power of labour unions and the welfare state dramatically weakened. While standard liberal economic theories present these transformations as necessary sacrifices for restoring post-war levels of growth in an age of economic globalization, the most recent economic crisis makes it clear that the Fordist crisis of profitability has never been resolved. The neoliberal reforms pioneered by conservative governments in the 1980s and continued by 'third way' social democrats in the Global North and international lending institutions in the Global South (free trade, financial capital, structural adjustment plans, austerity budgets, etc.) did not bring back steady economic growth. What they did was, in a complete betrayal of democratic principles, erode the wealth and political leverage of workers across the globe and privatize the goods they are supposed to hold in common, from their government services to their natural resources. If the dream of economic development and the fantasy of a middle-class existence is still alive today it is because over the past three or four decades it has been financed through rising public and private debt (mortgages, student debt, pension funds, pay day loans, etc.). It is becoming increasingly evident now that this arrangement is utterly unsustainable and even predatory.

By far the most sweeping changes in the transition from Fordism to post-Fordism took place in the world of production, but they immediately reflected and refracted onto education. It has become commonplace today to mourn

94 *Entrepreneurial education in Ghana*

the classic idea of the university – the university as a refuge from parental authority and market discipline, without financial worries, with free experimentation, communal living and a reasonable amount of leisure time (Read 2009b). The image is an attractive one, although inherently inaccurate. Until the 1960s this bohemian sanctuary was limited to the upper echelons of society who had the privilege to pursue non-utilitarian humanist ideals of free inquiry, civic virtue and national culture (Readings 1993). The working classes along with racial minorities, immigrants and women were never part of this arrangement. They only required minimal training for the deskilled, highly surveilled and stultifying jobs they would exercise for most of their lives. With the shift from industrial production to a service- and knowledge-based economy, however, higher education had to be both democratized and professionalized to produce the white-collar workers and 'mental labourers' (scientists, technologists, professionals, managers, educators and social workers) needed for the new economy (Barker 2001: 50). Wider access to post-secondary learning institutions should be saluted were it not tied to the condition that the university reformed itself 'in the interests of efficiency through flexibilization' (Olssen 2006: 222). The university would have to turn from a disinterested site for the pursuit of knowledge into a training ground for future workers. In other words, it had to be integrated much tighter into the field of social reproduction.

American universities, mostly as a result of the GI bill that provided free higher education to Second World War veterans but also due to pressures exerted by the civil rights and feminist movement, expanded massively in the post-war era. All industrialized nations followed suit (Barker 2001: 50–53). Unfortunately, however, flexibilized labour markets, where secure jobs are disappearing, social services are being dismantled and competition is rampant, have systematically undermined the professional promises of higher education. Despite constant invocations of the knowledge economy requiring adaptable workers endowed with advanced cognitive and communicative skills, many university graduates find themselves having to do free internships, work part time, or take out more student loans to pursue a second, more 'lucrative' degree before they can actually find a job. This is not so much an 'absorption problem', a mismatch between the supply of university graduates and the demand for their labour power. In fact, students are already productive workers. They are thoroughly integrated within the production process, as low-wage workers on campus or in internships, as consumers targeted through on-campus corporate sponsorships, or as financial subjects taking out student loans and placing their future labour power as collateral. The problem is that student labour power is valuable only when unpaid and unprotected. As soon as their degrees entitle students to decent working conditions, they cease to be needed (Dyer-Whiteford 2005; Bousquet 2008). As the manifesto of the California student occupation movement from 2009 cogently observed:

> [T]he jobs we work toward are the jobs we already have. Close to three quarters of students work while in school, many full-time; for most, the

Entrepreneurial education in Ghana   95

level of employment we obtain while students is the same that awaits after graduation. Meanwhile, what we acquire isn't education; it's debt. We work to make money we have already spent and our future labour has already been sold on the worst market around.

(Research and Destroy 2009)

Still, post-secondary education has not become entirely irrelevant or lost its value, as some free-market gurus are trying to convince us, mainly because the implications of not going to university are far more disastrous than being an unpaid intern. While one can argue that the university has been downgraded to a 'paper mill' that issues professional certification in assembly-line fashion, and that these certificates are no longer a guarantee for social mobility, university education remains the only *hope* for future economic security, at least for those who can afford it. The minimum academic credentials required to qualify for certain jobs are constantly inflating (jobs that once required a Bachelors, now demand a Masters degree), leaving people without university training entirely out of the race. But hope is an elusive thing, which is why it has to be complemented with strategically planned extra-curricular activities, work-related experience, foreign language knowledge and social skills. This model of 'enterprise education' or 'enterprise curriculum' strays away both from the original humanist ambition of open-ended knowledge pursuit and from the social-democratic language of 'equality of opportunity' (Peters 2001: 65–66). Its goal is not even the progressive accumulation of knowledge and skills. Since employees are no longer expected to be 'organization men', diligently following managerial orders, but creative, risk-taking individuals able to go above and beyond their job description, the goal of higher education is to teach translatable and transferrable talents that belong to a 'borderless neoliberal ethos' (Ong 2006: 148).

Volunteer tourism fits particularly well in this pedagogical model, where every course or extracurricular activity becomes an investment in one's human capital assessed in terms of future returns (Read 2009b: 152). As we will see in the remainder of this chapter, even when lacking in professional value, these transnational excursions manage to invest students with social skills and cultural competencies that can be easily packaged into a 'narrative of employability' (Brooks 2006: 279). Volunteering in developing countries most Westerners would not dare travel to, not to mention make it their temporary home, can set participants apart from everyone else in the race. Volunteers stand out as mobile and adaptable workers able to perform in a leaner, flatter and more globally integrated world with fluid territorial, linguistic and professional boundaries. Not surprisingly, the practice has quickly become an almost standard requirement for higher education and career development (Simpson 2005). Even if the merit of volunteering is temporally deferred (paying to volunteer abroad is more of a promise or bet on future returns than an investment with secure earnings), its pedagogical value remains unharmed because, ultimately, preparing young adults to thrive in a contingent labour market is about teaching them that the contradictions of capital are natural, ineluctable facts of life.

96 *Entrepreneurial education in Ghana*

It is easy to dismiss volunteer tourism as a humanitarian sham that appeals only to enterprising elites. But, while it is true that volunteer tourism is not a natural, spontaneous reaction to global poverty, the image of the careerist volunteer conceals the ways in which recent socio-economic mutations expose students and graduates to unprecedented levels of professional competition and insecurity. Flexible workers are expected to complement their professional expertise with linguistic abilities, interpersonal skills and a certain level of creativity and resourcefulness. What makes volunteer tourism such an attractive venue for investing in one's human capital is precisely its seemingly anti-utilitarian orientation. Volunteer tourism enjoys a virtuous aura because it does not look like an entirely premeditated response to economic flexibilization, but a disinterested manifestation of civility, social responsibility and cosmopolitan citizenship. Still, in a service-based knowledge economy that extracts value from knowledge, sociality and affect, even such seemingly universal values become points of access for economic profitability.

Useless education?

When I met Sandra in Ghana, she was already on her third volunteering trip. At the age of 23 she had earned a Bachelor of Science, had volunteered in an orphanage in Nepal, an HIV clinic in Zambia and with Projects Abroad in Ghana. On top of that, she had worked numerous community-oriented part-time jobs at home in Washington, DC and had written her MCAT test twice – all in the hope of getting into medical school. Sandra was the only volunteer I met in Ho who thought that the trip was a success.

> Ghana was the first volunteering trip where I was actually able to get placed in a hospital and a clinic that would let me do some hands-on work. At the Ho Polyclinic they did have me do some busy work like recording a list of patients with their complaints, but they also let me play in the lab, talk to patients one-on-one (once I picked up a little Ewe), let me take vitals, etc. Taking vital signs and talking one-on-one with patients is something that just wouldn't happen in the US (at least not in big cities, no idea about super rural areas) because of the liability. ... At Volta Regional hospital I was holding babies and taking notes on patient interviews in the paediatric department and I got to watch an amazing range of surgeries (that would *never* happen here, that alone made the trip worth it medical experience-wise).

In an email Sandra wrote to me a few months after the trip ended she confesses that her plan was to use volunteer tourism to compensate for a not-so-competitive MCAT score.

> Jobs and schools are crazy competitive and you have to have something that makes you stand out whether it's winning an award, having some insane

talent, or doing something like volunteer in a third world country in conditions that most people in this part of the world would not want to put up with. You have to have something like that on your resume/application, because everyone – this is especially true in medicine – has perfect grades, research experience, appropriate job experience and awesome test scores. I find it amusing (in a sick way) that there is a growing shortage of physicians in this country (just to add to the health care problems that we already are dealing with) and yet they make it close to impossible to get into medical school. Obviously you have to be driven, somewhat intelligent and dedicated to making it happen – but I really think that too much is based on numbers.

Within a year after returning from Ghana Sandra had applied to 15 medical schools and three osteopathic medicine schools. She was rejected by most of the former and accepted by all the latter:

For DOs, who aren't as number crazy, it showed them that I am dedicated and willing to get medical experience even if I have to go to extreme lengths. Another major bonus is that all of the trips are great topics of conversation during interviews, the stories I have from all three trips have helped me keep the flow of the interviews going as well as keep the interviewer interested.

Sandra's story is only unique in how clearly she sees the connection between her volunteering experience abroad and the possibility of professional success. But the driven, calculated approach she adopts towards her future career is true for all volunteers. With a few exceptions, most volunteers borrowed or received money for the trip from their parents on account of the fact that volunteering in Ghana was going to be a lucrative investment in their education. As Katherine, another American pre-med student from a working-class background explains, 'the only way I could justify doing it in my father's eyes was if it would contribute something to my future'. In coming to Ghana, all volunteers had a two-fold ambition: 'make a difference' in the lives of the people they were going to live and work with, and add some professional experience to their education. In fact, this is the double advantage most volunteer tourism programmes promise: you can do something for yourself and for others at the same time. But despite the exorbitant price difference, the programme in Ghana was equally ineffective, both in developmental and professional terms, as that in Guatemala. With Sandra's exception, most volunteers left disappointed. Whether they were placed in schools or in hospitals, volunteers grew bored and disillusioned within the first couple of weeks of their stay.

Over half of the 15 or so volunteers working with Projects Abroad during my stay in Ho were either in medical school or preparing to apply to medical school. The ones already in medical school or about to begin their medical studies were generally from the UK, where admission requirements are more

98   *Entrepreneurial education in Ghana*

lax and students can begin their studies immediately after high school. In the US, on the other hand, entrance to medical school is far more competitive, costly and requires a completed Bachelor of Science degree. Understandably, then, American pre-med volunteers were far more determined to turn their volunteering experience into professionally worthwhile credentials. Projects Abroad offered them a choice of two hospitals and several clinics to volunteer in. It also organized regular outreach programmes in nearby villages where volunteers could distribute medical supplies and treat wounds. For the remaining volunteers, the professional rewards of doing charitable work in Ghana were less straightforward. They wanted to 'take time off' their hectic and routinized schedules at home, 'experience Africa' in a useful and worthwhile way and experiment with various professional roles, which at Projects Abroad meant they volunteered as teachers in primary schools or caretakers in orphanages.

Ghana, much like the rest of Africa, suffers from a dire need of qualified medical staff, something that the brochure discourse exploits to justify the need for medical volunteers. What these programmes fail to mention though is that even in Ghana non-certified staff are not allowed to handle patients, which means that, to their surprise, volunteers were limited to doing administrative and observational work. While one might ungenerously argue that medical volunteers in Africa are 'basically paying to do medical things that you couldn't do in the US' or 'using people who are less well off to get medical experience', as an American medical student working with a women's health organization in Ho put it, most Projects Abroad volunteers found their placements 'boring as hell' and 'got no sense of achievement out of it at all'. Even Eric, who was a certified paramedic in the US, complained that 'the bureaucracy [in Ghana] didn't allow [him] to work to his full potential'. His medical expertise was more useful to fellow volunteers, who would periodically injure themselves or develop flu symptoms, than to the Ghanaian healthcare system.

Eric, for whom volunteering was supposed to be a 'perfect mix of adrenalin and humanitarianism', had come to Ghana hoping to gather the necessary medical and travel experience to eventually join medical relief teams in conflict zones across Africa. It became clear to him, after only a few weeks of being in Ho, that Projects Abroad had neither any relevant training to offer him nor the element of excitement to compensate for it. Nonetheless, he remained determined to make the most out of his trip, leaving the hospital to teach high school, do medical outreaches and travel extensively through Ghana:

> Fifty percent was about my own growth. [...] There were moments when what I wanted did not match with what Ghana wants or needs. At first I was very frustrated about it but I'm glad to have stuck it out because I learned a lot through frustration.

For Eric, Projects Abroad had clearly been 'the wrong choice'. But, in a slightly dismissive gesture, he admits that for 'people fresh out of high school', people with less travel and work experience than him, the programme could be instructive. It could provide them 'with their first overseas experience without having a shock'. Even though this is probably true, only Sandra saw 'volunteer tourism [as] a safe learning environment to get experience, which is so hard to get in the countries where we come from'. For all other volunteers the programme had been a bitter and costly disappointment. Patricia, a 19-year-old white South African high school graduate who came to Ghana to explore the medical profession, despite pronounced racial anxieties, had perhaps the harshest words:

> I don't think I've helped anyone while I was here. Only I benefited. I changed but I don't think I initiated any change. After I leave I'd have made a difference to myself but not to anyone else. This bothered me to a crazy extent in the beginning. I was coming all the way across Africa and paid a lot to be here when I could have stayed home, eat my own food, sleep in my own bed, be with my friends and family and still work in an orphanage down the road every day. I could have saved money and been more useful. It is misleading to think you can volunteer in the hospital because the placement is mostly observatory. It's for you and you only. For instance, one day you are asked to take vitals. If it's not you taking them, someone else would. I don't help at the hospital, I observe. I felt Projects Abroad was a bit to blame. They make it sound as if you weren't here, Ghana would fall apart, as if your presence is sought for. They painted a picture that's not in any way correct.

While this clearly shows a sentiment of frustration, of having been duped by false advertising, of having paid a lot of money for a product (an experience) that did not exist, there is more at work here. Volunteer tourism is not a clear-cut bait and switch. It offers all sorts of opportunities for self-growth and self-affirmation, but because these are limited to the cultural and personal realm they only make the separation between doing something for others and doing something for your own good more apparent and unsettling for volunteers. Mark and Katherine, students from the UK and the Netherlands, respectively, capture this tension well:

> Volunteering is more self-indulgent than you would think. It's more for your own reasons than for saving Africa. You see and do things that you want to do and also help a bit. I'd still tell people to do it, but realistically you can't change anything. It's almost a guilt thing. I feel like I could do something so I should. I have much more than them, so I should help and I get a really rewarding thing out of it as well. Being here ends up being far more about you than you'd imagine.
>
> When I first came, I was thinking I was going to create more of an impact than I have. I understand now that you cannot expect huge impacts in such a short time. You must learn to appreciate small changes.

It is a well-known fact that charitable work will lend people a greater sense of civic purpose and personal meaning, which is why the brochure discourse presents selflessness and self-growth in natural harmony with each other. But when personal growth comes not from helping others, but at the expense of other people's misery and suffering, when it is simply the result of having survived the 'culture shock' of Africa, not of having made a contribution to other people's welfare, it becomes an uncomfortable sort of achievement.

Even Sandra, who felt like she had gotten 'the experience [she] came here for', was aware of the one-sided exchange at the heart of volunteer tourism:

> Volunteering is more of a selfish thing than giving back. It might open up perspectives for yourself, not make a difference. I have issues with saying you're making a difference, unless you're here for a long time. Two months is more selfish: you experience, you grow. I've made some friendships and if they have made a difference to someone, I'm glad but it bothers me when people come here thinking they're going to change things. I used to think that on my first trip.

But she thought the imbalance could be redressed if volunteers took a more proactive role in their interaction with locals, if they worked harder at establishing relations of trust and cooperation with the local staff, rather than expect to be automatically welcomed as some long-awaited benefactor:

> I have a very different mind set than most. A lot of people were stand offish in the beginning. You have to do a bunch of bullshit in the first week so they see you're trustworthy. I didn't know how to do anything, but you jump in and try it. Most people get scared and don't want to do anything. You're nice to patients and they start trusting you even more. I learned how to take blood pressure and a few key phrases in Ewe. Patients think you know what you're doing because you're white. By the end of it they were letting me take medical histories, which only the head nurse could do.

In schools the situation was slightly different. Volunteers were encouraged from the very beginning to teach as many classes and whatever subjects they wanted. Local teachers were understaffed and drastically underpaid and, as a result, happy to see us ease their workload. Many of them were also poorly trained and apathetic or brutal in their pedagogical tactics, making us volunteers only more eager to replace them. The work was demanding. We were teaching six to eight hours a day, reorganizing the curriculum and leading sports and extra-curricular activities. But the enthusiasm and affection of our students energized us. Still, many feared the fruits of their labour would be short-lived.

The case of Christina and Judith is illustrative. One from the Netherlands, the other from Germany, they got in touch with each other well before coming to Ghana to coordinate what gifts and donations they would bring to the day-care centre they were going to volunteer at. Each of them organized fundraisers in their own communities and used the proceeds to buy suitcases full of handicrafts and musical instruments, repaint the school and purchase new tables

Entrepreneurial education in Ghana   101

and chairs. They also made substantial changes to the curriculum. When they arrived at the daycare, they found 50 children crammed into one room with little supervision and no activities. They opened up another room and separated the babies from the toddlers. For the latter they organized a daily schedule divided into crafts, singing and playtime. The daycare staff were very grateful for their efforts and even threw a party in their honor before they left. To us, Christina and Judith were 'ideal volunteers': engaged, committed and creative. And, yet, their contribution would not last. The objects would stay but the changes they had made to the curriculum and the new teaching methods they had introduced would be abandoned only days after their departure. The local daycare staff could not afford to give children as much individual attention as the volunteers had because they had other domestic duties to attend to. We took this as a cautionary tale. It taught us that even when we were invited to make a meaningful contribution, the impact of our work would remain limited.

Certainly, Projects Abroad was partly to blame for these disappointments. From a strictly logistical point of view, they were not actively involved in managing work placements, communicating with local staff or following up with volunteers. Except for providing a host family, a local liaison and a free tee-shirt, they left volunteers to their own devices. Often placements were poorly chosen, according to some cliché fantasy of humanitarian assistance rather than based on actual local needs and conditions. Non-transparent finances only exacerbated this problem. Volunteers paid approximately $2,500/month, of which the host family received only $350. Most volunteers did not find this price discrepancy unfair, but they would have preferred a clearer breakdown of what the remaining money was being used for. Sara, a political science student from Australia, describes the problem accurately:

> I'd like to know what projects it goes to. I know that a majority goes to recruitment – fairs and expos – but I would have appreciated a better breakdown than just a percentage pie chart in a guidebook which was global, not even broken down by country. It seemed like a token gesture to appease people. I'd like the money to go to the projects where I am. Maybe not in my placement, but in my town so I can go and see it. Volunteers should have a say in this. Make me feel that I'm not only helping in terms on time, but also monetarily.

Projects Abroad was very much aware of these complaints and, at the time of my research, was planning to introduce a so-called 'worthwhileness campaign' that would screen volunteers and placements to better match their skills and interests. But even so, as Tina, a staff member from the Accra office, explained, the key to avoiding disappointment is for volunteers to adjust their expectations of how much impact their work can have.

> Some people want to come to Africa and save the world, some want to gain experience. Many come thinking 'I want to change the life of children in

102   *Entrepreneurial education in Ghana*

Africa. I always wanted to go to Africa', not being realistic or thinking that they don't need saving. The job of PA staff is to manage these expectations and weigh them against the realistic possibilities on the ground because in the past there have been volunteers who complained that their stay has been a complete waste of time and money. Volunteers can make a small difference. You cannot have revolutionary expectations because your experiences will be disappointing.

On top of social, economic and cultural differences, which can weigh down on the impact and relevance of development work, as Charles points out, there are also very concrete bureaucratic and legal barriers to volunteering in a foreign country:

> From the medical side, legally they are limited. If it is for learning purposes, it is good, but legally they cannot help. Hospitals would not like to take the risk. They would need someone to work but not someone who is not legally allowed to do it. Those legal restraints, maybe it is possible to remove them because doctors are needed in Ghana.

Meaningful volunteering placements are complex and fragile social arrangements. For volunteers to feel needed, it is not enough to provide them with a task from nine to five. The work must also feel rewarding and fulfilling, it must incorporate volunteers' skills and talents, integrate them into a group effort and at the same time give them the freedom to take initiative and assume responsibility. Plus the work must make a visible change in local people's lives. This is not easy to achieve. Sustainable change requires trust, cooperation and a general understanding of the local culture and socio-economic conditions, clear goals and long-term commitment, local language skills and professional expertise and, above all, a shared vision of the possibilities and limitations of social change. All of these are things for-profit volunteer tourism providers are not well-equipped to offer. If, initially, many volunteers (and their parents) felt that having a reputable, trustworthy organization like Projects Abroad guide them through their first trip to Africa was essential, by the end of their trip, most volunteers realized that Ho and Ghana in general was actually a peaceful and relatively stable place, that did not require an overpriced chaperone. You did not need to join an organization to volunteer. You could find dozens of opportunities to get involved in by just making some local contacts.

It is not an exaggeration to claim that volunteering abroad is an overpriced holiday. Projects Abroad is quite sincere about this. Aware of the limited developmental impact their programmes have, they chose to actively focus on making sure volunteers enjoyed 'the beaches and nightclubs in a different country without having any problems', as Charles described his job responsibilities. In theory, the *Ghana Handbook* discourages travel during work placements, but it is clear from the Projects Abroad website that exploring the cultural sites, major market towns and wildlife Ghana has to offer is very much part of the appeal

Entrepreneurial education in Ghana 103

of this destination. In fact, the website spends more time describing the country's touristic attractions than explaining why Ghana needs the help of international volunteers.

> In Accra or Kumasi you can visit the bustling African markets selling everything from shoes and batteries to traditional cloth and carvings. Then a tailor in the street will transform your wood-cut prints into skirts and shirts for a couple of pounds. You can relax on some great palm-lined beaches along the coast, watch monkeys in Kakum Rainforest Reserve near Cape Coast and go mountain biking in the Akuapem Hills. If you want to party, Accra and Kumasi have lots of bars, clubs and restaurants – none of our volunteers ever fails to have a good social life here.
>
> During the weekends, you can get together and travel to places such as Ada in the Volta Delta or Kakum National Park. During your weeks off you may think about traveling to Mole National Park to see elephants close up and on foot, or get some more stamps in your passport by visiting Benin or Burkina Faso – and some even make it as far as Timbuktu!
>
> (Projects Abroad 2008b)

Ghana has no shortage of attractive tourist destinations. For white people, hungry for Western food, entertainment and service standards, Ghana offers an endless variety to choose from with the added bonus of a warm climate, servile people and lax law enforcement. There was Osu, Accra's upscale neighbourhood, where internet access was fast, shops carried all of our favourite products (at exorbitant prices) and nightclubs were abundant. There were also sport bars and swimming pools in five-star hotels peppered all across the capital and beach resorts immediately outside of it. It was a weekend ritual to leave Ho by Friday afternoon, catch a tro-tro ride south towards the Atlantic and spend the weekend in one of these heavens in the company of volunteers from other organizations, foreign students, Western aid workers, Middle Eastern and South Asian entrepreneurs and members of the comprador elite. More intrepid travellers would also venture beyond the tourist trail, into the northern hinterland, or neighbouring Togo, Ivory Coast and Burkina Faso. But most of us avoided these itineraries because they presented too many discomforts, like spending dozens of hours on public transport, eating only local food, staying in rudimentary guesthouses and having to put up with the eccentricity of being the only white person in sight.

Like in Guatemala, then, volunteering in Ghana did not have the expected results. Volunteers in medical placements were limited by legal constraints to observational and administrative roles, while teaching volunteers found their otherwise challenging work efforts to be short-lived. With small exceptions, everyone on the trip realized that, although they could still use overseas volunteering to bolster their résumés, on the ground their work remained ineffectual. Volunteers neither contributed to the welfare of local people in any significant way, nor did they gain any relevant professional skills. Still, as the

104 *Entrepreneurial education in Ghana*

next section demonstrates, the experience was not devoid of educational opportunities. Even when volunteers behaved like glorified tourists, simply living in a radically different culture without local language skills, modern amenities or the comfort of loved ones allowed young adults to develop personal skills and sensibilities valuable in the new economy. Phrases like 'expand your horizons', 'fulfil your potential' or 'come back a changed individual' may sound like empty platitudes, but they, in fact, capture the sincere pedagogical ambition of volunteer tourism.

Racial tensions

We saw in the previous chapter on Guatemala that, when the charitable and pedagogical ambitions of volunteer tourism fall short, volunteers try to establish an intimate connection to local people and culture to make up for their overwhelming sensation of boredom and frustration. Almost overnight, volunteers become tourists or amateur anthropologists observing and even participating in the local way of life. Yet the romantic fantasies and multicultural sensibilities we saw unfold in Guatemala were not present in Ghana. Although volunteers invariably came to appreciate the town of Ho, treating it as their home away from home, rarely did they celebrate its unspoilt charm or try to protect it from the forces of modernization. Similarly, volunteers found it difficult to forge coalitions of sympathy akin to those witnessed in Guatemala with their host families and larger community. Relations with locals were mostly friendly, with the occasional domestic dispute between volunteers and host families, but never sentimental or patronizing. Why this discrepancy? The answer lies in the overtly racialized language and behaviour used in Ghana. The Ghanaian habit of making white bodies visible either through close scrutiny or excessive admiration made volunteers feel uneasy about their relative position of privilege to the point of seeing themselves as victims of 'reverse racism'.

The *Handbook* distributed by Projects Abroad describes Ghanaians 'as some of the friendliest [people] in Africa':

> [P]rovided you show them respect, you will be welcomed with open arms. At times you will be frustrated by the culture, but there is a lot to be learned here. If you are tolerant, respectful and always remember that you have been welcomed visitors, you will spend some of the best months of your life here.
>
> (2008: 3)

This is true. Ghana is one of the most hospitable countries I ever visited. But the reasons for this are complicated. On the one hand, Western tourists perceive Ghana as such a welcoming place because there are obvious advantages to being white in this country. You always get the best seat on the bus, the biggest plate of food, the place in front of the line. If you are white, someone will guide you, share their food with you or buy you a drink. If you are lost,

Entrepreneurial education in Ghana   105

someone will help you handle your logistical problems without expecting any-thing in return. If you are upset, someone will cheer you up. If you are white, Ghana is one huge resort where almost everyone works as your personal entertainer. It is rare for anyone in Ghana to be indifferent to white bodies.

My relation with Charles, our coordinator, is illustrative of this peculiar fascination with whiteness. Charles had made it clear that he regarded me as the bearer of some secret knowledge that he wanted to gain access to. One day, for instance, he invited me for a drink at the White House, our favourite hangout spot and asked me to 'teach him everything I knew that he didn't know'. The request baffled me and I immediately changed the subject to his job at Projects Abroad. He explained that although the work was exhausting and exploitative (it was essentially free labour), he enjoyed it because it gave him a chance to 'hang out with volunteers, sharing ideas, learning new things, espe-cially about social issues', such as homosexuality, which he had grown more tolerant of through his interaction with volunteers. 'Maybe I'm limiting my mind to my own cultural values and not responding to other possibilities'. When I asked him why the words of a white person 'carry a different weight' in Ghana, Charles explained that the country's colonial 'mentality' causes Ghanaians to blame the country's inferior place in history on their own (racial) failures:

> Ghanaians believe whites are well off and with their money they can help by buying their drinks, eating their food, sleeping in their hotels. Gha-naians like visitors more than their own. If you are white it means you are well to do and you get lots of attentions. The eyes are on you always: some are waiting for you to make a mistake or some are waiting for you to make a friendly gesture. This is a colonial mentality. In pre-colonial society, our local kings were considered superior beings. With colonization, whites took over our kings. This had a strong impact on most Ghanaians. Also the kind of inventions they have made and the kinds of things they've been able to do with their lives. The people admire that. Although Ghana is politically independent, economically it still depends upon foreign loans, policies and imports. You cannot support your body fully. White people are in power and you look for help from them. ... Ghanaians think whites will bring innovation. It is a general mentality here. Their presence helps put so many things in place.

But with this misplaced reverence for white bodies comes intense curiosity and scrutiny. As a white person in Ghana you are constantly on display: people shout 'yevu' or 'obruni' (white person in Ewe and Twi, respectively) after you in the street, they touch your skin and stroke your hair to check for a difference in texture, they watch your dress and manners, reprimand you for your smoking, they ask for your name and contact information, or want their picture taken with you and they assume you are wealthy and expect you to pay 'white prices'. Eventually, all this attention and attending (the proverbial Ghanaian friend-liness) becomes unbearable. Marion, a quiet 20-year-old girl from Switzerland

106   *Entrepreneurial education in Ghana*

who spent most of her time in Ghana hanging out with Judith and Katherine, but saw herself forced to travel on her own after these two left for home, had to cut her trip short by two weeks because she was 'not strong enough' to handle the racial tensions.

> What is frustrating about traveling through Ghana is the constant haggle over taxi and tro-tro prices where you are cheated because you're white. I understand the idea but I can't stand it anymore. I'm getting tired. At the end of our trip [my friend] Judith had to calm me down because I couldn't take it anymore. And it is more or less everywhere like this: in the market, in tros, it's always about the price. At first, everything was new. But step by step I hate the feeling of having to repeat myself. You lose a lot of time and energy. And it's the same with Ghanaian boys. The first time they ask you 'can you take me home?' You joke that there is no room in your luggage. But after three months I overreact because I don't want to have this conversation again and again. They want to be your friend but that is not how you make friends. It's too easy to have friends here because I'm white, not because I'm interesting or I'm nice, only because I'm white. Being white can be funny, but I'm bored with it.

Even Mark, a jovial British volunteer whose friendly and relaxed attitude served as a model for us all, felt exhausted by the local fascination with whiteness:

> Being white in Ghana is strange. It gets you so much attention. If there's anything I'd want to do, I could do it here. It doesn't matter if it's illegal or I'm not trained to do it. But the tension can get annoying sometimes. If you want to walk or sit in a bar everyone wants to talk to you.

Some, like Sandra and Vanessa, were deeply uncomfortable with or outright angered at the exaggerated reverence their white bodies earned them in Ghana:

> My biggest fear is that I allow myself to take the advantages that they give me because I'm white: cut in line, get served first, or get the best of everything.
>
> I have no desire to come back to Ghana for all the cultural things I've experienced. Neo-imperialistic, that's what it is. They are so thankful for everything whites do. This undeserved level of respect ... it's welcoming and at the same time overly subservient. I don't deserve that. I'm sick of being idolized. My goal in ten years is that no one will have to travel to volunteer. There will be universal gratitude.

This is where Ho acted as a refuge. The point of leaving Ho on the weekends was to escape the tedium and deprivations of living in a small town in West Africa. Inevitably, however, after a few days on the road we would feel relieved to return to what we endearingly referred to as 'home sweet Ho'. With time, even the more sceptical of us learned to 'love' Ho. Despite its small-town feel and occasional afternoon boredom, Ho had many things to offer: its manageable size, safe atmosphere and the familiarity we had developed with shopkeepers, vendors, cab drivers, tailors and the rest of the white community confirmed that we had made Africa, the place everyone associates with extreme poverty, distress and chaos, our temporary home. There was something very satisfying about being able to say 'I live here' as opposed to 'I am staying at this hotel' or 'I am passing through.' It gave us a much longed for sense of belonging. Most importantly, though, Ho offered respite from the racial tensions we were confronted with everywhere else in Ghana. Mark remarked that he 'wouldn't want to be anywhere else' in Ghana except for Ho:

> It's friendlier. People are so much nicer here. You don't get hassled or begged. In Accra or Kumasi people constantly ask you for money or food. It's homely – you can feel at home here.

Similarly, Sandra saw Ho as a throwback to a better, simpler time, when people knew their neighbours by name and were content with the little they had.

> It's different in Ho: how friendly everyone is, how safe it is. I understand now that when people say 'yevu' it's a loving term in Ho, not to hassle or get money out of you. Ho is one of those innocent places, like America in the 1950s. My mom used to tell me how everything used to cost a nickel, you could go out at night without being shot or raped, you didn't have to have your guard up all the time. But you can feel how it's changing. In ten years it's going to be a completely different town because everyone wants the same benefits as the rest of the world. This is good as far as hygiene, sanitation and healthcare is concerned, but you also see people caring about name brand clothes, new cars ... You see the same dumb obsessions they care about in the rest of the world infiltrate a sleepy little town like this.

I do not doubt that having a place to call home has a reassuring effect on volunteers, but we have to be suspicious of these romantic ascriptions. The reason why Ho seemed such a welcoming place to volunteers was not necessarily because of its manageable size or safety, but rather because the large expat community in Ho helped shelter volunteers from the inquisitive gaze of locals. Getting together at the White House, for instance, every day after work gave us a chance 'to vent [and] let out our frustrations about Ghana and Ghanaians', as Carey put it. Over beers and pizza we would complain about local amenities or lack thereof, and exchange stories of cultural shock and bewilderment. By far our favourite past time was to mock Ghanaian English. Its colonial-type phrases and peculiar accents were an endless source of amusement to us. Quite problematically all of these conversations would take place in English despite the fact that the objects of our mockery, seated all around us or serving us, were just as fluent in English as we were. But we assumed

108   *Entrepreneurial education in Ghana*

that when spoken with a foreign accent, versatile vocabulary and abundant cultural references it would be hard for locals to follow our 'white' English. It would be easy to see this as an act of racial prejudice, but I am more inclined to attribute it to the curiosity, puzzlement and humour with which people from radically different cultural backgrounds inevitably approach each other. One could argue that this is exactly what Ghanaians were doing when gazing at 'yevu' or 'obruni' bodies and modes of conduct, except that volunteers perceived these acts as signs of discrimination – 'reverse racism'. I reproduce here two of the most exasperated statements from Eric and Carey, who after having spent extensive time on the continent saw their racialization as a failure to be taken seriously as individuals and build genuine relations with local people.

> In Ethiopia people would just want to be your friend to discuss your culture. In Ghana there are genuine people, who befriend you with no ulterior motives and then there are those who just want something from you. In Ho you stand out as a white person because there are not so many white people here. It was a novelty to me the first month, hated it the second month and got used to it the third month. In the beginning, people used to call me 'yevu' and I would go to them on the street and strike up a conversation only to discover they wanted something for me. I find this reverse racism frustrating. I couldn't understand if people were trying to rip me off just to spite me or because they were opportunists and wanted to make more money off me.
>
> I'm tired of being seen as a foreigner when I've lived here for so long [seven months], not being recognized by my neighbours, not being recognized in stores, being just a blank face, just another volunteer. They call you 'yevu' and are not interested in your name. For some reason they feel the need to identify you as a foreigner and share that with everyone else on the street. It is very frustrating, especially when parents teach their kids that. If I confront them about it, I'm not being taken seriously. They think it's funny because you're white. They don't see it as racism. They keep telling me 'yevu' is not a bad thing. They look up to you. They have a saying in Ewe that 'the white man is close to God' or that 'if you're going to church and you see a white man on the way, you can go home because you've seen God'. I don't know if they come up with it on their own or someone's teaching them, but there needs to be some sort of intervention. They have really warped conceptions about what skin color means and this rises from slavery times. My neighbours still call me 'yevu' after I've lived here for so long [seven months]. I got so mad [one day] that I yelled at them: 'I've been living here for seven months. I am no longer a yevu.' He answered: 'You've been living her for seven months and you still can't speak Ewe.'

What vexed volunteers was not simply the scrutiny they were subjected to but the markedly racial orientation of this gaze. Coming from Western liberal democracies, where systemic racism is well-hidden behind a veneer of colour blindness, volunteers were uncomfortable with overt racial appellations and nominal racial identities. To refer to someone as 'black' or 'white' is often seen as bad form in the West because liberal multiculturalism teaches us not to deduce race from biological markers and behavioural traits. Race is not a reflection of skin color, the most sophisticated of race theories argue, but gains substance through the learned yet forgotten repetition of certain attitudes, dispositions, performances, lifestyle choices, consumption preferences and so on. Unfortunately, many take this logic to its extreme and assume that just because race is constructed it does not exist or that it is a matter of personal choice. This is far from true. Racial identity acquires substance only when recognized by others in a dialogical process of 'racialization'. The terms of this exchange are not open-ended or equal, but take place within already-existing power structures and cultural conventions, which in modern times have always privileged white bodies and modes of life over all other forms of being. The constructedness of racial identities does not make racism passé. It bears concrete implications for what a body can do, how it can move through space, what kinds of socio-economic opportunities it enjoys, what worlds are open to it and which ones remain closed off (Ahmed 2006: 134). By accusing Ghanaians of 'reverse racism', however, volunteers chose to ignore this. In fact this is the very purpose of the term 'reverse discrimination', which was coined in response to affirmative action policies introduced in the 1960s: to obscure the racism sedimented in our socio-economic structures and politico-legal institutions and present middle-class whites as equally vulnerable to discrimination. What volunteers witnessed in Ghana was inter-personal racial prejudice, which can go either way, but in no way is it commensurate to the systematic exclusion and stigmatization of dark bodies modernity is founded upon.

I would argue that the fascination for the epidermal as well as the cultural properties of whiteness is less a form of 'racism' than the racialization of whiteness. Franz Fanon famously argued that whiteness is the universal human condition against which all other experiences are assessed. Only white bodies represent a concrete form of life. Blackness is a type of non-being or non-life for which the only concretization is to become white: '[f]or the black man there is only one destiny. And it is white' (Fanon 1967: 10). Sara Ahmed agrees: whiteness is the standard of reference by which all other positions are assessed as either desirable or deviant. To be outside this centre 'is to inhabit the negative: it is to be "not"' (2006: 139). But she takes Fanon's idea a step further to explain that the mechanism through which whiteness makes its privilege felt is not through its all-eclipsing presence, but through absence.

Historically, the privilege of whiteness derives from its ability to act as the invisible and unmarked centre of humanity. This is not simply due to skin colour, but the effect of concrete historical processes (slavery, colonialism, modern science, cultural representations) that placed white bodies 'in line' with standards of civilization, progress and beauty. Modern history since Columbus' arrival on the American continent in 1492 can be seen as a sustained attempt to design material and semiotic arrangements hospitable to white bodies. Whites

110 *Entrepreneurial education in Ghana*

are not only predominant in cultural and political representations, they are also the norm for what it means to be human. To be 'just' human is a position of extraordinary power because it allows you to speak and act for humanity as a whole rather than only for a segment of it. It allows white people to occupy a place of universality while keeping their privilege unnoticed. Not surprisingly, white bodies can do more than others. They are comfortable and confident in their own skin, their surrounding space is an extension of their own shape and their unmarked racial identity is always a door opener, never an obstacle. Meanwhile, all other bodies are made to feel at odds. Their shape and conduct must be inspected and their movement in space policed.

What Ghanaians effectively were doing by calling white bodies 'white' was to make this racial dynamic visible. Gazing at the natives is a well-known touristic pastime, especially in a place as foreign and exotic as 'black Africa'. But when this gaze is returned, in the starkest way possible, tourists become uneasy with their newly exposed position of privilege. Most of us volunteers had been unaware of our racial construction until coming to Ghana. In Guatemala, for instance, race was never an issue, despite the fact that both Latinos and Indios are heavily racialized bodies, because locals did not overtly bring up the subject. Although they referred to us as 'gringos', we usually (wrongly) assumed the term meant American or foreigner, not white person. This linguistic confusion allowed for race to be swept under the carpet so to speak. In Ghana, however, there was no escaping. Local language and cultural conduct were designed to make our racial identity visible. To suddenly have our white bodies made public for everyone to see, touch and assess was bound to generate some anxiety. For the first time in our lives we felt physically limited in what our bodies could do. We were confined in space, placed under intense observation and constant scrutiny, and made to feel particular and peculiar. No wonder most of us were overwhelmed and exasperated by the experience.

As confrontational as these techniques of racialization may seem they can be highly effective in provincializing whiteness, something postcolonial theory (Chakrabarty 2000) considers imperative for unsettling the privileged position of white European tradition. But I am not convinced that in this case racialization produced the desired pedagogical effect. Towards the end of their trip volunteers started talking about the transformative impact the experience had on them. Despite the technical shortcomings of the programme, many, like Marion, felt the trip had made them 'stronger': 'I learned how to live without my parents. I learned English. And how to live without my organized life in Switzerland. In all, I learned how to be stronger'. Living and travelling on their own, making multinational friends, learning how to survive without modern amenities, narrating their daily adventures in a blog and especially handling unnerving and somewhat traumatic cultural encounters, like the ones described above, helped test the character, push the tolerance limits and widen the horizons of otherwise sheltered young adults. Katherine, an Australian nurse who had quite some trouble in the beginning adapting to Ghanaian modes of conduct and standards of living, captures this transformation well:

Entrepreneurial education in Ghana 111

> When you're uncomfortable you grow the most. I was put in a situation that was completely different from the lifestyle I have at home – that's what I mean by uncomfortable. The water was not always running; I was eating different foods; I was sleeping in a different bed; I did not know what the communication would be like before I came here; I was living in a place where people still sleep on the street or at the place of their work. I'll be going home a more appreciative person: excited for a healthcare system that's trustworthy, understanding that having clean water and electricity at all times is not something that we can take for granted, knowing what a child with malnutrition looks like.

This narrative of self-discovery and personal growth is a classic trope of travel literature. Immature and incompetent Westerners are promised they will discover independence, autonomy and maturity through contact with less modern natives and adventure abroad. Or they are invited to get in touch with older, more authentic values long lost in the West, like in Sandra's case:

> Every trip changes you and I'm not talking about making a difference. It's always changed me in a good way. I go home with a very different mindset every time. It's like when you step away from a situation and everything seems easier or clearer. I don't agree with a lot of views in America: the obsession with appearance, money, big houses. But a lot of times you get sucked in. You can come here and have a good time and be yourself. A lot of times I'm more myself here than at home. Sometimes I put on a front at home. Of course this 'new me' mindset is difficult to maintain at home, but the value of traveling is still indisputable. Travel helps you gain perspective. When you settle in you become comfortable. When you're in new situations, you learn and grow. On this trip I learned where I want to fit in the medical field. If you never expose yourself to new situations, you get really boring. My dad's job made a lasting impression upon me. I blame Shell for my urge to travel. But trips in the developed world don't really interest me. I don't see it as travel, but visiting previous home towns and family. They're not as enriching as here where you have the complete difference in culture. I find it really important to understand different cultural perspectives, to see every side of the story. It will make me a better physician. I will understand things better than the regular Joe. I'm a care-taker. My family thinks this is a dangerous personality trait.

The problem with this narrative of personal transformation, however, is that it is entirely one-sided. It suggests that the racial tensions encountered in Ghana, even though potentially productive, were better suited at producing flexible and worldly citizen-workers unencumbered by sovereign boundaries and national culture than at unsettling the white privilege this subjectivity rests upon. Again, Sara Ahmed's work can be of help here. She points out that making whiteness visible is not in and of itself a sufficient gesture for launching a critique of

112 *Entrepreneurial education in Ghana*

race. Seeing the mark of white privilege does not necessarily translate into unlearning that privilege. More often than not it will result in a strange cultural politics of emotion where 'feeling bad' about one's racial privilege becomes a way of 'feeling good' about oneself again. Feelings of guilt and shame are essentially restorative and redemptive. They demonstrate that the gap between wrongdoing and the ideal of justice is only temporary, and allow the subject to reassert a secure identity position (Ahmed 2005). What is more, decentering whiteness risks aggravating white people's growing sense of victimization. If white bodies are seen as one minority among many, then we must also accept complaints about white people, their cultures and values, being under attack as legitimate (Ahmed 2004).

In conclusion, the racial tensions volunteers encountered in Ghana were more useful in restoring the pedagogical value of volunteer tourism than in provincializing whiteness. Even when volunteering in Ghana was nothing more than an overpriced travel package, emotionally trying encounters and nervous conditions helped turn the experience into an opportunity for self-transformation. To enjoy their time abroad *despite* racial tensions, material deprivation and geographical distance volunteers had to mobilize a great deal of endurance and patience as well as learn to manage various cultural anxieties and nervous conditions. It required them to develop a series of social and affective skills, like self-reliance, initiative, endurance, innovation, adaptability and resourcefulness, which are also competencies expected from today's creative workers. Unfortunately, the unequal global distribution of political rights and economic resources across the globe makes this a profoundly unequal exchange. Volunteers are not oblivious to this, which makes them highly uneasy. They realize they are the only ones who stand to benefit from this encounter: make the world their home, increase their social capital, employability and mobility status against the backdrop of supposedly timeless, rooted people like those usually associated with Africa.

'Africa' as training ground

Whether it is by allowing volunteers to experiment with various professional personas or gather the necessary linguistic and cultural competencies to confidently navigate a foreign setting, volunteering in the Global South is ripe with affective and aesthetic lessons that can be easily translated into entrepreneurial skills. Africa plays an essential function in this process. Its material dispossession and semiotic foreignness represent a boot-camp-like training ground for tomorrow's professional elites. Even when all we did was go out for drinks at the White House or read books by the pool, even when we slacked or quit our work placements altogether to tour the country's resorts and expat hangout places, we were still doing something almost no one we knew had done. Mark, for instance, who 'comes from a very rural part of England', explains that for the people back home volunteering in Africa 'is kind of a big deal. No one I know went to Africa. A lot of people never leave town, let alone come to Africa. Older people are happy and admiring'. Invariably, friends and relatives see overseas volunteering as a confirmation of their sons and daughters' exceptional courage and generosity. Vanessa's parents think she is 'an angel for sacrificing [herself] to help needy Ghanaians'.

> Only my parents would like me to come home and get a job instead of helping Africans who are naturally lazy and can't help themselves. ... But it's cool to be unselfish. Being self-centered is so terrifying. You can be more content if you do stuff that's not for yourself. And it's fun. I think the greatest deed is the deed you don't get credit for.

Not even the nagging suspicion that volunteers might, in fact, be pursuing careerist ambitions can detract from the virtuous appeal of volunteer tourism. 'Yes', Sara admits, 'I get to put it on my CV, but this is a very minor thing. I've paid to do this. Most people could do this. But when you're at home it could seem quite daunting to go around the world and help. They say what I'm doing is great but they would never be able to do it themselves'. Because it comes from a place of awe and admiration, being called 'crazy', something which volunteers often get to hear, does not offend them. It only confirms they are exceptional people, whose spirit of sacrifice and heroism exceed what is usually considered 'normal' in the individualistic and consumerist West. 'Some think I'm crazy', Katherine explains, 'but they respect me for what I'm doing. A lot of them have done exchanges in Australia or Britain but I was the first one to go to Africa, to the Third World in general. They say I'm brave but I needed to do it'. Modesty is not a forte for volunteers who, like Christina and Eric, see volunteering as a natural calling, an organic reaction to global poverty and injustice, which they were meant for all along.

> All my female friends are proud of the work I'm doing with the local children. But I don't know why because, for me, this has been a normal step in my life. It fits in with my life. I've always spoken of doing something like this. Occasionally there are people who say I'm crazy because they live in a secure environment they are used to and are afraid of giving that up. They don't understand how I can leave my life behind. Or they are scared that I might get sick.
> Before I came to Ghana, I got a text message from my friends saying how cool they think it is that I'm going to Ghana. But I don't see anything special about it. Although everyone admires and is proud of what I've been doing in Africa, I cannot see what the big deal is because this has been my plan since grade four. I was raised with the thought that this is something I was going to do ... like being raised with a family business.

Patricia, on the other hand, was uncomfortable with the praise she received from home because she was painfully aware of how ineffectual her contribution had been and also realized that a lot of her friends and family's admiration

114 *Entrepreneurial education in Ghana*

was based on a series of distorted, even racist assumptions about life in Ghana and Africa in general.

> At home everyone's so proud. Everyone I've ever known in my life has called my mom to ask whether I'm still in Ghana. But what's there to be proud of? If I wasn't here, no one would care. But although I may not be needed, coming to Ghana by myself is a big step for me. I'm only 18 and have proven during this trip that I have the independence and the self-control not to go crazy. My friends and family have an incorrect perception of what my time here is like. Ghana is not like the rest of Africa. And Projects Abroad is a big security. If I came here alone, it would be a bigger deal.

In all cases, however, what was admired were not the effects of volunteering, which were never assessed or questioned, but the fact that the altruism of these young adults had extended to a space outside modernity, a space that in the Western imagination is usually associated with chaos and danger – Africa. Being able to say 'I lived in Ghana' bears such purchase in the minds of friends, relatives, Facebook audiences and also admission and recruitment officers back home, that even when someone recognizes the futility of volunteering abroad they can still not cut their trip short.

Carey's story is a case in point. Following her parents' example, she joined the American Field Service to complete her senior year at a high school in Ghana. She was supposed to attend classes in Ho for nine months but graduated much earlier than expected. She then tried volunteering at a school for a while but was quickly disillusioned with the meagre results of her work. When I met Carey, she used to spend most of her days at the White House listening to music, reading, keeping track of the arrivals and departures of other whites. Disappointed with her stagnant routine, she told me, 'I went from being a student to being a teacher to doing nothing'. Still, she had to stay in Ghana to prove, especially to her father, that she had the strength and stamina to 'hold out until the end'.

Carey was not alone in this position of limbo. Several other volunteers felt that Ghana would 'not have fallen apart' had they not been there. Life in Ghana was far less exciting and exotic than they had been led to believe. Social conventions were often strict and conservative and everyday life, once you had mastered the challenges of culture shock, was fairly uneventful. Many volunteers resented having spent their savings on a trip that felt more and more like an overpriced vacation than a mix of 'adrenalin and humanitarianism', as Eric described volunteer tourism. The situation was even more apparent for the Projects Abroad staff in Accra, Tina and Elli, two twentysomethings from Canada and the UK, respectively. They were painfully aware of the tedium of their work but had decided to sign one-year contracts in the hopes of acquiring 'international work experience'. It is important to draw a distinction here between 'work experience' as a quantitative measure of time spent in the workforce, which is what volunteering offers regardless of its qualitative value and professional

Entrepreneurial education in Ghana   115

skills, which the formula has trouble providing. Sometimes, the former is enough. At least it allows young workers to overcome the paradox of already having to have a job in order to be eligible for one. This contradiction is paralyzing for recent graduates, who then, like Sandra, end up having to pay to work in order to eventually secure paid work: 'All jobs I look at online, you need an MA, a PhD or several years working experience'.

Unfortunately, most of the 'excitement' of living in Ghana revolved around hostile encounters and traumatic experiences. More than once I witnessed volunteers engage in fights over money with host families and street vendors, aggressively tell off beggars and children, make racially charged observations, or simply break down in tears exhausted and exasperated with the unintelligible world around them. My roommate, for instance, a 19-year-old Dutch volunteer from a well-to-do family, was constantly dissatisfied with the food our host family served us, especially the lack of milk for breakfast, which in Ghana costs $3/liter, something very few people can afford on a $2/day income. When one of the children in our family got a bicycle for his birthday she openly accused our host family of pocketing the money they had received from Projects Abroad for our accommodation.

Stories such as these would then be funnelled into larger complaints about local food, rudimentary living conditions and local customs during our get-togethers at the White House. Having 'done their part' by spending a hefty sum of money to do charity work in Ghana, volunteers often felt entitled to act in this assertive and arrogant manner even if it made them have serious doubts about their own ethicality. But none of these anxieties could have made them interrupt their trip. Going home early would have meant admitting that Ghana was less extraordinary than people at home imagined or too difficult to handle. It would have meant giving up on some of the esteem and admiration family and friends reserved for them.

If volunteers and foreign workers are prepared to tolerate the monotony and frustrations of being 'mandatory tourists' in Ghana, then, we should probably ask: what irreplaceable good can Ghana and Africa in general, offer people in liberal capitalist societies? Is there a function or a lack only Africa can fill? At first this might seem like a bizarre question. What could a place, which in the modern imagination is associated with lack and abject need, have to offer the West? The answer is quite counterintuitive. It is precisely because Africa, just like the black bodies populating it, is a non-being whose greatest quality is 'to be nothing at all' (Mbembe 2001: 4) that the trope can supply whatever the West thinks it misses. It can function as a final frontier for adventure, a spiritual resource for self-actualization, a cultural repository for meaningful lessons, or 'the training ground for citizens of empire' (Mathers and Hubbard 2006: 212).

In geographic terms 'real' or 'black' Africa, which is where volunteers wanted to travel when they chose Ghana as their destination, excludes both South Africa, with its considerable white minority and advanced market economy, and the Maghreb, with its preponderantly Muslim population and fragile

116   *Entrepreneurial education in Ghana*

geopolitical position in the War on Terror. It is an umbrella term for a multitude of political, linguistic and cultural groups, living without history and outside modernity somewhere in sub-Saharan Africa. This Africa is a colonial fantasy about timeless cultures, moral simplicity, communitarian values, ecological harmony, religious mysticism and historical stagnation. It is a product of the modern discourse on race, which designates Africa as the radical other of Western 'constructions of civilization, enlightenment, progress, development, modernity and, indeed, history' (Ferguson 2006: 2).

What fascinates Western tourists about Africa is that, despite successive encounters with agents of modernity (explorers, missionaries, colonial administrators, adventurers, development workers, tourists, volunteers and celebrities), Africa seems to have remained impervious to foreign influences. It is *unmodernizable*. For some this denotes the heroic resilience of African people to defend their ancestral ways of life. For others it demonstrates their incorrigible (lazy, corrupt and duplicitous) nature. Either way, Africa is seen as stagnant and timeless, not only in cultural terms, which guarantees that cultural encounters with African people are always authentic because tourists can never arrive *too* late, but also in socio-economic terms, where Africa is associated with economic contingency and organizational chaos. Strangely enough, contingency, crisis and cultural diversity are also the keywords of neoliberal capital. This similarity, which is rather a statement about the crisis-prone nature of capital than a reflection of Africa's state of development, is why places like Ghana can act as a classroom for tomorrow's mobile and versatile workforce. A sojourn in Africa can teach young adults how to become the resourceful and self-reliant citizen-workers needed in this globalized and volatile regime of accumulation.

What is taught in volunteer tourism are not concrete professional skills, but 'intercultural competence', what management studies describes as the 'complex of abilities needed to perform *effectively* and *appropriately* when interacting with others who are linguistically and culturally different from oneself' (Fantini cited in Sinicrope, Norris and Watanabe 2007: 1, original emphasis). The concept first emerged in education and the healthcare sector to accommodate a growingly diverse society in the 1960s and 1970s. From there it made its way into human resources, business, development and public administration, where it has now established itself as a credible model for effective performance and even ethical conduct: 'The acquisition of such competencies may be important not only for individual enrichment and communicative proficiency but also for providing future educators, professionals and leaders with the capabilities necessary for promoting successful collaboration across cultures' (ibid.). In management studies, where the buzzword has been most successful, cultural competence is now a full-fledged area of research with its own nomenclature, scientific models, professional associations (International Association of Cross-Cultural Competence and Management), journals (*European Journal of Cross-Cultural Competence and Management*), study courses (MBAs in Intercultural Management) and an impressive number of researchers and publications. Despite working with a limited understanding of culture, which has long fallen into disrepute in anthropology for its tendency to reduce culture to efficiency calculations and market rules, the appeal of cultural competence is that it offers practical tools (detailed steps and models) for realizing the larger goal of multiculturalism: it can solve labour disputes and shortages, mediate conflicts between special interest groups and prepare workers to navigate the complexities of multinational capital. In doing so, it has become an asset employers, educators and administrators actively look for in their workers, students and citizens. Projects Abroad volunteers and office staff have remained oblivious to this and are, like Elli, eager to demonstrate they have the necessary skills to enter the borderless professional class:

> There is a lot that I can gain from it, not from the job itself but from living and working overseas in a foreign country. It stands out. ... It shows that you're adaptable, you can hold your own in various situations, you are willing to travel, easy-going and laid-back. Also, the logistics of going abroad, you have to be organized and proactive. All of these are good qualities for future employers.

The initial goal of multicultural education was to prepare liberal democracies for a more diverse and tolerant social reality. In time, however, study abroad programmes, language courses, internships and volunteering programmes were introduced to prepare workers to operate in multicultural settings at home or away. Borders, geographical distances, class and racial differences could no longer stand in the way of transnational capital. This is reflected in the shift in higher education from 'a focus on political liberalism and multicultural diversity at home to one on neoliberalism and borderless entrepreneurial subjects abroad' (Ong 2006: 140). But against this dream of unencumbered geographical mobility stands the stark reality of stagnating social mobility, which not even higher education can offset anymore. This is the painful reminder about the limits of capitalist growth, which the constant expansion of one's human capital through entrepreneurial education schemes is supposed to conceal or compensate for. Of course, precarious economic times make it impossible to predict whether any of these investments will actually result in secure employment. Yet the model of entrepreneurial education persists. In fact, it only grows more inventive as our prospects for economic justice grow thinner because, ultimately, creative bets against the future such as volunteer tourism are strategies for coping with the stress, fear and anxiety associated with living like a self-reliant *homo oeconomicus* (Read 2009b: 153).

Conclusion

Increasingly economic and political rights are being granted in a 'graduated' fashion depending on individual abilities to creatively navigate the demands of flexible capital (Ong 2005: 698). Students and graduates are at the forefront of this race for status and privilege. Having only their education as an asset,

118 *Entrepreneurial education in Ghana*

they must participate in all sorts of extra-curricular activities and 'continuing education' programmes to ensure a smooth transition from reserve army of labour to professional middle class. Volunteer tourism is one such strategy.

This chapter has argued that, despite the apparent uselessness of overseas volunteering projects, the practice remains instructive. It exposes young adults from the Global North to cultural, emotional and interpersonal challenges that endow them with the necessary skills and resources needed to perform in multicultural settings and flexible work conditions. Whereas, in Guatemala, tourists found it easy to develop an affective relation with the 'friendly' locals and their 'authentic' culture because their foreignness was not explicitly racialized, in Ghana, racial tensions frequently interrupted such sentimental effusions. But instead of determining volunteers to break off their travels, these moments of frustration, anger and sheer exasperation only augmented volunteers' sense of personal growth and self-development. This narrative of becoming was only strengthened by friends and family back home who revered volunteers for having the courage to travel to a place as dangerous and destitute as 'black Africa'. The same is true for educators and employers, who have also discovered the importance of travelling and working abroad to cultivate the cognitive and communicative skills necessary for effective conduct in a multicultural society and multinational capital. At the end of the day, though, volunteer tourism can only remain a promise of employability, never a guarantee. Despite the conceit of capitalism to govern uncertainty through investment, insurance and risk assessment, the future remains the only dimension of time for which there is no historical evidence (Brook 2004: 2). The little we can intimate about the future is that it bears no reason for celebration. Neoliberal capital is gradually making it more contingent and less sustainable, introducing a competitive, highly polarized political regime that betrays our aspirations for democratic rule and universal dignity.

5 Conclusion

International political life

Overseas volunteering draws its strength from communitarian and cosmopolitan principles that value transnational cooperation, mutual assistance and cross-cultural exchange. The twin goals of giving back to the developing world and learning from traditional cultures are cited in every brochure on volunteer tourism, and are mentioned by volunteers as the primary reasons for enrolling on these costly trips. This book has been mostly concerned with showing how events on the ground complicate these aspirations, arguing that the experience of volunteering always somehow gets brought back into the fold of capitalist value production. I have argued in this book that volunteer tourism is one of several contemporary practices (along with flexible production, ethical consumption, corporate social responsibility, social entrepreneurship and urban regeneration) meant to provide capital with the 'forms of sociality and subjectivity' it needs to reproduce itself (Read 2003: 135). It does so by cultivating emotional and communicative competencies required from adaptable workers and transgressive entrepreneurs. Still, the discourse of charity, community and compassion mobilized here is more than just window dressing. Volunteer tourism expresses a genuine desire for community, mutual aid and cosmopolitan sociality that neoliberal government does not know how to accommodate, other than by packaging it as a luxury commodity with feel-good value.

It might seem peculiar to witness such a widespread embrace of communitarian and cosmopolitan values just as the War on Terror is placing public spaces and cross-border movement under increasing police surveillance, and neoliberal capital is eroding the social and environmental basis for collective survival. If we look at it from the opposite perspective, however, this makes perfect sense. Precisely because sovereign power is impeding the free movement and peaceful assembly of people, and global capital is auctioning off our common goods and resources, we find more and more people trying to resist the hyperindividualist effects of consumer capitalism. Neoliberal rule has not missed out on the fact that there is always a 'potential for a kind of spontaneous and elementary communism' (Hardt and Negri 2000: 294) at work in capitalism, which is why it seeks to subsume our penchant for communication, cooperation and friendship to the logic of scarcity and profitability. Under the combined pressures of competitive job markets, uncertain economic conditions

120   *Conclusion*

and managerial surveillance, these potentially commonist impulses are turned into their opposites. The desire to meet new people, learn about other cultures, understand the causes of global poverty, gain new skills and experience, travel and become involved in community affairs are stripped down of their excess creativity, knowledge and sociality and reduced to strategic assets and branding techniques that individuals must collect in the race for social mobility and status.

In this final chapter I want to establish a closer dialogue between Foucault's theory of subject formation, which has been the main source of inspiration in this book, and the autonomist Marxist critique of capital. My intent is to show how neoliberalism introduces sharp differentiations between various subject positions depending on their respective abilities to conform to the dictates of the market. I begin the chapter with a summary of the arguments presented so far. In the second section, I turn to Aihwa Ong's concept of 'flexible citizenship' (1999, 2005, 2006, 2007a, 2007b) to illustrate how volunteer tourism produces hierarchical and uneven forms of being and acting in the world. Finally, I close the book by reflecting on whether the most recent global economic crisis, which calls into question the ability of capital to continue delivering the goods, might detract from the legitimacy and value of entrepreneurial strategies like volunteer tourism and, instead, open the door to non-market based experiments of living in common.

Giving back in neoliberal times

The ambition of this project has been to explore the means through which volunteer tourism produces subjects and social relations congruent with the entrepreneurial spirit of neoliberal capital. My approach has been most heavily indebted to Foucauldian theories on neoliberal governmentality. According to Foucault, neoliberalism is more complex than just a generalized laissez-faire economy. It describes an entire mode of social organization, which in using market principles to optimize the productivity, longevity and security of a population subsumes the entire social field to market imperatives. The reason why neoliberalism has proven so resilient despite successive waves of crisis is because it has been successfully embedded in adequate institutions, social conventions, identity structures, class relations, norms and values (Cahill 2011). Government intervention is not only necessary for this task, contrary to what neoliberal dogma regarding a self-regulating market society may suggest, it is also not limited to the institutions and power networks of the state. The primary task of neoliberal government is not about regulating or embedding the destructive tendencies of the market, but about making sure the social field contains the necessary values, tastes and attitudes for a free market economy to operate smoothly.

A core focus of this research project has been to understand how neoliberalism creates the subjects and social relations it needs to effortlessly reproduce its rule. The example of volunteer tourism in the Global South seemed not

Conclusion 121

only fitting, but also provocative. The innovative combination of leisure and labour, enjoyment and entrepreneurship, charity and careerism proves that the logic of neoliberalism is not exhausted by economic rationalizations and dispassionate utility calculations, as it is often caricatured. While entrepreneurship and competition remain foundational modes of neoliberal conduct, neoliberalism places an equal emphasis on associational values of mutual aid, care and responsibility. Volunteer tourism unites these two registers. On the one hand, it offers young adults the opportunity to enhance their professional skills and overall employability by living and working in foreign environments, often under difficult circumstances. On the other hand, it taps into people's genuine desire to do good, learn about foreign cultures and experience ways of being in the world that the rational, individualistic West has made impossible.

If these rather communitarian or cosmopolitan aspirations never fully escape the logic of entrepreneurship, but are repeatedly translated into useful professional assets and work competencies, as I found it to be the case in my study, it is because neoliberalism is quite skilled at incorporating dissenting attitudes and affects into its fold. Neoliberalism needs to include elements external or even inimical to its logic to generate public legitimacy and, more concretely, counteract the anxiety and despair produced by the gradual erosion of collective bonds and social protections at the hands of the market. With its mix of economic rationality and social responsibility, volunteer tourism is perfectly poised to teach young adults both how to succeed in a globalized market economy and how to govern themselves and others in the absence of direct government intervention and spending. In other words, volunteer tourism seizes upon people's longing for community and sociality to teach individuals how to apply entrepreneurial talents to fill the void left by a shrinking welfare state.

The conclusion I drew from volunteering with a grassroots nature conservation project in rural Guatemala and a teaching programme in Ghana is that, even when volunteer tourism falls short of its idealistic and pragmatic promises, even when it does nothing to contribute to local development or the professional education of volunteers, the formula continues to invest participants with the cognitive, communicative and affective competencies expected from entrepreneurial workers and responsible citizens. While spending time in foreign cultures and unfamiliar situations, volunteers are invited to use every experience as an opportunity for self-growth and personal transformation. This pedagogical tool, which is ultimately a strategy of subjectivization, is never for naught. Whether they develop their tolerance for local culture and people or they pick up social and communicative skills to better cope with the challenges of culture shock, overseas volunteering is consistently beneficial to Western tourists.

In Guatemala, I was surprised that the charitable souls, appealed to in the brochure literature, were nowhere to be found. After only a couple of weeks in San Andres, volunteers already lost interest in the seemingly inefficient and unrewarding programmes offered by Volunteer Peten, and began focusing on socializing with the 'friendly' locals and getting to know the 'authentic'

122 *Conclusion*

culture instead. These more culturally oriented activities helped volunteers compensate for the nagging feeling of not being useful and, more importantly, allowed them to demonstrate their affective credentials in ways that strict volunteer work could not. The volunteering program may not have been able to offer participants any meaningful social roles in the community, leaving many frustrated about having 'wasted' their vacation time and money. However, in staging a temporary escape from modern mass society, volunteering in Guatemala managed to retain its legitimacy and appeal. Volunteers were happy to interact with local people, broaden their cultural horizons, live in close proximity to nature and enjoy the small pleasures of life. The town of San Andres was essential to the ultimate success of this experience. According to volunteers the town was not 'poor enough' to require humanitarian assistance, but was at least small and quaint enough to allow tourists to 'fall in love' with the local population and culture. What this demonstrates is that what motivates volunteering in the Global South is less a humanitarian impulse to do good than a romantic longing for the traditional structures of meaning the West has supposedly sacrificed on the altar of modernization: community, authenticity and spirituality.

This romantic quest for authentic meaning and spiritual renewal is not endemic to volunteer tourism. It is foundational to the temporal self-constitution of the West, which prides itself on having overcome the irrationality and despotism of primitive cultures, while also mourning the lost spiritual richness and natural harmony of earlier civilizations. We find this narrative of loss and rupture in a variety of places: in Orientalist representations of subaltern people it takes the shape of a constant switching back and forth between denigrating and idealizing the other, between the systematic discrimination of racialized populations and the celebration of cultural diversity; in critiques of capitalism, from the Industrial Revolution all the way to the Internet Revolution, it focuses overwhelmingly on the alienating and stultifying effects of industrial modernity; and in liberal strategies of government from the 1990s (like 'community government', 'good governance', humanitarianism and the post-development doctrine) the romantic ethos mobilizes social democratic and cosmopolitan principles not to reign in the effects of flexible accumulation but to cultivate a civic spirit that can bear the cost of rolled back public spending and social services. All of these romantic impulses betray a deep dissatisfaction with the rationalism and individualism of modern capitalist societies. Unfortunately, however, community and collective autonomy alone cannot unsettle the status quo. In refusing to directly confront questions of material redistribution and social justice, aspirations of dignity, romantic appeals to self-determination, autonomy and authentic meaning have worked better at making accumulation more tolerable rather than more just.

We see a similar problem with the romantic narrative underlying volunteer tourism. The formula takes its force from a legitimate discontent volunteers have with industrial modernity. Dissatisfied with the consumerist and homogenizing effect of Western culture, volunteers are eager to learn about and *from* foreign cultures by living with local families, observing and participating in their everyday routines, house chores, festivities and local dialect. This is a genuine desire. Declaring their tolerance and appreciation for local culture and people is a way for volunteers to profess their solidarity with people in radical positions of inequality and counteract painful feelings of boredom and uselessness. In the absence of a political pedagogy, however, the economic and environmental exploitation that banishes places like San Andres to the back-water of modernity is overlooked in favour of a misguided appreciation for the 'poor-but-happy' lifestyle of local people. When multicultural sensibilities are not anchored in an understanding of the material and historic roots of difference, they actually end up denying local people's claims to development, progress and equality. Multiculturalism then becomes a strategy for managing diversity, not for advancing a cosmopolitan vision of justice. The only ones who stand to gain from this exchange are volunteers. By charging themselves with the responsibility of protecting traditional cultures from corrupting modern influences volunteers appear as worldly, generous souls. But this profession of moral superiority only functions at the expense of developing populations who cannot afford the luxuries of transnational travel and working class people at home who cannot participate in such acts of ethical consumption. This is romanticism at its worst: a rejuvenation of consumer capitalism through Orientalist fantasies of difference that earns white middle-class people additional social capital.

In Ghana most of these romantic aspirations were thwarted by difficult racial encounters. Like in Guatemala volunteers were mostly disappointed with the loose organization of volunteering projects and the limited impact these had on the local community. But since the Projects Abroad trip cost three times as much as that offered by Volunteer Peten, volunteers remained determined to gather professional skills and relevant work experience despite all odds. While the placements themselves fell short of these expectations, simply 'living' in Ghana, without the material comforts and emotional support of home, helped students and graduates develop sought-after cognitive, communicative and affective skills.

Of great use in this context were the racial tensions unfolding between volunteers and their hosts. Ghanaians have a habit of making white bodies visible by shouting 'white man' after tourists in the street, touching their skin and hair and observing their every move. Although this scrutinizing gaze usually comes from a place of intense admiration and reverence for white bodies, it still made volunteers feel highly uncomfortable and even anxious about their relative position of privilege to the point where they saw themselves as victims of 'reverse racism'. Critical race literature considers the racialization or pro-vincialization of whiteness to be a necessary step for helping white bodies unlearn their privilege. The reason white bodies can do more (they are more mobile, esteemed, versatile) than others is because our dominant cultural representations and politico-legal structures systematically place whiteness at the centre of humanity. Provincializing whiteness is supposed to show that the

124   Conclusion

latter too is a racially constructed identity position like any other. In Ghana, however, this exercise did not produce the desired pedagogical effect. It only caused volunteers to use what they thought were acts of racial discrimination directed against them as another opportunity to assert their independent, assertive sovereign self. These stressful and exasperating encounters taught volunteers how to cope with cultural anxieties and nervous conditions, mediate cross-cultural conflicts and communicate more effectively. It did not encourage them to critically reflect upon their racial privilege or pursue deeper relations with the local population. In effect, racial tensions were better at producing the flexible and employable citizen-workers required in a multicultural society and a multinational economy than at unsettling the white privilege this subjectivity rests upon.

Because of its exorbitant price, volunteering in Ghana was seen as an investment in the future or an insurance policy against an increasingly flexible and fickle job market. This is not to say that volunteers are purely interested in boosting their résumés, only to recognize that the exigencies of neoliberal capital are such that individuals need to treat all areas of life, even leisure time, like work or an investment in one's future ability to work. This is particularly true in a knowledge economy where higher education no longer functions as a guarantee of secure employment or social mobility but is nevertheless an indispensable requirement for entering the professional class. The larger contradiction here is that capital no longer needs many of the workers it trains. To negotiate this paradox, students have to take their education beyond the classroom by working part-time jobs, doing internships, learning foreign languages, participating in study abroad programmes, volunteering, travelling and constantly gathering international experience. It may seem absurd or wasteful to pay $2,500 for one month of volunteering in Ghana but, for those who can afford it, the experience represents an institutionally accepted and professionally valuable asset.

Volunteers are well aware of the symbolic weight overseas volunteering carries with it, especially in the eyes of friends, family, recruitment agents, educators and employers back home. It is precisely because the merits of volunteer tourism are assessed at home and not on the ground, that the formula can retain its aura of moral virtue and professional relevance despite contrary evidence. Most people in the West who have never been to Africa entertain a colonial fantasy of the continent. They imagine Africa to be the flipside of modernity, a huge expanse of poverty and disease, which only the bravest and most self-sacrificing of travellers can withstand. This designates Africa as either the final frontier of adventure, a spiritual repository of meaningful lessons or, in this case, the ideal classroom for learning how to navigate the challenges and complexities of globalization. Although volunteers quickly learn that life in Ghana is far less dangerous and exotic than they had expected, this does not determine them to cut their trip short. They continue attending to their unrewarding work placements and mundane routines because they do not want to risk the admiration they gathered at home. Ultimately, even boredom

Conclusion 125

can function as an opportunity for self-growth. Africa, with its proverbial contingency, chaos and cultural diversity, acts as a mirror image to neoliberal capital. The skills one needs to navigate this uncertain terrain are the same skills one needs to perform in a globalized economy with no hard rules or guarantees. The rule-breaking adventurer in Africa becomes the risk-taking entrepreneur in casino capitalism.

Uneven fields of possibility

In this final chapter I want to place Foucault's theory of subject formation in a more direct conversation with the autonomist Marxist critique of capital. The reason for doing so is that, while I agree with Foucault that power is a ubiquitous social relation that produces (not only subordinates) subjectivity, not all subjects are produced equally. While the Foucauldian concept of subjectivity describes a historically situated and potentially open-ended process of individuation that can, in theory, assume an endless number of shapes, neoliberal government complicates this picture by assigning normative value and economic privilege to entrepreneurially oriented subjects while treating others as suspect and dangerous. Neoliberal government, then, makes as much room for spontaneity and gratification as it does for unevenness and exclusion. Responsible, self-reliant individuals, who can provide for their own welfare and even that of their fellow citizens without the help of public assistance, will enjoy greater economic benefits and political rights than other political subjects. Foucault is not oblivious to this process of 'normalization' (1977), but his analysis is not sufficiently attuned to the material conditions that underpin this hierarchical order. In *The Birth of Biopolitics* (2008), for instance, Foucault systematically shies away from making an explicit connection between the neoliberal art of government and the capitalist identities, class relations and institutions this mode of rule produces and legitimizes. This is where autonomist Marxism can come in handy.

The Marxist critique of capital recognizes that there has always been an 'intimate relationship between capital and subjectivity' (Read 2002: 125). Capital, as Marx recognized, is less an enclosed economic system than a social relation, whose primary goal is to produce hospitable class identities and property relations that facilitate the extraction of surplus value. The smooth extraction of wealth could not be achieved without an adequate ideological, cultural and subjective groundwork. For example, the successful transition from feudalism to capitalism required that collective and self-sufficient modes of agricultural production be replaced, in many instances forcefully, with the habits, routines and identities of the industrial working class. A similar transformation at the level of political subjectivity is needed every time capital changes its mode of production or encloses substantial components of our social fabric, leaving us with no option but to embrace capitalist property relations and forms of social cooperation. Particularly, in a flexible knowledge economy where value is no longer extracted from the mass production and consumption of

126   *Conclusion*

material goods, but through what David Harvey (2003) calls 'accumulation through dispossession', the reproduction of market-friendly subjects and social relations becomes all the more important since this is what guarantees that individuals acquiesce to a system that appropriates the value of their creative energies. If Marx generally relegated this task to the superstructure, the sphere of education, media, public institutions, ideology and culture, autonomist Marxists point out that in cognitive capital the production of subjects becomes indistinguishable from that of objects (Read 2002: 130).

In contemporary capitalism, the value created through the extraction of raw materials and the production of finished goods has decreased considerably. As a result, production has been automated and de-proletarianized, meaning we either do not require as many people to work in production or those still employed in this sector are so poorly rewarded that they come to be seen as financial liabilities rather than profitable consumers or potent citizens. Capitalism increasingly generates wealth by enclosing and monetizing people's inherent inclinations towards language, friendship and creativity through things like branding, advertising, copyright legislation, gentrification and widespread commodification. This does not mean that workers have lost their relevance. On the contrary, the more capital detaches itself from the 'real' economy, the more its survival comes to depend on the production of producers. The advantage of mobile, adaptable and entrepreneurial individuals is that they can bear the cost for the 'externalities' neoliberal capital no longer wants to be responsible for (education, healthcare, old age). Plus, they are willing to accept the precarity and contingency of this arrangement as a natural fact of life. This is essential for manufacturing consent with a mode of accumulation that has become entirely parasitical on energies and talents entirely outside its control (Hardt and Negri 2009). Instead of liberating work from its enslavement to value production or at least reducing work, cognitive capitalism erases the distinctions between labour and leisure time, extending the injunction to work to the fields of social reproduction, culture production and consumption. The result is what autonomists have called the 'social factory', a condition in which work becomes the subjective orientation we apply to all temporalities and domains of life (see Virno and Hardt 1996).

Foucault touches only briefly upon these developments in his discussion of 'human capital' (2008: 219–20), a concept developed by the Chicago school of neoliberal economics, but also related to Bourdieu's 'social capital' (1984). Neoliberal economic theory recognizes that people are the main driving force behind economic growth, not only in abstract terms that reduce labour power to hours of work, as held by classical political economy as well as scientific Marxism, but also as concrete social beings with complex capacities and desires. Yet instead of decoupling work from the need to produce surplus wealth, the concept of 'human capital' only further extends economic rationality to areas previously deemed as non-economic. It functions as an activating discourse designed to produce the entrepreneurial subject neoliberalism has set as its ideal. Within the parlance of 'human capital' the sociality of workers, their

Conclusion 127

informal knowledge, communicative skills, emotional competencies and overall personalities, are treated as strategic skills and assets for raising the bottom line. The object of work is no longer the external world, but the workers themselves and their capacity to work on short notice, under flexible conditions, across borders.

The original ambition behind the call to flexibilize Fordist institutions and social arrangements was to make room for more diverse and accountable forms of organization and greater opportunities for personal satisfaction and self-determination. This was the demand voiced by the student movements and worker struggles associated with the New Left: down with sclerotic organizational structures, repetitive jobs and conformist cultural conventions! Down with the welfare–warfare state, whose greatest achievement had been to satisfy the consumerist drives of white middle-class people at the expense of racial minorities at home and developing nations abroad! Although many leftists today, especially of the neo-Keynesian variety, mourn the social protections and government regulations of the post-war era, if we consider the political exclusions and human sacrifices the Fordist social compact was built upon, there is not much we need to be nostalgic about (Shukaitis 2007; Holmes 2011). Plus, as the New Left has been busy showing since the 1960s, all attempts at restoring the Fordist compromise by demanding better working conditions and higher wages fall short of emancipation. Any compromise between workers and capital, no matter how generous, is ultimately designed to make sure that the former continue to perform as the passive and docile servants of the latter. In contradistinction, an emancipatory politics should focus on escaping alienated work altogether. It should refuse to reduce human life to the poverty, both material and spiritual, of a working-class existence. As Harry Cleaver, the forefather of autonomist Marxism, put it: '[t]he aim of the mass worker is to cease to be a worker, not to make a religion of work' (1979: 69).

Neoliberal 'reformers' have done a great job of adopting this language of freedom and human dignity, popular both with radical activists in the West and anti-communist dissidents in the East, to suggest that dismantling the 'rigidities' of the old regime would make work more rewarding, sovereign power less interventionist, social norms less oppressive and life in general more self-directed and satisfying (Harvey 2005: 5). In reality, however, what replaced the Fordist compromise and its Keynesian mode of social regulation made the post-war era look like the Golden Age of capitalism. Neoliberalism introduced a series of cosmetic changes to our management routines, organizational structures, urban spaces, consumption patterns, citizenship practices and aesthetic styles. In exchange, it enclosed our collaborative and communitarian drives to justify overwork, boost private consumption and decouple communities from public assistance.

How could it have been otherwise? As a revanchist project meant to restore class domination, neoliberalism defines freedom as the ability to amass unlimited private wealth and privilege, not as the ability of people to pursue collective self-determination in the absence of sovereign power and market rule

128   *Conclusion*

(Smith 1996; Harvey 2005). Neoliberal dogma professes that anyone able to unleash their entrepreneurial skills and talents can access the American Dream. Free-market society is a world of equal opportunity because there is no pre-determined ruling class. In reality, however, this promise for colossal social mobility and personal realization unfolds against the constant threat of radical economic insecurity. To succeed under these conditions, an unrestrained spirit of competition has to be applied to all areas of social life, from the distribution of material wealth and resources to the allocation of rights, privileges and freedoms. Everything from the job you have, to the goods you buy, all the way to the emotions you demonstrate becomes a potential source of capital and an expression of social status. The subjective condition is not exempt from this logic of competition and social stratification. It is precisely where the link to neoliberal ideology is forged.

Foucault saw 'the work of turning human beings into subjects' (Dean 1994: 297) as an inevitable fact of modern power. Subjection is the process through which individuals come to understand themselves, their position and possibilities for action in the world. Without the work of subjection reality would not cohere around singular normative definitions as those imposed by capital or the state. But while for Foucault this was an inherently constructed and malleable process, I would like to put greater emphasis on the unevenness and differentiation that neoliberal government introduces into subject formation. It is probably true that post-Fordist capitalism offers us more diverse options for expressing our individuality, but becoming a liberal subject free from want, stigma and supervision is less a matter of universal rights than the outcome of competitive performance. When subjectivity comes to occupy a strategic role in the reproduction of capital and the extraction of immaterial value, it is bound to be judged by the same criteria of entrepreneurship and competition that apply to any other professional activity. This resembles the condition described in the famous *Animal Farm* phrase: 'we are all equal, but some of us are more equal'.

The outcome is a growing polarization between people like volunteer tourists who can afford to do fun jobs, combine lifelong learning with leisure, engage in ethical consumption and aesthetic politics and subaltern populations or the working poor who are not creative and mobile enough to keep up with the race for innovation, and who also lack the material wealth and security to assume the risks of participating in this race. This is not just the old economic distinction between haves and have-nots endemic to capitalist relations of production. It is also a normative distinction between individuals able to organize their lives according to the exceedingly demanding criteria of entrepreneurship and those unable to conform to sanctioned rationalities of government. The former come to enjoy ever more possibilities for action in terms of political rights and consumer freedoms, while the latter are *de-subjectified* – included only by virtue of their exclusion from social protections and democratic participation (Neal 2008: 51). As the lifestyles of the poor are made the object of surveillance, compassion and even criminalization, their 'choices' for

Conclusion   129

where to work, live, shop and move become increasingly constraining and punitive (Piven 1993; Peck 2001; Ehrenreich 2009; Wacquant 2009; Ilcan and Lacey 2011). To make matters even worse, the dividing line between the have-nots and varying degrees of haves is mutable and arbitrary because the normalizing power of neoliberalism is not based on a quantitative measure of skill or merit, but is 'conditional on conduct' (Rose 2000: 1408), conditional on our individual abilities to embody the values, habits and consumer tastes of flexible capital.

Aihwa Ong's work on 'flexible citizenship' (1999, 2005, 2006, 2007a, 2007b) is a great illustration of this condition. With the historical disintegration of territorial sovereignty under the pressures of global capital, Ong argues, citizenship disintegrates from a bundle of rights and freedoms distributed equally across all members of a territorial community into a commercialized, market-based privilege accorded in hierarchical fashion. An increasingly loose relation between political membership and territorial belonging introduces zones of 'graduated sovereignty' that follow the mobile and transient paths of capital (global cities, cyberspace, refugee camps, regional labour markets, high-tech districts, etc.) (Ong 2005). These flows create localities and conditions that make it possible for the rights of citizenship to be claimed outside state territory and national legislature, under conditions that contravene the fundamental principles of national representative democracy. As a result, the criteria for citizenship are recombined to reward those who can respond opportunistically and creatively to the demands of flexible accumulation (ibid.: 698). Because government is no longer interested in or able to provide for the welfare of its entire population, 'the security of citizens, their well-being and quality of life, are increasingly dependent on their own capacities as free individuals to confront globalized insecurities by making calculations and investments in their lives' (Ong 2006: 501). Those who cannot meet these expectations are automatically marginalized as deviant or labelled as security threats that must be contained (ibid.: 502). In conclusion, what was once a legal prerogative is now a scarce good to be earned depending on merit, conduct and market value under increasingly competitive and confining terms.

To illustrate this transformation, Ong draws on the example of the mega-city, which she defines not based on size, but on its ability to attract and capture inherently footloose capital, services, cultural products, experts and artists (2007b). Foreign professionals, in particular, are highly prized goods who promise to attach speculative value to a certain locale. The responsibility of global cities is to lure these 'pieds-à-terres' into becoming residents by offering them prestigious housing, tax breaks, maids and entertainment to facilitate an international lifestyle. Meanwhile, 'old' citizens have to fight off the side-effects of real-estate speculation, urban agglomeration and political disenfranchisement brought on by these patterns of 'gentrification'. In this context, citizenship becomes a strategic category for valorizing the membership of some populations over others. Those who possess the skill, talent, symbolic capital, market value and self-enterprise to creatively adapt to global conditions and

130   *Conclusion*

transnational processes will be rewarded with a growing number of passports, residence permits and mobility incentives as well as increasing access to job markets, housing options and cultural goods around the world. Those who fail to conform will be demoted to second-order citizens, confined to slums and ghettos, doomed to perform low-skilled and tedious jobs, with little possibility of escape. Their citizenship rights will be claimed through appeals to biological survival, rather than universal human rights and will be granted only by the grace of humanitarian organizations, foundations and charities. While some are accorded all the rights and privileges of citizenship, others have to claim them through struggle.

In volunteer tourism we find a similarly unequal competition over political subjectivity. Because the practice is predicated on an unequal global distribution of political rights and economic resources, volunteers are invited to expand their 'field of possibilities' (Foucault 2001: 343) at the expense of static and suspect local populations. Subjectivity is a more ineffable category than citizenship, but to the extent that it shapes people's understanding of the world and their possibilities for action in it, it has a variety of concrete political implications that cannot be ignored.

My research has shown that, regardless of the actual merits of overseas volunteering in terms of professional training or humanitarian assistance, simply having lived and worked in places the West considers destitute and dangerous earns volunteers a flexible seal of quality. By developing multicultural sensibilities or mastering cultural tensions, volunteers distinguish themselves as mature, magnanimous and mobile subjects unencumbered by sovereign borders and cultural boundaries. In a way, this has been the function of travelling to the 'heart of darkness' since colonial times: to establish the moral superiority of white bodies (Stoler 1995, 1997, 2002; McClintock 1995; Cook 2005, 2007, 2008). What is distinct about volunteer tourism is that, suddenly, conforming to Western standards of progress and civility is imbued with market value. Being 'at home in the world' is no longer the mark of the cosmopolitan aristocracy, like in the days of the nineteenth-century Grand Tour, but a requirement for all workers who wish to enter the ranks of the middle class. Because it places young adults in trying circumstances and foreign settings, volunteer tourism, more so than university education or other forms of credentialed training, can help individuals amass scarce social capital, demonstrate their cognitive and communicative skills and become the transgressive, risk-taking subjectivities multinational capital thrives on.

But there is also another advantage to volunteer tourism not captured by this rather economistic explanation. Recently, volunteer tourism has also been recognized as an important tool for reinvigorating the social fabric eroded by the Thatcherite logic that insisted 'there is no society ... only individuals and their families'. Adding the language of social responsibility to the ethos of entrepreneurship, volunteer tourism is thought to help individuals cultivate the civic values and communitarian ethos needed to fill the void left by the fragmentation of wage labour and social bonds. Seeing how neoliberal globalization

Conclusion   131

is forcing nation states to devolve more and more of their public responsibilities onto private shoulders, individuals are called on to assume a more active role in their communities. Using the language of local empowerment and community government, responsible citizens are expected to unleash their entrepreneurial talents to make up for the demise of Keynesian social regulation through things like volunteerism, charities and social enterprises.

It is no small irony that in 2010, just as the British government was preparing to introduce some of its most drastic spending cuts, Prime Minister David Cameron launched the International Citizen Service (ICS), otherwise known as 'the Big Society without borders' (Birdwell 2011). The programme, which is still in its pilot phase, is planning to send 1,000 people aged 18–22 on three-month aid and development trips to countries across Latin America, West Africa and the occupied territories in Palestine. The groundbreaking element about this initiative is that, unlike the for-profit volunteer tourism industry, it will give 'thousands of our young people, who could otherwise not afford it, the chance to see the world and serve others' (cited in ibid.: 15). People from households with an annual income lower than £25,000 will be able to enrol for free. The rest will have to pay between £1,000–2,000 depending on income.

It may seem paradoxical that in these times of economic austerity the British government would 'contribute to helping reduce poverty overseas as well as to broaden the horizons of the young volunteers and develop skills such as team working and communications' (Department of International Development 2011). What is even more surprising is that David Cameron would set up a free education programme for students from lower income families just when the tuition hikes introduced by his own government are drastically eroding the ability of these very same students to access higher education in Britain.

To untangle this contradiction we need to remind ourselves that the International Citizen Service is not a selfless gesture of cosmopolitan responsibility. It is not about the British government boosting its foreign aid and development spending. Rather, the ICS is an investment strategy designed to expand the labour power and civic spirit of young British nationals. As the website explains, by giving participants a chance to help the world's poor 'as a global citizen', the programme is a lifetime opportunity to 'develop important skills as teamworking, communication and decision-making: really important for finding a job and building your future' (Department of International Development 2011).

Programmes like the International Citizen Service or the Big Society, more broadly, should not be mistaken for 'handouts' of the Keynesian variety. They are the hallmark of the 'roll-out' phase of neoliberal government. If in the initial 'roll-back' phase neoliberalism destroyed and discredited Fordist institutions, modes of regulation and social bonds, in its second phase, neoliberal government rolls out 'neoliberalized state forms, modes of governance and regulatory relations' to better anchor free market capitalism in appropriate institutions, social relations and modes of life (Peck and Tickell 2002: 384). This is also known as the Third Way of liberal government, which tries to 're-regulate' laissez-faire economic policies through social democratic principles. It is not

132 *Conclusion*

so much that the welfare state has withered away at the hands of neoliberal market rule or the forces of economic globalization. Rather, the 'caring' welfare state of the mid-twentieth century, organized around the figure of the male industrial worker and the state-sponsored reality of high growth and full employment, has given way to an 'activating' welfare state where citizens must provide for their own well-being and that of their surrounding community (Vogel 2009). The neoliberal subject presented here is at the same time strongly individualized and keenly socialized. It is a subject expected to make a difference while also making a profit out of it (Lessernich 2009).

These are no easy tasks to fulfill. Individuals who can live up to the twin injunctions of economic rationality and social responsibility experience an expansion of their possibilities for action and participation as full members of the global society. They become norm-setting subjects with organization forms, institutions, communities, living spaces and cultural norms created in their image. Those who fail will 'not simply ... be thought ill of, looked down upon or devalued in others' attitudes, beliefs or representations, [they will also be] denied the status of a full partner in social interaction' (Fraser 2000: 113–14). Pedagogical tools like volunteer tourism can go a long way in this selection process. Overseas volunteering programmes may not be able to prepare workers for the changing needs of capital in the same way that higher education does, but it can disseminate ineffable work competencies like self-confidence, self-reliance, motivation, communication, teamwork and leadership skills, along with a sense of civic and political responsibility (Birdwell 2011: 11). These social and emotional skills alone cannot guarantee professional success or social mobility, but they prepare individuals to assume the risks and the costs associated with a flexible labour market and a shrinking welfare state.

What this unequal distribution of social status demonstrates is that neoliberalism is less a unified reality that stretches over the entire world than a normative ideal of progress and civility against which all other forms of community and subjectivity have to be measured. If there is any doubt about its hegemony, we must only look at the forcefulness with which the neoliberal ideal arranges subjects and social relations into hierarchies of inclusion and exclusion. If certain bodies or places are excluded from the neoliberal cartography that doesn't mean that they exist 'beyond' market relations. Those who fall outside the liberal parameters of order, rationality and progress are seen as existential threats to be contained through foreign intervention of either the military or the humanitarian sort (Jahn 2005; Dillon and Reid 2009). Of course, volunteers cannot be held directly responsible for this stratification of political subjectivity. Whatever the technical problems of volunteering programmes, young adults joining these trips are ultimately also victims of larger socio-economic transformations (the corporatization and professionalization of higher education, stagnating wages and rising joblessness, reduced government funding and social services and the dissolution of Fordist social bonds and collective frameworks of meaning) desperately trying to live up to the requirements of neoliberal subjectivity.

Conclusion   133

Getting stuck in neoliberal times

The arguments presented in this book, in particular the idea that volunteer tourism can enhance the employability and expand the political subjectivity of young adults, have been based on the assumption that neoliberal society rewards those who conform and even surpass its exigencies. If you go to the right school, do the right internships and learn the right languages, the market will repay you in material privileges and social status. But what if this turns out to be an empty promise? What if capital is no longer able to deliver the goods, as the progression of the most recent financial crisis into its fifth year of slow growth and high unemployment seems to indicate? What if volunteering in the Global South, along with all the other instruments of entrepreneurial education and responsible citizenship, does not help young people achieve the kind of prestige and social mobility associated with a middle-class existence?

In my research I did not interview volunteers after returning home from their trips to find out whether the experience actually helped them find better jobs or get into the school of their choice. This was a conscious choice with both technical and theoretical justifications. The concrete benefits of volunteering abroad are inherently future oriented and can take years to materialize. Conducting post-trip interviews would have only stalled the completion of the project, with no concrete guarantee of reliable results. What is more, the advantage volunteer tourism bestows upon participants cannot be easily reduced to material privilege. Even if economic security and social mobility are the ultimate goal of enrolling on a volunteering trip, the immediate appeal of the formula is to allow participants to become 'full members of society' unencumbered by national borders or cultural boundaries (Fraser 2000: 113). The expectations of personal growth young people have from volunteering in the developing world are better assessed in terms of the cultural value and improved self-perception the experience affords than according to job opportunities. Material rewards should not be excluded from this account, only better situated within larger conditions for gaining institutional, legal and cultural access to social interaction. What frustrates this frame of analysis, though, is the crisis of capital unfolding before our eyes, which suggests that neoliberal prescriptions for how one should conduct and govern oneself are naked instruments of discipline with little economic bearing.

Contra Foucault, Marxist scholars like David Harvey (2005), Gérard Duménil and Dominique Lévy (2011) and Jodi Dean (2011) have argues that neoliberalism is essentially a strategy of class domination that uses the tools of sovereign power, often in contravention of the principles of representative democracy, to promote and protect the interests of the wealthy. Rather than focusing only on the governmental or, rather, the *mental* aspect of neoliberalism, as Foucault does, Marxists encourage us to be explicit about its class character (ibid.). What defines neoliberal government, they argue, is not the dissemination of a coherent economic rationality across the entire social body to help the market reach its most efficient form, but a series of disparate and often chaotic (crisis-prone)

134　*Conclusion*

instruments for restoring elite power even at the expense of the ideal of a self-regulating market. If an economic logic prioritizing efficiency, cost–benefit analysis and competition were indeed the overarching rationality of neoliberal government we 'would have incentivized productive investment rather than consumption and debt'. Instead, neoliberalism has systematically eroded the productivist base of the economy through tax cuts, financial deregulation, manipulative and fraudulent lending practices, austerity measures, stagnating wages, debt bondage and sustained attacks on labour power, inviting a type of wealth extraction based purely on 'society-wide exploitation' (ibid.). This is an exploitation no longer limited to labour time. It extends to public goods, natural resources, social relations, cognitive and creative energies, emotions and fantasies. It includes both the things we already own in common and the social and ecological foundations for future production (Hardt and Negri 2009).

Surely we cannot blame Foucault for not anticipating the disastrous and distorted effects neoliberalism would produce in the decades to come. Written in 1978–79, *The Birth of Biopolitics* impresses in its ability to grasp the neoliberal logic of rule even before the political sea change introduced by Reaganomics and Thatcherism. But, as Jodi Dean rightfully notes, to privilege this interpretation over the Marxist analysis of capital, is to miss out on the 'crucial anti-economic component of neoliberalism that is inextricable from its class character' (2011). There is a world of difference between the idealistic prescriptions of neoliberal theory (idealistic not in the sense of utopia but in terms of the project's unattainability), which see no role for the state in regulating an otherwise rational, effective and harmonious market and actually existing neoliberalism, which requires increasingly undemocratic and inevitably brutal forms of state intervention to sustain its monopolies, ponzi schemes, government bailouts, rent extractions, corporate lobbyists and complicit politicians (Peck 2010b; Cahill 2011). We need to give up on the fantasy that we live in a free-market society. Neoliberalism is not about a disembedding of the market from mechanisms of social regulation or a triumph of market society over national sovereignty. To the extent that neoliberal capital has been able to withstand successive rounds of crisis and critique it is because its logic of operation is firmly lodged in social relations, institutions, legal norms and cultural values that lend itself well to the unequal and predatory accumulation of wealth.

Actually existing neoliberalism also complicates Foucault's analysis of the *discourse* of neoliberalism. While Foucault is correct to suggest that neoliberal government employs discursive strategies to generalize entrepreneurial and competitive modes of conduct across the entire social field, the most recent economic crisis indicates that these discursive devices are in fact disciplinary tools with no economic merit. Free-market capitalism does not unfold according to some coherent design that will 'naturally' satisfy collective needs and reward industrious individuals. Rather, the mechanisms through which neoliberalism promotes the interests of financial and managerial elites manipulate the supposed rationalism of the market, turning it into an erratic and arbitrary lottery game. 'Neoliberalism doesn't make us little entrepreneurs; it makes us

Conclusion 135

contestants' (Dean 2011) in a game with limited and uncertain odds. No matter how adaptable, flexible and calculating we are, we can still end up as debt-driven, job-seeking individuals who can barely make ends meet (Southwood 2011: 4). This is the message of the 'We Are the 99%' (http: //wearethe99percent.tumblr. com/) campaign blog, which features thousands of testimonies from people who made all the 'correct' calculations about their future and still ended up without a job, a home, or health insurance. What more and more people are coming to realize after the 2008 economic crisis is that the *homo oeconomicus* discourse touted by neoliberalism as an infallible recipe for success has in fact little bearing on actual economic performance. Its primary goal is to enlist our compliance with a system designed to benefit only a small number of winners.

Particularly hard hit by this crisis of capital is the population volunteer tourists are recruited from – overeducated, underemployed students. The situation is perhaps most glaring in the United States, but the UK is closely following suit. Exorbitant tuition increases are forcing students to take out massive government-backed loans on the vague promise that some day they may be able to find decent employment. What is essentially a condition of indentured labour, where people literally have to pay money to earn the 'privilege' to work (Ross 2011), has powerful institutional and subjective effects upon the idea of education. The university is turned from a site dedicated to the pursuit of knowledge into a factory-like training ground for future workers. It is no longer a space for living in common beyond the authority of parents or bosses, with the freedom to explore intellectual interests and talents, enjoy lots of free time and experiment with new forms of living. This experience is placed under attack when students are forced to live at home, take part-time jobs, drastically reduce their free time, assess the profitability of their degrees and participate only in extracurricular activities with high added value (Read 2009b: 151–52). On top of that, after finishing university, these workers in waiting cannot even be sure that their sacrifices will pay off: degrees are losing their market value, rewarding and well-remunerated jobs are few, student debt is skyrocketing, wages are stagnating or plummeting, benefits are vanishing, working hours are getting longer and the American Dream is out the window. Many young people today cannot expect to recreate the standard of living their parents enjoyed, although they probably struggled harder for it than any previous generation:

'I did everything I was supposed to! I worked hard, studied hard, got into college. Now I'm unemployed, with no prospects and $50 to $80,000.00 in debt.' These were kids who played by the rules and were rewarded by a future of constant harassment, of being told they were worthless deadbeats by agents of those very financial institutions who – after having spectacularly failed to play by the rules and crashing the world economy as a result, were saved and coddled by the government in all the ways that ordinary Americans such as themselves, equally spectacularly, were not.

(Graeber 2011)

136 *Conclusion*

Seeing how this so-called 'lost generation' is best positioned to grasp the contradictions of neoliberal capital, it is important to ask whether these feelings of anxiety and despair might engender an exodus from the discipline of capital. Is it possible that the chronic underemployment and reduced social mobility threatening young graduates today might erode some of the confidence these people have in neoliberal values, dispositions and modes of action? Could it be that, in time, entrepreneurial education strategies like volunteer tourism will lose their value and appeal only to be replaced by forms of community and solidarity that contradict the logic of the market?

It might take years before we see any significant impact on commercial volunteer tourism. For now, we can observe people, inspired by the year of revolt that swept the world in 2011 (the Arab Spring, anti-austerity protests in Southern Europe, university struggles in Britain and Chile, the indignados movement and Occupy Wall Street), slowly rediscovering the pleasures of being together after decades of consumer individualism, political apathy and economic nihilism. Centred loosely on a broad critique of global capital and its distortion of democratic politics, these movements exploded in size and sophistication to spread into university campuses, schools, homes and communities. Indebted, overworked and discouraged, young people everywhere have been at the forefront of these struggles, not only because activists are usually recruited from this age group, but mainly because their overeducated, underemployed condition is a blatant example of the contradictions of neoliberal capital. The political pedagogy of this experience is to teach people the beauty as well as the challenges of organizing life in common beyond the strictures of market capitalism. This is not entirely opposed to the spirit of volunteer tourism, which also searches for communion with others to counteract the hyperindividualism and quotidian nihilism of modern existence. In both instances we find the 'surplus knowledge, surplus creativity, surplus sociality and surplus relationality' (Haiven 2011) autonomist Marxists warned us cognitive capitalism would produce but not know how to contain. But whereas the latter is a for-profit instrument that reduces our longing for community and self-determination to economic assets, the former uses principles of mutual responsibility and transnational cooperation to stage a dramatic exit from capitalism.

How is such a transition from complicity to exodus from capital to be achieved? I have been asked numerous times, during the course of this research, by educators, parents, past and future volunteers, whether I would advise people to enroll in volunteering trips. This book provides no definitive answers to this question because the decision is essentially a personal one, with the mention that even the personal is intensely governed (Rose 1991: 1). We cannot demand that people 'come out' and get involved in politics or 'make a difference' through non-market avenues. These moralistic appeals to personal and even social responsibility can only exacerbate people's sense of guilt and fear of their own potentials. We are all complicit with the violence, economic dispossession and natural destruction we see around us, if not by actually causing these, then at least by not being able to extricate ourselves from the conditions that make them

Conclusion   137

necessary: all of us eat food produced in dubious conditions, engage in wasteful consumption practices, work for predatory bosses and purchase our dreams through finance capital. A neoliberal art of government that draws our genuine aspirations for autonomy, community and self-government into its logic of profit extraction makes it very difficult to 'be the change you want to see in the world'. It is not that we have passively submitted to neoliberalism so much as we have become emotionally invested in it. With these complications in mind, this book has been animated by a rather modest ambition: to encourage a level of theoretical literacy that will allow us to practice a rigorous (self-) examination of our deepest emotional and political investments. This is what Foucault called a 'critical ontology of ourselves' – a sceptical attitude 'in which the critique of what we are is at one and the same time the historical analysis of the limits that are imposed on us and an experiment with the possibility of going beyond them' (1997c: 132).

Bibliography

CBC Radio (2009) 'Voluntourism', *The Sunday Edition*, 1 February.

'Communique from an Absent Future' (2009) Online. Available HTTP: http://wewante verything.wordpress.com/2009/09/24/communique-from-an-absent-future/ (accessed 30 October 2011).

Agamben, G. (1998) *Homo Sacer: Sovereign Power and Bare Life*, Stanford, CA: Stanford University Press.

Agathangelou, M. A., Bassichis, D. M. and Spira, T. L. (2008) 'Intimate Investments: Homonormativity, Global Lockdown, and the Seductions of Empire', *Radical History Review*, 100: 120–43.

Ahmed, S. (2004) 'Declarations of Whiteness: The Non-Performativity of Anti-Racism', *borderlands ejournal* 3.2. Online. Available HTTP: www.borderlands.net.au/vol3no2_2004/ahmed_declarations.htm (accessed 27 December 2011).

——(2005) 'The Politics of Feeling Bad', *Australian Critical Race and Whiteness Studies Association Journal*, 1: 72–84.

——(2006) *Queer Phenomenology: Orientations, Objects, Others*, Durham, NC: Duke University Press.

Allon, F., Anderson, K. and Bushell, R. (2008) 'Mutant Mobilities: Backpacker Tourism in "Global" Sydney', *Mobilities* 3: 73–94.

Anand, D. (2007) *Geopolitical Exotica: Tibet in Western Imagination*, Minneapolis: Minnesota University Press.

Andresky, F. J. (2001) *White-Collar Sweatshop: The Deterioration of Work and Its Rewards in Corporate America*, New York: W. W. Norton.

Ashley, R. and Walker, R. B. J. (eds) (1990) 'Speaking the Language of Exile: Dissidence in International Studies', *International Studies Quarterly*, 34: 259–417.

Badone, E. (2004) 'Crossing Boundaries: Exploring the Borderlands of Ethnography, Tourism and Pilgrimage', in E. Badone and S. R. Roseman (eds), *Intersecting Journeys: The Anthropology of Pilgrimage and Tourism*, Champaign, IL: University of Illinois Press.

Barker, C. (2001) 'Some Reflections on Student Movements of the 1960s and Early 1970s', *Revista Critica de Ciecias Sociais*, 81: 43–91.

Barry, A., Osborne, T. and Rose, N. (eds) (1996) *Foucault and Political Reason: Liberalism, Neo-Liberalism and Rationalities of Government*, Chicago: University of Chicago Press.

Bauman, Z. (1998) *Globalization: The Human Consequences*, Cambridge: Polity Press.

Bayart, J. F. (2008) *Global Subjects: A Political Critique of Globalization*, New York: Polity Press.

Behar, R. (1996) *The Vulnerable Observer: Anthropology that Breaks Your Heart*, Boston: Beacon Press.

Bibliography 139

——(2003) 'Ethnography and the Book that Was Lost', *Ethnography*, 4: 15–39.

Behrent, C. M. (2009) 'Liberalism without Humanism: Michel Foucault and the Free-Market Creed, 1976–79', *Modern Intellectual History*, 6: 539–68.

Beier, M. J. and Arnold, S. (2005) 'Becoming Undisciplined: Toward the Supradisciplinary Study of Security', *International Studies Review*, 7: 41–62.

Berlant, L. (2004) 'Introduction', in L. Berlant (ed.) *Compassion: The Culture and Politics of an Emotion*, New York: Routledge.

Birdwell, J. (2011) *Service International*, London: Demos.

Birrell, J. (2010) 'Before You Pay to Volunteer Abroad, Think of the Harm You Might Do.' *The Guardian*, 14 November 2010. Online. Available HTTP: www.guardian.co.uk/commentisfree/2010/nov/14/orphans-cambodia-aids-holidays-madonna (accessed 15 June 2011).

Boden, S. and Williams, S. J. (2002) 'Consumption and Emotion: The Romantic Ethic Revisited', *Sociology*, 36: 493–512.

Boltanski, L. and Chiapello, E. (2005) *The New Spirit of Capitalism*, New York: Verso.

Bourdieu, P. (1984) *Distinction: A Social Critique of the Judgement of Taste*, Cambridge, MA: Harvard University Press.

Bousquet, M. (2008) *How the University Works: Higher Education and the Low-Wage Nation*, New York: New York University Press.

Brennan, T. (2005) 'The Empire's New Clothes', *Critical Inquiry*, 29: 337–67.

Broad, S. (2003) 'Living the Thai Life: A Case Study of Volunteer Tourism at the Gibbon Rehabilitation Project, Thailand', *Tourism Recreation Research*, 28: 63–72.

Bröckling, U. (2007) *Das unternehmerische Selbst: Soziologie einer Subjektivierungsform*, Frankfurt: Suhrkamp.

Brook, T. (2004) 'Violence as Historical Time', Working Paper Series, Institute on Globalization and the Human Condition, McMaster University. August 2004. Online. Available HTTP: www.socialsciences.mcmaster.ca/institute-on-globalization-and-the-human-condition/documents/IGHC-WPS_04-4_Brook.pdf (accessed 27 December 2011).

Brooks, D. (2000) *Bobos in Paradise: The New Upper Class and How They Got There*, New York: Simon & Schuster.

Brooks, P. (2011) 'Our Universities: How Bad? How Good?' *New York Review of Books*. 24 March 2011. Online. Available HTTP: www.nybooks.com/articles/archives/2011/mar/24/our-universities-how-bad-how-good/?pagination=false (accessed 27 December 2011).

Brooks, R. (2006) 'Learning and Work in the Lives of Young Adults', *International Journal of Lifelong Education*, 25: 271–89.

Brown, W. (2003) 'Neo-Liberalism and the End of Liberal Democracy', *Theory & Event*, 7.

——(2006) *Regulating Aversion: Tolerance in the Age of Identity and Empire*, Princeton, NJ: Princeton University Press.

Bruner, E. M. (2005) *Culture on Tour: Ethnographies of Travel*, Chicago: University of Chicago Press.

Buden, B. (2011) 'Dislocation of Utopia: In Between Capitalism and Socialism', paper presented at the Institute for Cultural Inquiry, Berlin, 16 June 2011.

Burchell, G. (1996) 'Liberal Government and Techniques of the Self', in A. Barry, T. Osborne and N. Rose (eds), *Foucault and Political Reason: Liberalism, Neo-Liberalism and Rationalities of Government*, Chicago: University of Chicago Press.

Butcher, J. (2003) '*The Moralisation of Tourism: Sun, Sand … and Saving the World?*' New York: Routledge.

140 *Bibliography*

——(2007) *Ecotourism, NGOs and Development*, New York: Routledge.

Butler, J. (1990) *Gender Trouble: Feminism and the Subversion of Identity*, New York: Routledge.

——(2003) 'What is Critique? An Essay on Foucault's Virtue', paper presented at University of California, Berkeley. Online. Available HTTP: www.law.berkeley.edu/centers/kadish/what%20is%20critique%20J%20Butler.pdf (accessed 30 July 2009).

——(2005) *Giving an Account of Oneself*, Bronx, NY: Fordham University Press.

Caffentzis, G. (1999) 'The End of Work or the Renaissance of Slavery? A Critique of Rifkin and Negri', *Common Sense*, 24: 20–38.

——(2005) 'Immeasurable Value? An Essay on Marx's Legacy', *The Commoner*, 10: 87–114.

Cahill, D. (2011) 'Beyond Neoliberalism? Crisis and the Prospects for Progressive Alternatives', *New Political Science*, 33: 479–92.

Campbell, C. (1987) *The Romantic Ethic and the Spirit of Modern Consumerism*, Oxford: Blackwell.

Campbell, L. and Smith, C. (2006) 'What Makes Them Pay? Values of Volunteer Tourists Working for Sea Turtle Conservation', *Environmental Management*, 38: 84–98.

Cerwonka, A. (2007) 'Nervous Conditions: The Stakes in Interdisciplinary Research', in A. Cerwonka and L. H. Malkki (eds) *Improvising Theory: Press and Temporality in Ethnographic Fieldwork*, Chicago: University of Chicago Press.

Cerwonka, A. and Malkki, L. H. (2007) *Improvising Theory: Press and Temporality in Ethnographic Fieldwork*, Chicago: University of Chicago Press.

Chakrabarty, D. (2000) *Provincializing Europe: Postcolonial Thought and Historical Difference*, Princeton, NJ: Princeton University Press.

Chandler, D. (2009) 'Critiquing Liberal Cosmopolitanism? The Limits of the Biopolitical Approach', *International Political Sociology*, 3: 53–70.

——(2010) 'Globalising Foucault: Turning Critique into Apologia – A Response to Kiersey and Rosenow', *Global Society*, 24: 135–42.

Chin, C. B. N. (1998) *In Service and Servitude: Foreign Female Domestic Workers and the Malaysian 'Modernity' Project*, New York: Columbia University Press.

Chow, R. (1993) *Writing Diaspora: Tactics of Intervention in Contemporary Cultural Studies*, Bloomington: Indiana University Press.

Chrisinger, C. K., Meijer-Irons, J. and Garshick-Kleit, R. (2009) 'Methods of Poverty Measurement', Evans School of Public Affairs, University of Washington. Online. Available HTTP: http://cvp.evans.washington.edu/ wp-content/uploads/2009/09/chrisinger_meijer-irons_kleit_2009.pdf (accessed 10 May 2010).

Clancy, M. (2001) *Exporting Paradise: Tourism and Development in Mexico*, London: Pergamon.

——(2009) *Brand New Ireland: Tourism, Development and National Identity in the Irish Republic*, London: Ashgate.

Cleaver, H. (1979) *Reading Capital Politically*, Brighton: Harvester Press, 1979.

Clemmons, D. (2009) 'Welcome Potential VolunTourists', www.voluntourism.org/travelers.htm (accessed 18 April 2012).

Clifford, J. (1983) 'On Ethnographic Authority', *Reprsentations* 2: 118–46.

——(1988) *On Ethnographic Authority. The Predicament of Culture*, Cambridge, MA: Harvard University Press.

——(1986a) 'Introduction: Partial Truths', in J. Clifford and G. E. Marcus (eds) *Writing Culture: The Politics and Politics of Ethnography*, Berkeley: University of Chicago Press.

Bibliography 141

——(1986b) 'On Ethnographic Allegory', in J. Clifford and G. E. Marcus (eds) *Writing Culture: The Politics and Politics of Ethnography*, Berkeley: University of Chicago Press.

Cohen, E. (1979) 'A Phenomenology of Tourist Experiences', *Sociology*, 13: 179–201.

Comaroff, J. and Comaroff, J. (1992) *Ethnography and the Historical Imagination*, Boulder, CO: Westview Press.

Cook, N. (2005) 'What to Wear, What to Wear? Western Women and Imperialism in Gilgit, Pakistan', Qualitative Sociology, 28: 349–67.

——(2007) Gender, Identity and Imperialism: Women Development Workers in Pakistan, New York: Palgrave Macmillan.

——(2008) 'Development Workers, Transcultural Interactions and Imperial Relations in Northern Pakistan', in W. Coleman and D. Brydon (eds) Globalization, Autonomy and Community, Vancouver: University of British Columbia Press.

Cox, W. R. (1983) 'Gramsci, Hegemony and International Relations: An Essay in Method', *Millennium: Journal of International Studies*, 12: 162–75.

Crick, M. (1985) 'Tracing the Anthropological Self: Quizzical Reflections on Field Work, Tourism, and the Ludic', *Social Analysis*, 17: 71–92.

——(1989) 'Representations of International Tourism in the Social Sciences: Sun, Sex, Sights, Savings, and Servility', *Annual Review of Anthropology*, 18: 307–44.

Cruikshank, B. (1999) *The Will to Empower: Democratic Citizens and Other Subjects*, Ithaca, NY: Cornell University Press.

Dalton, A. (2008) 'Voluntourism Trips for Do-Gooders: When Sipping Margaritas, Sunburning Yourself Poolside Looses its Luster', *MSNBC.com*, 4 February. Online. Available HTTP: www.msnbc.msn.com/id/19314446/ (accessed 18 May 2008).

Dauphinee, E. and Masters, C. (eds) (2007) *The Logics of Biopower and the War on Terror: Living, Dying, Surviving*, Houndsmill: Palgrave Macmillan.

Dean, J. (2011) 'Three Theses on Neoliberalism (Or Contestants not Entrepreneurs)', paper presented at the annual meeting of the American Political Science Association, Seattle, September 2011.

Dean, M. (1994) 'Foucault's Obsession with Western Modernity', in B. Smart (ed.) *Michel Foucault: Critical Assessments*, New York: Routledge.

——(1999) *'Governmentality: Power and Rule in Modern Society'*, London: Sage.

Deleuze, G. (1988) *Foucault*, New York: Continuum.

Department for International Development (2011) www.dfid.gov.uk/Media-Room/Press-releases/2011/Young-people-to-make-a-difference-to-the-worlds-poorest-Internationonal-Citizen-Service-opens/ (accessed 17 April 2012).

Dillon, M. (2007) 'Governing Terror: The State of Emergency of Biopolitical Emergence', *International Political Sociology*, 1: 7–28.

Dillon, M. and Neal, A. W. (eds) (2008) *'Foucault on Politics, Security and War'*, Basingstoke: Palgrave Macmillan.

Dillon, M. and Reid, J. (2001) 'Global Liberal Governance: Biopolitics, Security and War', *Millennium: Journal of International Studies*, 20: 41–66.

——(2009) *The Liberal Way of War: Killing to Make Life Live*, New York: Routledge.

Duffield, M. (2009) 'The Fortified Aid Compound: Risk Management, Security Training and Urban Pathology', Global Insecurities Centre, University of Bristol. Online. Available HTTP: www.bris.ac.uk/politics/gic/files/fortifiedaidcompound.doc (accessed 20 November 2009).

Duménil, G. and Lévy, D. (2011) *The Crisis of Neoliberalism*, Cambridge, MA: Harvard University Press.

142 *Bibliography*

Dyer-Whiteford, N. (1999) *Cyber-Marx: Cycles and Circuits of Struggle in High Technology Capitalism*, Chicago: University of Illinois Press.

——(2005) 'Cognitive Capitalism and the Contested Campus', in G. Cox and J. Krysa (eds) *Engineering Culture: On the Author as (Digital) Producer*, New York: Autonomedia. Online. Available HTTP: www.anti-thesis.net/contents/texts/DB/DB02/DyerWitheford.pdf (accessed 27 December 2011)

Edkins, J. (2003) *Trauma and the Memory of Politics*, Cambridge: Cambridge University Press.

Edkins, J. and Pin-Fat, V. (2004) 'Introduction: Life, Power, Resistance', in J. Edkins, V. Pin-Fat and M. J. Shapiro (eds) *Sovereign Lives: Power in Global Politics*, New York: Routledge.

Ehrenreich, B. (2005) *Bait and Switch: The (Futile) Pursuit of the American Dream*, New York: Metropolitan Books.

——(2009) 'Is It Now a Crime to be Poor?' *New York Times*, 8 August. Online. Available HTTP: www.nytimes.com/2009/08/09/opinion/09ehrenreich.html?pagewanted=all (accessed 27 December 2011).

Fabian, J. (1983) *Time and the Other: How Anthropology Makes Its Objects*, New York: Columbia University Press.

——(1991) *Time and the Work of Anthropology: Critical Essays 1971–1991*, Philadelphia: Harwood Academic Publishers.

Fanon, F. (1961) *The Wretched of the Earth*, New York: Grove Press.

Federici, S. (2004) *Caliban and the Witch: Women, the Body and Primitive Accumulation*, Brooklyn: Autonomedia.

——(2011) 'Precarious Labor: A Feminist Viewpoint', lecture given on October 2006 at Bluestockings Radical Bookstore in New York. Online. Available HTTP: www.scribd.com/full/3108724?access_key=key-27agtedsy1ivn8j2ycc1 (accessed 21 July 2011).

Ferguson, J. (2006) *Global Shadows: Africa in the Neoliberal World Order*, Durham, NC: Duke University Press.

Florida, R. (2002) *The Rise of the Creative Class and How It's Transforming Work, Leisure, Community and Everyday Life*, New York: Basic Books.

——(2008) *Who's Your City: How the Creative Economy Is Making Where to Live the Most Important Decision of Your Life*, New York: Basic Books.

Foley, D. and Valenzuela, A. (2005) 'Critical Ethnography: The Politics of Collaboration', in N. K. Denzin and Y. S. Lincoln (eds) *The Sage Handbook of Qualitative Research*, 3rd ed. Thousand Oaks, CA: Sage.

Fortier, A.-M. (2010) 'Proximity by design? Affective citizenship and the management of unease', *Citizenship Studies* 14(1): 17–30.

Foucault, M. (1977) *Discipline and Punish*, New York: Vintage Books.

——(1980) *Power/Knowledge: Selected Interviews and Other Writings 1972–1977*, Colin Gordon (ed.) New York: Pantheon Books.

——(1976) *The History of Sexuality: An Introduction*, New York: Vintage Books.

——(1997a) 'Technologies of the Self', in M. Foucault and P. Rabinow (eds) *Essential Works of Foucault 1954–1984. Volume I: Ethics, Subjectivity and Truth*, New York: The New Press.

——(1997b) 'The Ethics of the Concern of the Self as a Practice of Freedom', in M. Foucault and P. Rabinow (eds) *Essential Works of Foucault 1954–1984. Volume I: Ethics, Subjectivity and Truth*, New York: The New Press.

——(1997c) 'What is Critique?', in S. Lotringer and L. Hochroth (eds) *The Politics of Truth*, New York: Semiotext(e).

Bibliography 143

——(2001) 'The Subject and Power', in J. D. Faubion (ed.) *Michel Foucault: Power. Essential Works of Foucault 1954–1984*, New York: The New Press.

——(2002) 'What Is Critique?', in D. Ingram (ed.) *The Political*, Malden, MA: Blackwell.

——(2007) *Security, Territory, Population: Lectures at the College de France 1977–1978*, New York: Palgrave, 2007.

——(2008) *The Birth of Biopolitics: Lectures at the Collège de France 1978–1979*, Hampshire: Macmillan.

Fowles, J. (1969) *The French Lieutenant's Woman*, London: Jonathan Cape.

Frank, T. and Weiland, M. (eds) (2002) *Commodify Your Dissent: Salvos from the Baffler*, New York: W. W. Norton & Company.

Franklin, A. and Crang, M. (2001) 'The Trouble with Tourism and Travel Theory?', *Tourist Studies*, 1: 5–22.

Fraser, N. (2000) 'Rethinking Recognition', *New Left Review*, 3: 107–20.

Fraser, N. *et al.* (2008) *Adding Insult to Injury: Nancy Fraser Debates Her Critics*, New York: Verso.

Frow, J. (1997) *Time & Commodity Culture: Essays in Cultural Theory and Postmodernity*, Oxford: Clarendon Press.

Fukuyama, F. (1992) *The End of History and the Last Man*, New York: Avon Books.

Fumagalli, A. and Mezzadra, S. (eds) (2010) *Crisis in the Global Economy: Financial Markets, Social Struggles and New Political Scenarios*, Los Angeles: Semiotext(e).

Galley, G. and Clifton, J. (2004) 'The Motivational and Demographic Characteristics of Research Ecotourists: Operation Wallacea Volunteers in Southeast Sulawesi, Indonesia', *Journal of Ecotourism*, 3: 69–82.

Geertz, C. (1988) *Works and Lives: The Anthropologist as Author*, Stanford: Stanford University Press.

Ghose, I. (1998) *Women Travellers in Colonial India: The Power of the Female Gaze*, New York: Oxford University Press.

Goldberg, T. D. (1993) *Racist Culture: Philosophy and the Politics of Meaning*, Oxford: Blackwell.

——(1994) 'Introduction', in D. T. Goldberg (ed.) *Multiculturalism: A Critical Reader*, Oxford: Blackwell.

Gordon, C. (1980) 'Afterword', in C. Gordon (ed.) *Power/Knowledge: Selected Interviews and Other Writings 1972–1977*, New York: Pantheon Books.

Gorz, A. (1999) *Reclaiming Work: Beyond the Wage-Based Society*, Cambridge: Polity Press.

Graeber, D. (2011) 'On Playing by the Rules – The Strange Success of #OccupyWallStreet', *Naked Capitalism*. October 2011. Online. Available HTTP: www.nakedcapitalism. com/2011/10/david-graeber-on-playing-by-the-rules-%E2%80%93-the-strange-success-of-occupy-wall-street.html (accessed 27 December 2011).

Grafton, A. (2011) 'Our Universities: Why Are They Failing?', *The New York Review of Books*, November 2011. Online. Available HTTP: www.nybooks.com/articles/ archives/2011/nov/24/our-universities-why-are-they-failing/?utm_source=feedburner&u tm_medium=feed&utm_campaign=Feed%3A+nybooks+%28The+New+York+Revie w+of+Books%29 (accessed 27 December 2011).

Grewal, I. (1997) *Home and Harem: Nation, Gender, Empire and the Culture of Travel*, Durham, NC: Duke University Press.

Gunew, S. (2001) 'Postcolonialism and Multiculturalism: Between Race and Ethnicity', in M. Danova (ed.) *Essays in American Studies: Cross-Cultural Perspectives*, Sofia: Polis.

144 *Bibliography*

Guttentag, D. (2009) 'The Possible Negative Impacts of Volunteer Tourism', *International Journal of Tourism Research*, 11: 537–51.

Haiven, M. (2011) 'From NYC: Oct 15 – Massive Marches, The University in the Streets, and Overcoming the Arrogance of the Left', Halifax Media Co-Op. October 2011. Online. Available HTTP: http://halifax.mediacoop.ca/blog/max-haiven/8418 (accessed 27 December 2011).

Hardt, M. (1996) 'Introduction: Laboratory Italy', in P. Virno and M. Hardt (eds), *Radical Thought in Italy: A Potential Politics*, Minneapolis: Minnesota University Press.

——(1999) 'Affective Labour', *Boundary*, 26: 89–100.

Hardt, M. and Negri, A. (2000) *Empire*, Cambridge, MA: Harvard University Press.

——(2004) *Multitude: War and Democracy in the Age of Empire*, New York: The Penguin Press.

——(2009) *Commonwealth*, Cambridge, MA: Belknap Press of Harvard University Press.

Harris, M. (2011) 'Bad Education', *n+1*, April 2011. Online. Available HTTP: http://nplusonemag.com/bad-education?utm_source=feedburner&utm_medium=feed&utm_campaign=Feed%3A+nplusonemag_main+%28n%2B1+magazine%29 (accessed 27 December 2011).

Harvey, D. (2003) *The New Imperialism*, Oxford: Oxford University Press.

——(2005) *A Brief History of Neoliberalism*, Oxford: Oxford University Press.

Hazbun, W. (2008) *Beaches, Ruins, Resorts: The Politics of Tourism in the Arab World*, Minneapolis: Minnesota University Press.

Henwood, D. (2003) *After the New Economy: The Binge … And the Hangover that Won't Go Away*, New York: New Press.

Heron, B. (2007) *Desire for Development: Whiteness, Gender, and the Helping Imperative*, Waterloo, ON: Wilfrid Laurier Press.

Higgins-Desbiolles, F. (2009) 'Indigenous ecotourism's role in transforming ecological consciousness', *Journal of Ecotourism*, 8(2): 144-160.

Hirschman, A. (1977) *The Passions and the Interests: Political Arguments for Capitalism before Its Triumph*, Princeton, NJ: Princeton University Press.

Hoffman, S. (1977) 'An American Social Science: International Relations', *Daedalus*, 106: 41–60.

Holmes, B. (2002) 'The Flexible Personality: For a New Cultural Critique', European Institute for Progressive Cultural Policies (eipcp). Online. Available HTTP: http://transform.eipcp.net/transversal/1106/holmes/en (accessed 27 December 2011).

——(2011) 'Keynesian Fordism as Global Social Compact', lecture presented as part of the seminar 'Three Crises: 30s–60s–Today', at Mess Hall, Chicago. Online. Available HTTP: http://brianholmes.wordpress.com/2011/10/19/american-dreams/ (accessed 27 December 2011).

Hudson Institute (2010) 'The Index of Global Philanthropy and Remittances 2010'. Hudson Institute Centre for Global Prosperity. Online. Available HTTP: www.hudson.org/files/pdf_upload/Index_of_Global_Philanthropy_and_Remittances_2010.pdf (accessed 13 May 2010).

Hutnyk, J. (1996) *The Rumor of Calcutta: Tourism, Charity and the Poverty of Representation*, New York: Zed Books.

——(2004) 'Photogenic Poverty: Souvenirs and Infantilism', *Journal of Visual Culture*, 3: 77–94.

——(2006) 'Trinketization: "Third-World" Tourism and the Manufacture of the Exotic', *Trinketization Blog*. Online. Available HTTP. http://hutnyk.blogspot.com/search/label/tourism (accessed 16 May 2008).

Bibliography 145

——(2007) 'Mind-Blogging Trinketization', *Trinketization Blog.* Online. Available HTTP. http://hutnyk.wordpress.com/2007/04/24/mind-boggling-trinketization/ (accessed 16 May 2008).

Huws, U. (2003) *The Making of a Cybertariat: Virtual Work in a Real World*, New York: Monthly Review Press.

Ilcan, S. and Lacey, A. (2011) *Governing the Poor: Exercises of Poverty Reduction, Practices of Global Aid*, Montreal, McGill University Press.

Illich, I. (1968) 'To Hell with Good Intentions', address to the Conference on Inter-American Student Projects (CIASP) in Cuernavaca, Mexico. Online. Available HTTP: www.swaraj.org/illich_hell.htm (accessed 27 December 2011).

Illouz, E. (1997) *Consuming the Romantic Utopia: Love and the Cultural Contradictions of Capitalism*, Berkeley: University of California Press.

——(2003) *Opray Winfrey and the Glamour of Misery: An Essay on Popular Culture*, New York: Columbia University Press.

——(2007) *Cold Intimacies: The Making of Emotional Capitalism*, Cambridge: Polity Press.

Inglehart, R. (1977) *The Silent Revolution: Changing Values and Political Styles among Western Publics*, Princeton, NJ: Princeton University Press.

Isin, E. (2000) *Democracy, Citizenship and the Global City*, New York: Routledge.

Jabri, V. (2006) 'War, Security and the Liberal State', *Security Dialogue*, 37: 47–64.

Jahn, B. (2005) 'Kant, Mill, and Illiberal Legacies in International Affairs', *International Organization*, 59: 177–207.

Jameson, F. (2000) 'Globalization and Political Strategy', *New Left Review*, 4: 49–68.

Joseph, J. (2009) 'Governmentality of What? Populations, States and International Organizations', *Global Society*, 23: 413–27.

——(2010a) 'The Limits of Governmentality: Social Theory and the International', *European Journal of International Relations*, 16: 223–46.

——(2010b) 'What Can Governmentality Do for IR?', *International Political Sociology*, 2: 202–4.

Kiersey, J. N. (2009) 'Neoliberal Political Economy and the Subjectivity of Crisis: Governmentality is Not Hollow', *Global Society*, 23: 363–86.

——(2011) 'Everyday Neoliberalism and the Subjectvity of Crisis: Post-Political Control in the Era of Financial Turmoil', *Journal of Critical Globalization Studies*, 1: 23–44.

Kiersey, J. N. and Weidner, J. R. (2009) 'Editorial Introduction', *Global Society*, 23: 353–61.

Kincaid, J. (1988) *A Small Place*, New York: Plume.

Kunkel, B. (2010) 'Into the Big Tent', *London Review of Books*, 32.8. Online. Available HTTP: www.lrb.co.uk/v32/n08/benjamin-kunkel/into-the-big-tent (accessed 24 April 2010).

Langley, P. (2008) *The Everyday Life of Global Finance: Saving and Borrowing in Anglo-America*, Oxford: Oxford University Press.

Larner, W. and Williams, W. (2004) 'Global Governmentality: Governing International Spaces', in W. Larner and W. Walters (eds) *Global Governmentality: Governing International Spaces*, New York: Routledge.

Lemke, T. (2001) '"The Birth of Bio-Politics" – Michel Foucault's Lecture at the Collège de France on Neo-Liberal Governmentality', *Economy & Society*, 30: 190–207.

——(2007) 'An Indigestible Meal? Foucault, Governmentality and State Theory', *Distinktion: Scandinavian Journal of Social Theory*, 15: 43–6.

Lessernich, S. (2008) *Die Neuerfindung des Sozialen: Der Sozialstaat im flexiblen Kapitalusmus*, Bielefeld: transcript Verlag.

146   Bibliography

——(2009) 'Mobilität und Kontrolle. Zur Dialektik der Aktivgesellschaft', in K. Dörre, S. Lessenich and H. Rosa (eds) *Soziologie. Kapitalismus. Kritik. Eine Debatte*, Frankfurt am Main: Suhrkamp.

Lipietz, A. (1992) *Towards a New Economic Order: Postfordism, Ecology and Democracy*, New York: Oxford University Press.

Lisle, D. (2006) *The Global Politics of Contemporary Travel Writing*, Cambridge: Cambridge University Press.

——(2010) 'Joyless Cosmopolitans: The Moral Economy of Ethical Tourism', in J. Best and M. Peterson (eds) *Cultural Political Economy*, New York: Routledge.

Lonely Planet (2007) *Guatemala*, London: Lonely Planet Publications.

——(2007) *Volunteer: A Traveller's Guide to Making a Difference Around the World*, London: Lonely Planet Publications.

Lotringer, S. (2009) 'In Theory', Frieze Art Fair. Online. Available HTTP: www. friezeartfair.com/podcasts/details/in_theory_sylvere_lotringer/ (accessed 27 December 2011).

Lotringer, S. and Marazzi, C. (eds) (2007) *Autonomia: Post-Political Politics*, Los Angelos: Semiotext(e).

MacCannell, D. (1973) 'Stages Authenticity: Arrangements of Social Space in Tourist Settings', *American Journal of Sociology*, 79: 589–603.

MacKinnon, J. B. (2009) 'The Dark Side of Volunteer Tourism', *UTNE Reader*, November–December 2009. Online. Available HTTP: www.utne.com/Politics/The-Dark-Side-of-Volunteer-Tourism-Voluntourism.aspx (accessed 15 June 2011).

Madison, S. D. (2005) *Critical Ethnography: Methods, Ethics, Performance*, New York: Sage.

Madra, M. Y. and Özselcuk, C. (2010) '*Juissance* and Antagonism in the Forms of the Commune: A Critique of Biopolitical Subjectivity', *Rethinking Marxism*, 22: 484–5.

Mahler, R. (1993) *Guatemala: A Natural Destination*, Santa Fe, NM: John Muir Publications.

Marcus, G. E. and Cushman, D. (1982) 'Ethnographies as Texts', *Annual Review of Anthropology*, 11: 25–69.

Marcuse, H. (2002[1964]) *One-Dimensional Man*, New York: Routledge.

Marazzi, C. (2008) *Capital and Language: From the New Economy to the War Economy*, Los Angeles: Semiotext(e).

——(2010) *The Violence of Financial Capitalism*, Los Angeles: Semiotext(e).

Mathers, K. and Hubbard, L. (2006) 'Doing Africa: Travelers, Adventurers, and American Conquest of Africa', in L. A. Vivanco and R. J. Gordon (eds) *Tarzan Was an Eco-Tourist ... and Other Tales in the Anthropology of Adventure*, New York: Berghahn Books.

Mazzarella, W. (2009) 'Affect: What Is It Good For?', in S. Dube (ed.) *Enchantments of Modernity: Empire, Nation, Globalization*, London: Routledge.

Mbembe, A. (2001) *On the Postcolony*, Berkeley: University of California Press.

McClintock, A. (1995) *Imperial Leather: Race, Gender, and Sexuality in the Colonial Contest*, New York: Routledge.

McGee, D. (1997) 'Post-Marxism: The Opiate of the Intellectuals', *Modern Language Quarterly*, 58: 201–25.

McGehee, N. and Santos, C. A. (2005) 'Social Change, Discourse and Volunteer Tourism', *Annals of Tourism Research*, 32: 760–79.

McNay, L. (2009) 'Self as Enterprise. Dilemmas of Control and Resistance in Foucault's Birth of Biopolitics', *Theory, Culture & Society*, 26: 55–77.

Bibliography 147

Mendleson, R. (2008) 'Helping the World. And Me: Is Volunteer Tourism about Saving the World or Enhancing a Résumé?', *Maclean's*, September. Online. Available HTTP: www.macleans.ca/culture/lifestyle/article.jsp?content=20080917_60473_60473 (accessed 12 May 2009).

Michaels, W.B. (2006) *The Trouble with Diversity: How We Learned to Love Identity and Ignore Inequality*, New York: Metropolitan Books.

——(2008) 'Against Diversity', *New Left Review*, 52: 33–36. Online. Available HTTP: www.newleftreview.org/?page=article&view=2731 (accessed 9 November 2009).

Mills, S. (1991) *Discourses of Difference: An Analysis of Women's Travel Writing and Colonialism*, London: Routledge.

Moore, Phoebe (2010) *The International Political Economy of Work and Employability*, London: Palgrave.

Muehlebach, A. (2010) 'On Affective Labor in Post-Fordist Italy', *Cultural Anthropology* 26(1): 59–82.

Neal, A. (2008) 'Goodbye War on Terror? Foucault and Butler on Discourses of Law, War, and Exceptionalism', in M. Dillon and A. W. Neal (eds) *Foucault on Politics, Security and War*, London: Palgrave.

Negri, A. (1989) *Marx beyond Marx: Lessons on the Grundrisse*, London: Autonomedia.

Neilson, B. and Rossiter, N. (2005) 'From Precarity to Precariousness and Back Again: Labour, Life and Unstable Networks', *Fibreculture* 5. Online. Available HTTP: http://journal.fibreculture.org/issue5/neilson_rossiter.html (accessed 21 July 2011).

——(2008) 'Precarity as a Political Concept, or, Fordism as Exception', *Theory, Culture & Society*, 25: 51–72.

Nelson, G. S. (2009) *Sovereignty and the Limits of the Liberal Imagination*, New York: Routledge.

Nyers, P. (2005) *Rethinking Refugees beyond States of Emergency*, New York: Routledge.

Olssen, M. (2006) 'Understanding the Mechanisms of Neoliberal Control: Lifelong Learning, Flexibility and Knowledge Capitalism', *International Journal of Lifelong Education*, 25: 213–30.

Ong, A. (1999) *Flexible Citizenship: The Cultural Logics of Transnationality*, Durham, NC: Duke University Press.

——(2005) '(Re)articulations of Citizenship', *PS: Political Science & Politics*, 38: 697–99.

——(2006) *Neoliberalism as Exception: Mutations in Citizenship and Sovereignty*, Durham, NC: Duke University Press.

——(2007a) 'Mutations in Citizenship', *Theory, Culture & Society*, 23: 499–505.

——(n.d.) 'Neoliberalism as a Mobile Technology', *Transactions of the Institute of British Geographers*, 32: 3–8.

——(2007b) 'Please Stay: Pied-à-Terre Subjects in the Megacity', *Citizenship Studies*, 11: 83–93.

Peck, J. (2001) *Workfare States*, New York: Guilford Press.

——(2005) 'Struggling with the Creative Class', *International Journal of Urban and Regional Development*, 29: 740–70.

——(2010a) 'Zombie Neoliberalism and the Ambidextrous State', *Theoretical Criminology* 14: 104–10.

——(2010b) *Constructions of Neoliberal Reason*, Oxford: Oxford University Press.

Peck, J. and Tickell, A. (2002) 'Neoliberalizing Space', *Antipode*, 34: 380–404.

Perlin, R. (2011) *Intern Nation: How to Learn Nothing and Earn Little in the Brave New Economy*, New York: Verso.

148   Bibliography

Peters, M. (2001) 'Education, Enterprise Culture and the Entrepreneurial Self: A Foucauldian Perspective', *Journal of Educational Enquiry*, 2: 58–71.

Piven, F. F. (1993) *Regulating the Poor: The Functions of Public Welfare*, New York: Vintage Books.

Pratt, M. L. (1992) *Imperial Eyes: Travel Writing and Transculturation*, New York: Routledge.

Projects Abroad (2008a) *Ghana Handbook*, London: Projects Abroad.

——(2008b) www.projects-abroad.org/destinations/ghana/ (accessed 17 April 2012).

Prozorov, S. (2007) 'The Unrequited Love of Power: Biopolitical Investment and the Refusal of Care', *Foucault Studies*, 4: 53–77.

Pupavac, V. (2010a) 'Weaving Postwar Reconstruction in Bosnia? The Attractions and Limitations of NGO Gender Development Approaches', *Journal of Intervention and Statebuilding*, 4: 475–93.

——(2010b) 'The Consumerism-Development-Security Nexus', *Security Dialogue*, 41: 691–713.

Rai, A. S.(2002) *Rule of Sympathy: Sentiment, Race, and Power, 1750–1850*, New York: Palgrave.

Ravensbergen, D. (2008) 'Be Nice to the "Creative Class"', *The Tyee*, August. Online. Available HTTP: http://thetyee.ca/Views/2008/08/05/CreativeClass/ (accessed 19 July 2011).

Read, J. (2002) 'A Fugitive Thread: The Production of Subjectivity in Marx', *Pli*, 13: 125–46.

——(2003) *The Micro-Politics of Capital: Marx and the Prehistory of the Present*, New York: State University of New York Press.

——(2009a) 'A Genealogy of Homo Economicus: Neoliberalism and the Production of Subjectivity', *Foucault Studies*, 6: 25–36.

——(2009b) 'University Experience: Neoliberalism against the Commons', in The Edu-factory Collective (eds) *Toward a Global Autonomous University: Cognitive Labor, the Production of Knowledge and Exodus from the Education Factory*, New York: Autonomedia.

Readings, B. (1993) *University in Ruins*, Cambridge, MA: Harvard University Press.

Reid, J. (2006) *The Biopolitics of the War on Terror: Life Struggles, Liberal Modernity and the Defence of Logistical Societies*, Manchester: Manchester University Press.

Research and Destroy (2009) 'Communiqué from an Absent Future', http: //wewantev erything.wordpress.com/2009/09/24/communique-from-an-absent-future/ (accessed 17 April 2012).

Richter, L. (2010) 'Inside the Thriving Industry of AIDS Orphan Tourism', *HSRC Review* 8.2. Online. Available HTTP: www.hsrc.ac.za/HSRC_Review_Article-195.phtml (accessed 15 June 2011).

Robbins, B. (2010) 'Multitude, Are You There?', *n+1*, December 2010. Online. Available HTTP: http://nplusonemag.com/multitude-are-you-there (accessed 20 July 2011).

Rosaldo, R. (1986) 'From the Door of His Tent: The Fieldworker and the Inquisitor', in J. Clifford and G. E. Marcus (eds) *Writing Culture: The Poetics and Politics of Ethnography*, Berkeley: University of Chicago Press.

Rose, N. (1991) '*Governing the Soul: The Shaping of the Private Self*', New York: Routledge.

——(1996) 'Governing "Advanced" Liberal Democracies', in A. Barry, T. Osborne and N. Rose (eds) *Foucault and Political Reason: Liberalism, Neo-Liberalism and Rationalities of Government*, Chicago: University of Chicago Press.

Bibliography   149

——(1999) *Powers of Freedom: Reframing Political Thought*, Cambridge: Cambridge University Press.

——(2000) 'Community, Citizenship, and the Third Way', *American Behavioral Scientist*, 43: 385–411.

——(2004) *Powers of Freedom: Reframing Political Thought*, Cambridge: Cambridge University Press.

Rose, N. and Miller, P. (1990) 'Governing Economic Life', *Economy & Society*, 19: 1–31.

——(1992) 'Political Power beyond the State: Problematics of Government', *The British Journal of Sociology*, 43: 173–205.

——(2003) *No-Collar: The Humane Workplace and Its Hidden Costs*, New York: Basic Books.

——(2009) *Nice Work If You Can Get It: Life and Labour in Precarious Times*, New York: New York University Press.

——(2011) 'Is Student Debt a Form of Indenture?', talk given at the open forum on student debt at Occupy Wall Street, New York. Online. Available HTTP: www.youtube.com/watch?v=MwDKZYMbZDc (accessed 27 December 2011).

Ross, A. (2003) *No-Collar: The Human Workplace and Its Hidden Costs: Behind the Myth of the New Office Utopia*, New York: Basic Books.

——(2009) *Nice Work If You Can Get It: Life and Labor in Precarious Times*, New York: New York University Press.

——(2011) Lecture at the Student Debt Forum of Occupy Wall Street, 19 October, www.youtube.com/watch?v=MwDKZYMbZDc (accessed 17 April 2012).

Said, W. E. (1979) *Orientalism*, New York: Vintage Books.

Schwartz, N. (1990) *Forest Society: A Social History of Petén, Guatemala*, Philadelphia: University of Pennsylvania Press.

Scott, J. C. (2009) *The Art of Not Being Governed: An Anarchist History of Upland Southeast Asia*, New Haven, CT: Yale University Press.

Scott, J. W. (1992) 'Experience', in J. Butler and J. W. Scott (eds) *Feminists Theorize the Political*, New York: Routledge.

Selby, J. (2007) 'Engaging Foucault: Discourse, Liberal Governance and the Limits of Foucauldian IR', *International Relations*, 21: 324–45.

Senellart, M. (2008) 'Course Context', in M. Foucault, *The Birth of Biopolitics, Lectures at the College de France 1978–1979*, New York: Palgrave.

Shapiro, M., Edkins, J. and Pin-Fat, V. (eds) (2004) *Sovereign Lives: Power in Global Politics*, New York: Routledge.

Shukaitis, S. (2007) 'Whose Precarity Is It Anyway?', *Fifth Estate* 41.3.

Simpson, K. (2004) 'Doing Development: The Gap Year, Volunteer-Tourists and a Popular Practice of Development', *Journal of International Development*, 16: 681–92.

——(2005) 'Dropping Out or Signing Up? The Professionalization of Youth Travel', *Antipode*, 37: 448–69.

Sinicrope, C., Norris, J. and Watanabe, Y. (2007) 'Understanding and Assessing Intercultural Competence: A Summary of Theory, Research and Practice', *Second Language Studies*, 26: 1–58.

Smith, N. (1996) *The New Urban Frontier: Gentrification and the Revanchist City*, New York: Routledge.

Soguk, N. (1993) 'Reflections on the "Orientalized Orientals"', *Alternatives*, 18: 361–84.

Söderman, N. and Snead, S. (2008) 'Opening the Gap: The Motivation of Gap Year Travellers to Volunteer in Latin America', in K. Lyons and S. Wearing (eds) *Journeys of Discovery in Volunteer Tourism*, Oxon: CABI Publishing.

150 Bibliography

Southwood, I. (2011) *Non-Stop Inertia*, London: Zero Books.

Stoddart, H. and Rogerson, C. (2004) 'Volunteer Tourism: The Case of Habitat for Humanity South Africa', *GeoJournal*, 60: 311–18.

Stoler, A. (1995) *Race and the Education of Desire: Foucault's History of Sexuality and the Colonial Order of Things*, Durham, NC: Duke University Press.

——(1997) *Tensions of Empire: Colonial Cultures in a Bourgeois World*, Berkeley: University of California Press.

——(2002) *Carnal Knowledge and Imperial Power: Race and the Intimate in Colonial Rule*, Berkeley: University of California Press.

Sundberg, J. (1998) 'NGO Landscapes in the Maya Biosphere Reserve, Guatemala', *Geographical Review*, 88: 388–412.

Szeman, I. and Cazdyn, E. (2011) *After Globalization*, New York: Blackwell.

Terranova, T. (2000) 'Producing Culture for the Digital Economy', *Social Text*, 18: 33–58.

——(2009) 'Another Life. The Nature of Political Economy in Foucault's Genealogy of Biopolitics', *Theory, Culture & Society*, 26: 234–62.

The Invisible Committee (2009) *The Coming Insurrection*, Los Angeles: Semiotext(e).

Todorov, T. (1992) *The Conquest of America: The Question of the Other*, New York: Harper Perennial.

van Maanen, J. (1988) *Tales of the Field: On Writing Ethnography*, Chicago: University of Chicago Press.

Virno, P. (2004) *Grammar of the Multitude: For an Analysis of Contemporary Forms of Life*, New York: Semiotext(e).

Virno, P. and Hardt, M. (eds) (1996) *Radical Thought in Italy: A Potential Politics*, Minnesota: University of Minnesota Press.

Vogel, B. (2009) *Wohlstandskonflikte. Soziale Fragen, die aus der Mitte kommen*, Hamburg: Hamburger Edition.

Vrasti, W. (2008) 'The Strange Case of Ethnography and International Relations', *Millennium: Journal of International Studies*, 37: 279–301.

——(2010) 'Dr. Strangelove or How I Learned to Stop Worrying about Methodology and Love Writing', *Millennium: Journal of International Studies*, 39(01): 79–88.

——(2011) 'Universal but Not Truly "Global": An Intervention in the Global Governmentality Debate', *Review of International Studies*, published online 30 November. Available HTTP: http://journals.cambridge.org/action/displayAbstract?fromPage=on line&aid=8444330&fulltextType=RA&fileId=S0260210511000568 (accessed 30 November 2011).

Wacquant, L. (2009) *Punishing the Poor: The Neoliberal Government of Social Insecurity*, Durham, NC: Duke University Press.

Walker, G. (2011) 'Primitive Accumulation and the Formation of Difference: On Marx and Schmitt', *Rethinking Marxism*, 23: 384–404.

Walker, R. B. J. (1993) *Inside/Outside: International Relations as Political Theory*, Cambridge: Cambridge University Press.

Walters, W. and Haahr, H. (2005) 'Governmentality and Political Studies', *European Political Science*, 4: 288–300.

Ward, L. (2007) 'You're Better off Backpacking – VSO Warns about Perils of "Voluntourism"', *The Guardian*, 14 August. Online. Available HTTP: www.guardian.co.uk/ uk/2007/aug/14/students.charitablegiving (accessed 13 March 2008).

Wearing, S. (2001) Volunteer Tourism: Experiences that Make a Difference, Oxon: CABI Publishing.

Bibliography 151

——(2002) 'Re-Centering the Self in Volunteer Tourism', in G. M. S. Dann (ed.) *The Tourist as a Metaphor of the Social World*, Oxon: CABI Publishing.

Wearing, S. and Neil, J. (2001) 'Refiguring Self and Identity through Volunteer Tourism', Loisir & Societe, 23: 387–419.

Wearing, S., Deville, A. and Lyons, K. (2008) 'The Volunteer's Journey Through Leisure into the Self', in K. Lyon and S. Wearing (eds) *Journeys of Discovery in Volunteer Tourism*, Cambridge, MA: CABI Publishing.

Weidner, J. (2009) 'Governmentality, Capitalism, and Subjectivity', *Global Society*, 23: 387–411.

Wright, S. (2005) 'Reality Check: Are We Living in an Immaterial World?', *Mute Magazine*, November. Online. Available HTTP: www.metamute.org/en/node/5594 (accessed 21 July 2011).

Zalewski, M. (1996) 'All These Theories yet the Bodies Keep Piling Up: Theory, Theorists, Theorizing', in K. Booth, S. Smith and M. Zalewski (eds) *International Relations: Positivism and Beyond*, Cambridge: Cambridge University Press.

Zizek, S. (1997) 'Multiculturalism, or the Cultural Logic of Multinational Capitalism', *New Left Review*, 225: 28–51.

——(1999) *The Ticklish Subject: The Absent Center of Political Ontology*, New York: Verso.

——(2001) 'Have Michael Hardt and Antonio Negri Rewritten the Communist Manifesto for the Twenty-First Century?', *Rethinking Marxism*, 13: 190–98.

——(2008a) 'Tolerance as an Ideological Category', *Critical Inquiry*, 34: 660–82.

——(2008b) *Violence: Six Sideways Reflections*, London: Profile Books.

——(2009) *First as Tragedy, Then as Farce*, New York: Verso.

Index

affectivity 21; cognitive capitalism 21; commodification of affect 26; economic rationality 46; emotional capitalism 45–46; entrepreneurship 44, 46; neoliberal subjectivity 16; neoliberal turn towards affect 14, 15, 30, 36, 41, 121; political subjectivity 27, 29, 83; sentimental education 15, 56; voluntourism, affective/ entrepreneurial competence 4, 15, 26, 28, 56, 83, 91, 112, 118, 119, 121, 122, 123, 130, 132

Agamben, Giogio 37, 38, 54; biopower 20–21

agency 19, 24, 25, 85; *see also* autonomy; freedom

Ahmed, Sara 82, 109, 111–12

aid assistance 10, 67, 68, 73, 84, 103

anthropology 6, 11, 13, 117; voluntourism 12, 22, 25, 80

archaeology 18–19

Autonomist Marxism 29, 42, 48–49, 50, 127, 136; bioeconomy 48; biopower 20; capital 45, 120, 125–27; capital/ subjectivity relationship 125; cognitive capitalism 48–49; criticism 49, 50, 51; Foucault's subject formation theory/ autonomist Marxist critique of capital 27, 120, 125–32, 133–34; neoliberalism 48–49; power 49; 'social factory' 48, 126; subject-as-capital 48–49, 126; *see also* Marx, Karl/ Marxism

autonomy 10, 20, 25, 26, 36; *see also* agency; freedom

Bayart, Jean-Francois 18

behaviourism 8, 16, 86

biopolitics 20–21, 30, 54; benevolent intent 37–38; bioeconomy 48; biopolitics/capital/subjectivity in neoliberal governmentality 3, 20–22, 26, 28–55; biopower 20–21, 24, 30, 38; *The Birth of Biopolitics* 20, 21, 32, 36–37, 41, 125, 134; capital accumulation 26, 37; capitalism 21; competition 37; definition 37; economic rationality 21, 26, 30, 36, 37; entrepreneurial form, universalization 37; governmentality 37–38; haves/have-nots division 54; normative nature 21, 37

Boltanski, L. 42, 45

Bourdieu, Pierre 52, 126

Bretton Woods system 30

brochure discourse 2, 4, 12, 14, 16, 65, 66, 98, 99–100, 119; *see also* literature; voluntourism.org

Butler, Judith 82

capital 125; Autonomist Marxism 45, 120, 125–27; biopolitics/capital/ subjectivity in neoliberal governmentality 3, 20–22, 26, 28–55; capital accumulation 26, 30, 31, 37, 45, 57, 71; capital/subjectivity relationship 125; flexible capital 4, 41, 43, 117, 129; Marx, Karl 3, 125; multiculturalism 21; subject-as-capital 47–54; transformation of 93, 125; *see also* capitalism; economic rationality; human capital; social capital

capitalism 38, 41; biopolitics 21; capitalist dystopia 40; 'caring' capitalism 29, 30, 41, 47, 132; cognitive capitalism 15, 16, 21, 48–49, 126 (knowledge economy 92, 94, 96,

Index 153

124, 125); consumerism 56, 71, 74; critique 3, 45, 85, 125, 133–36; devoid of moral logic 38, 45; emotional capitalism 45–46; ethico-political confusions 29; feudalism/capitalism transition 81–82, 125; flexible capitalism 41, 43; free-market capitalism 31, 128; Marx, Karl 48, 125–26; multiculturalism 77, 79, 81–82; post-Fordist capitalism 29; racism 81; romantic sensibility 71, 122, 123; tourism industry 72–73; utopia within capitalism 43; voluntourism 12, 15, 56–57, 119; *see also* capital; economic rationality; Fordism; neoliberalism; post-Fordism

care 14, 16, 38, 55, 56, 66, 121; 'caring' capitalism 29, 30, 41, 47, 132; *see also* charity; compassion

charity 10, 52, 119, 121; charitable work 2, 14, 50, 72, 98, 99–100

Chiapello, E. 42, 45

Chicago School of Economics 31, 126

citizenship 53; ethopolitics 46–47; flexible citizenship 120, 124, 129–30, 132; host community 22; voluntourism 12

class: bourgeoisie 23, 25, 48, 83–84; creative class 43, 51; haves/have-nots division 54, 57, 128–29; neoliberalism, class character 47, 133–35; norm-setting class 23, 43, 51, 132; social mobility 23, 53, 117, 128, 133, 136; *see also* inequality; white middle-class people

Cleaver, Harry 127

Clifford, James 13

colonialism 12; Ghana, colonial mentality 105, 108; postcolonial theory 10, 81 (provincializing whiteness 110); travel writing 10; voluntourism 5, 9, 56–57, 79, 116

commodity 8, 20, 49, 71, 74, 80; commodification of intellect, affect and sociality 26, 30, 126; voluntourism 57, 68, 74, 78, 82, 119; *see also* consumption

communism 49, 119–20; 'liberal communists' 44

compassion 14–15, 16, 21, 28, 52, 53, 56, 67, 69, 119; *see also* care; charity

competition 30, 34; biopolitics 37; education 96–97; labour 96–97, 119, 128; neoliberalism 30, 34, 36, 41, 47,

121, 128; political subjectivity 30, 47, 53; *see also* economic rationality; entrepreneurship

constructivism 16, 24, 34

consumption 12, 43, 45; consumer politics 74–75; consumerism 40, 42, 47, 85, 127 (capitalism 56, 71, 74; romantic sensibility 71–72, 73, 122); critique of 44; ethical consumption 1, 3, 26, 54, 72, 74, 84, 119, 123, 128; mass consumption 6, 29; post-Fordism 27, 56, 74; pseudo-political relevance 74; San Andres, consuming a 'small place' 56, 69–75; *see also* commodity

Cook,Thomas 7, 72

cooptation 42, 44, 45–46, 49

cosmopolitanism 1, 2, 12, 130; cosmopolitan values 12, 119, 122; multiculturalism 81

critical theory 4, 8, 19, 23, 25, 40, 71, 76; critical IR 24; multiculturalism 76; voluntourism 10

Dean, Jodi 133, 134

democracy 24, 30, 37, 50, 118; democratic distemper 41, 42–47; Fordist crisis 93; neoliberalism 133, 134

economic rationality 14, 32, 34, 48, 62, 71, 126; affectivity 46; biopolitics 21, 26, 30, 36, 37; economic rationality/ moral responsibility mix 50, 121, 132; entrepreneurship 44; neoliberal governmentality 29, 36, 133–34; *see also* capital; capitalism; competition; entrepreneurship

economy: bioeconomy 48; creative economy 43–44; economic crisis 27, 116, 120, 133, 134, 135 (Fordist crisis 30–31, 42, 93); economic liberalism 21, 38–39, 50; *homo oeconomicus* 14, 21, 37, 39–41; knowledge economy 92, 94, 96, 124, 125 (cognitive capitalism 15, 16, 21, 48, 126); market economy 29, 33, 39; neoliberalism, anti-economic component 133–35; new economy 43, 91–92 (skills needed in 15, 94, 96, 104); political economy 33, 34, 39; *see also* capital; capitalism; economic rationality; neoliberalism

education: competition 96–97; entrepreneurial education 87, 95, 117; Fordism/post-Fordism transition

154 *Index*

93–94; Ghana 27, 90, 96–104, 112, 124; Guatemala 63–64; intercultural competence 116–17; post-secondary education 93, 94, 95; sentimental education 15, 56; teaching volunteering 14, 98, 100–101, 103; voluntourism 1, 7, 15, 27, 50, 82, 86–87, 95, 104, 118, 121, 124, 132 (moral/technical education 27); *see also* higher education

employment 22; employability and work versatility 27, 87, 95, 96–97, 112, 116, 118, 121, 124, 133; underemployment 22, 92, 135, 136; unemployment 30, 35, 58, 133, 135; *see also* labour

entrepreneurship 1, 3, 21, 26; affectivity 44, 46; biopolitics 37; competition 47; economic rationality 44; entrepreneurial competence 22, 27, 44; entrepreneurial education 87, 95, 117; entrepreneurial form, universalization 36, 37, 41; neoliberal subjectivity 16; neoliberalism 26, 29, 36, 47, 121, 134; new entrepreneur 44; 'philantrepreneurs' 44; political subjectivity 27, 29, 44; self as enterprise 47, 54, 55; social responsibility 130; voluntourism, affective/entrepreneurial competence 4, 15, 26, 28, 56, 83, 91, 112, 118, 119, 121, 122, 123, 130, 132; *see also* competition; economic rationality

ethics 55; capitalism, devoid of moral logic 38, 45; economic rationality/ moral responsibility mix 50, 121, 132; ethical consumption 1, 3, 26, 54, 72, 74, 84, 119, 123, 128; ethical/ entrepreneurial self 55; ethico-political confusions 29; ethopolitics 46–47; moral/technical education 27; non-market-based experiments of living in common 27, 120, 136–37; voluntourism, moral appeal 2, 4, 7, 15, 96, 113; white middle-class people, moral superiority 26, 57, 123, 130

ethnography 12; 'deep hanging out' 12; ethnographic improvisation 17; 'ethnographilia' 13; ethnography/ archaeology merging 18–19; methodology 3, 11, 12–20; reflexivity 12; subject formation 16; subjectivity 16; *see also* methodology

Eurocentrism 1, 12, 73, 76

Fabian, Johannes 80
Fanon, Franz 109
Federici, Sylvia 81
Ferguson, James 81
flexibilization 50, 87, 94, 96, 125–26, 127; flexible capital 4, 41, 43, 117, 129; flexible citizenship 120, 124, 129–30, 132; flexible higher education 94; flexible labour 42, 94, 96, 124; flexible market 20, 57, 132; flexible production 29, 93, 119; flexible subjectivity 83, 111, 126–27

Florida, Richard 16, 43–44, 51, 53; creative class: the norm-setting class 43, 51; *The Rise of the Creative Class* 43; utopia within capitalism 43; *Who's Your City* 43

Fordism 30, 31, 35, 42, 127; 1960s' revolts 21, 41, 42–47, 67, 73, 93; Fordism/post-Fordism transition 42–47, 93–94; *see also* post-Fordism

Foucault, Michel 24, 38; archaeological method/analytics of government 18; *The Birth of Biopolitics* 20, 21, 32, 36–37, 41, 125, 134; 'critical ontology of the self' 20, 54, 137; criticism 50; Foucault's subject formation theory/ autonomist Marxist critique of capital 27, 120, 125–32, 133–34; governmentality 20, 33–35, 40; *homo oeconomicus* 14, 21, 37, 39–41; human capital 126; neoliberalism 26, 29, 32–33, 40, 45, 47–48, 120, 134; power 24, 25; subject formation 3, 52, 120, 125, 128; subjection 52, 128; subjectivity 22, 40–41, 49, 125; *see also* neoliberal governmentality; subject formation; subjectivity

Fowles, John 23
freedom 68; definition 127; neoliberalism 26, 36, 42–43, 54, 127, 135

Friedman, Milton 31

gap year 2, 60, 87
gentrification 126, 129
geography 5, 11, 22, 63, 82
Germany: German Ordoliberal School 34; Frankfurt School 29, 71; Schröder, Gerhard 35
Ghana 3, 15, 25, 27, 86–118, 123–25; Africa as training ground 88, 112–17, 124–25; education 27, 90, 96–104, 112, 124; employability and work

Index   155

versatility 27, 87, 95, 96–97, 112, 116, 124; entrepreneurial education 87, 95, 117; Ho 14, 90–91, 104, 106–7; human capital 27, 95; intercultural competence 116; multiculturalism 88, 91, 124; poverty 14, 91; racial tensions 15, 27, 87–88, 91, 104–12, 118, 123–24 ('reverse racism' 15, 27, 104, 108, 109, 123); theoretical framework 87, 91–96; volunteers 91, 95–96, 98, 117, 123–24 (affective/entrepreneurial competence 4, 27, 112, 118, 123; benefits 27, 87, 98–99, 114, 124; dissatisfaction 87, 91, 97, 98–99, 101–2, 103, 114, 115, 118, 123; home, support/admiration 87, 91, 112–15, 118, 124; overpriced holiday 102, 112, 114, 123, 124; slacking and local involvement/exploration 86, 91, 98, 102–3, 104, 108, 112, 114, 118); see also Projects Abroad

'giving back' 2, 14, 26, 28, 100, 119; giving back in neoliberal times 120–25

globalization 20, 42, 81, 107, 124, 130–31, 132; effects 7, 92; global governmentality 50–52; global liberalism 50; global politics 22

government: 'government through community' 46, 68; subjectivity 47; see also governmentality; neoliberal governmentality

governmentality 33–35; biopolitics 37–38; Foucault, Michel 20, 33–35, 40; liberal rule 35; power 20; see also neoliberal governmentality

Grand Tour 1, 7, 130

grassroots organization 56, 60, 67–68, 88, 90, 121

Guatemala 3, 14, 25, 26, 56–85, 121–23; affective competence 26, 56, 83, 122; care/compassion 56, 67; consuming a 'small place' 56, 69–75; education 63–64; longing for authentic meaning 56, 122; longing for unspoiled nature, tradition, cultural diversity 1, 57, 69, 78, 122; multiculturalism 15, 56, 75–84, 85, 123; post-Fordist consumption 27, 56; poverty 14, 58, 65–66, 84; racism 110; San Andres 14, 15, 56, 57–58, 65, 69, 78, 122; volunteers 59, 60, 84, 121–23 (benefits 27, 82–84; complains 56, 62–64, 65, 67, 69, 83, 84; frustration 63–64, 69, 84, 122; slacking and local

involvement/exploration 62, 64, 69–70, 80, 83, 118, 121–22); see also Volunteer Peten

Hardt, Michael 20, 51

Harvey, David 32, 47, 49, 126, 133; A Brief History of Neoliberalism 30–31

Hayek, Friedrich van 31, 36

health issues 24–25, 37, 38; medical volunteering 96, 98, 100, 102, 103

higher education 92–98, 117, 124, 135; corporatization of 92, 93, 132; flexible higher education 94; internship 1, 91–92, 94, 117, 124, 133; investment in future ability to work 86–87, 92, 95, 97, 117, 124, 135; labour 92–93, 94–95, 117–18, 124, 135; medical school 96, 97–98; new economy 92–93, 94, 124; overeducated students 92, 135, 136; volunteering 95, 96–98, 118; see also education

Hirschman, Albert: The Passions and the Interests 39

homo oeconomicus 14, 21, 37, 39, 40–41, 117, 135; see also Foucault, Michel

hospitality 74, 78; hospitality studies 6, 8, 12, 16

host community 5, 25–26; citizenship 22; stuck between romanticisation and denigration 27; subjectivity 22; voluntourism, benefits 6, 9, 101; voluntourism, impact on 9, 26, 53, 89, 99, 101–2, 103

human capital 4, 21, 40, 27, 95; subject formation 126–27; subjectivization 40; see also skill; social capital

Illich, Ivan 11

Illouz, Eva 45–46

imperialism 1, 12, 23

inequality 6, 12, 29, 34, 42; see also class

international relations (IR) 22–26; critical IR 24; identity formation 22–23; methodology 11; transnational tourism 11; voluntourism, contribution to IR research 22–26

Keynesianism 31, 36, 127, 131

labour 42, 53; Autonomist Marxism 49, 51; competition 96–97, 119, 128; cooptation 45; flexible labour 42, 94, 96, 124; higher education and labour 92–93, 94–95, 117–18, 124, 135;

156 *Index*

immaterial labour 44, 51; internship 1, 91–92, 94, 117, 124, 133; investment in future ability to work 86–87, 92, 95, 97, 117, 124, 135; new economy 91–92; volunteers are already workers 95–96, 114–15; work experience 3, 87, 114–15, 123; *see also* employment

the Left 29, 42; New Left 42, 68, 77, 127; Old Left 77

liberalism 33, 35, 39; economic liberalism 21, 38–39, 50; global liberalism 50; hegemony 36, 51; 'liberal communists' 44; liberal democracy 30, 37, 50; liberal multiculturalism 15, 109; political/economic liberalism transition 33; *see also* neoliberal governmentality; neoliberalism

Lisle, Debbie 11, 22; *The Global Politics of Contemporary Travel Writing* 11–12

literature: brochure discourse 2, 4, 12, 14, 16, 65, 66, 98, 99–100, 119; promotional literature 4–5; scholarly literature 6–12

'making a difference' 2, 7, 10, 14, 26, 28, 65, 99, 100, 111

market 39; competition 34; flexible market 20, 57, 132; free-market capitalism 31, 128; market economy 29, 33, 39; market logics and political subjectivity 26; neoliberalism 20, 26, 29, 35, 36, 120, 121; non-market-based experiments of living in common 27, 120, 136–37; 'technology of the self' 39; *see also* economy; economic rationality; neoliberalism

Marx, Karl/Marxism 21; capital 125; capitalism 38, 48, 125–26; critique of capital 3, 125; effects of self-making 3; multiculturalism 76–78; neoliberalism 32, 38, 40, 45, 47–48, 133; political subjectivity change 44–45; subject formation 126; *see also* Autonomist Marxism

methodology 17; ethnography 3, 11, 12–20; Foucault, archaeological method 18; politics 26; subjectivity 16; tourism research 11; *see also* ethnography

modernity 1, 7, 73, 85; Africa, *unmodernizable* 116; critique of 57, 70–71, 75, 84, 122; discontent with

modernity 4, 29, 61, 73, 74, 75; modernization. 7, 66, 69, 70, 73, 79–80, 104, 122; *see also* romantic sensibility

monetarism 31

multiculturalism 1, 12, 44, 123; capital 21; capitalism 77, 79, 81–82; critical theory 76; criticism 56, 76–78, 123; culturalization of politics 78–79; depoliticization 26, 57, 78, 82, 84; Ghana 88, 91, 124; Guatemala 15, 56, 75–84, 85, 123; intercultural competence 116–17; the Left 77; liberal multiculturalism 15, 109; Marxism 76–78; Michaels, Walter Benn: *The Trouble with Diversity* 79; neoliberalism 15, 109, 116; reification of culture 79–82; resistance 85; romanticism 75–76, 78, 79–80, 84, 123; social capital 82–84, 123; tolerance 44, 76, 81, 123

Negri, Antonio 20, 51

neoliberal governmentality 3, 15, 16, 32, 39–40, 45, 48, 120, 137; biopolitics/capital/subjectivity 3, 20–22, 26, 28–55; commodification of intellect, affect, sociality 26, 30; definition 20, 133–34; discipline and distemper 42–47; economic rationality 29, 36, 133–34; entrepreneurial form, universalization 36, 41; global governmentality 50–52; market 20, 36, 120; paradox 36; subject formation 128; subjectivity 3, 20–22, 125; tools 36–41; turn towards affect 14, 15, 30, 36, 41, 121; voluntourism 49–50; *see also* Foucault, Michel; governmentality; neoliberalism

neoliberalism 39, 54, 118, 126; anti-economic component 133–35; Autonomist Marxism 48–49; bohemian values/dissident language 14, 21, 26, 30, 44, 45, 47, 53, 94, 127; capitalist dystopia 40, 116; class character 47, 133–35; competition 30, 34, 36, 41, 47, 121, 128; criticism 41, 133–36; definition 26, 32, 34; democracy 133, 134; discipline and distemper 42–47; entrepreneurship 26, 29, 36, 47, 121, 134; Fordist crisis 93–94, 127; Foucault, Michel 26, 29, 32–33, 40, 45, 47–48, 120, 134; Foucault's subject formation theory/

autonomist Marxist critique of capital
27, 120, 125–32, 133–34; freedom 26,
36, 42–43, 54, 127, 135; hegemony 31,
50, 51, 53, 132; 'humane'
neoliberalism 29, 30, 47, 53;
investment in future ability to work
86–87, 92, 95, 97, 117, 124, 135;
market 20, 26, 29, 35, 36, 120, 121;
Marxism 32, 38, 40, 45, 47–48, 133;
multiculturalism 15, 109, 116;
neoliberal subjectivity 16, 30, 54, 132;
normative nature 4, 38–39, 54, 125,
128, 132, 133, 134; political/economic
liberalism transition 33; resistance to
119; responsibility 121; roll-out/Third
Way phase 35, 45, 93, 131–32; short
story of 30–36; sociality 15, 20, 30,
41, 121; subject formation 12, 21, 48,
120, 126–27; turn towards intellect,
affect, sociality 15, 30, 41, 121;
voluntourism 49–50, 120–21; *see also*
capitalism; economic rationality;
neoliberal governmentality
NGOs 4, 5, 58, 90
norm/normative issues: biopolitics 21,
37; capitalism 38–39; creative class 43,
51; haves/have-nots division 54, 57,
128–29; neoliberalism 4, 38–39, 54,
125, 128, 132, 133, 134; norm-setting
class 43, 51, 132; subjectivity,
'normalization' 125

Ong, Aihwa: flexible citizenship 120,
129–30
Orientalism 3, 10, 79, 56, 73, 122, 123;
Said, Edward 10, 56, 79; Soguk,
Nevzat 81
Orwell, George: *Animal Farm* 52, 128

Perlin, Ross *Intern Nation: How to
Learn Nothing and Earn Little in the
Brave New Economy* 91–92
philanthropy 10, 48, 68, 73, 83, 85;
'philantrepreneurs' 44
political economy 11, 49, 126;
neoliberalism 33, 34, 39
political subjectivity 4, 21–22, 27, 44;
affectivity 27, 29, 83; competition 30,
47, 53; competitive/hierarchical
struggle for subjectivity 53–54;
'conditional on conduct' 47, 57, 129;
entrepreneurship 27, 29, 44;
expanding the 'field of possibilities'
27, 29, 130; hierarchical/uneven forms

of 27, 83, 120, 129; market logics and
political subjectivity 26; political
subjectivity change 44–45, 47, 125;
privilege 44, 47; self as enterprise 47;
voluntourism 4, 27, 29, 83, 84, 130,
133; *see also* subject formation;
subjectivity
politics 68, 85; aid assistance 68;
consumer politics 74–75;
culturalization of politics 78–79;
depoliticization 67–68, 73, 74–75, 85
(multiculturalism 26, 57, 78, 82, 84);
emancipatory politics 127;
ethopolitics 46–47; global politics 22;
liberalism 33; market logics and
political subjectivity 26; voluntourism,
criticism 11; world politics 23; *see also*
biopolitics; political subjectivity
post-Fordism 29, 128; consumption 27,
56, 74; modes of production 27; *see
also* capitalism; Fordism
post-structuralism 17, 18
poverty 2, 7, 66, 84; *de-subjectified*
individual 53, 128; Ghana 14, 91;
haves/have-nots division 54, 57,
128–29; San Andres 14, 58, 65–66, 84;
a social construct 66
power: Autonomist Marxism 49;
biopower 20–21, 24, 30, 38; Foucault,
Michel 24, 25; governmentality 20;
productive function of 24, 25;
sovereign power 32, 33, 34, 36, 37,
119, 127, 133; subject formation 125,
128; subjectivity 20 (power/resistance
struggle 16, 54)
privilege 19, 22, 23, 94; 'conditional on
conduct' 47, 57, 129; neoliberalism
54; political subjectivity 44, 47;
whiteness 109–10, 111–12, 123–24
Projects Abroad 14, 87, 88–91, 114, 123;
bad-structured placements 101, 102,
123; customer service 88–89; Ghana
89–90; *Ghana Handbook* 89, 102, 104;
medical volunteering 96, 98, 100, 102,
103; price 87, 88, 89, 91, 101, 102,
112, 114, 123, 124; professionalism
88, 91, 97; staff 88, 102, 114, 117;
teaching volunteering 14, 98,
100–101, 103; *see also* Ghana

racism 15, 108–9, 116, 122; capitalism
81; Ghana, racial tensions 15, 27,
87–88, 91, 104–12, 118, 123–24
(reverse racism 15, 27, 104, 108, 109,

158 *Index*

123); Guatemala 110; racial privilege 109–10, 111–12, 123–24; racialization 108, 109, 110, 123; whiteness 27, 105, 106, 109–10, 111–12, 123–24 (provincializing whiteness 110, 112, 123–24); *see also* Ghana

reflexivity 12, 13, 23

resistance 23, 25, 48; multiculturalism 85; neoliberalism 119; subjectivity, power/resistance struggle 16, 54

responsibility 121; economic rationality/ moral responsibility mix 50, 121, 132; entrepreneurship 130; individual responsibility 2, 21, 47 (voluntourism 5, 7, 130–31; welfare 32, 39, 46, 125, 129, 132); responsible tourism 8, 72, 82; social responsibility 1, 5, 44, 96, 119, 121, 130, 132, 136; *see also* welfare

romantic sensibility 1, 70, 75, 83, 122; Campbell, Colin: *The Romantic Ethic and the Spirit of Modern Consumerism* 71; capitalism 71, 122, 123; consumerism 71–72, 73, 122; longing for authentic meaning 56, 71, 72, 122; longing for unspoiled nature, tradition, cultural diversity 1, 57, 69, 71, 78, 122; multiculturalism 75–76, 78, 79–80, 84, 123; romantic distemper 47; romantic retro-utopia 85; voluntourism 56, 57, 69, 71–73, 78, 122–23; *see also* modernity

Rose, Nikolas 46–47, 68

skill: entrepreneurial competence 22, 27, 44; immaterial skill 15, 27, 53; intercultural competence 116–17; new economy, skills needed in 15, 94, 96, 104; social networking skill 44; subject formation 127; voluntourism, affective/entrepreneurial competence 4, 15, 26, 28, 56, 83, 91, 112, 118, 119, 121, 122, 123, 130, 132; voluntourism, skills acquisition/career development 8–9, 27, 29, 82–83, 84, 86–87, 95, 96–97, 103; *see also* human capital; social capital

social capital 23, 126; multiculturalism as social capital 82–84, 123; social networking skill 44; superior social capital through ethical consumption 3, 26, 123; volunteer 2, 3, 4, 9, 22, 78, 123 (social capital increase 52–53, 82–84, 112, 130); *see also* human capital; skill; sociality

sociality 85; commodification of 26; government 47; neoliberalism 15, 20, 30, 41, 121; 'social factory' 48, 126; voluntourism 119, 121; *see also* social capital

sociology 6, 8, 11, 22, 23; MacCannell, Dean 6–7

state 35, 36; liberal theory 33, 34; sovereign power 32, 33–34, 36, 37, 119, 127, 133; weak welfare state 50, 93, 121, 129, 132; *see also* government; governmentality

subject formation 15, 18–19, 25; affirmation of the self 3; cognitive capitalism 15, 16; ethnography 16; Foucault, Michel 3, 52, 120, 125, 128; Foucault's subject formation theory/ autonomist Marxist critique of capital 27, 120, 125–32, 133–34; human capital 126–27; identity formation 22–23; *kulturlos* subject 83; market, 'technology of the self' 39; neoliberal governmentality 128; neoliberalism 12, 21, 48, 120, 126–27; power 125, 128; self as enterprise 47, 54, 55; self-growth 72, 87, 99, 100, 111, 114, 118, 121, 125, 133; 'social factory' 48, 126; subjection 52, 128; subjectivization 18, 21, 40, 41, 83, 121; voluntourism 120–21; *see also* Foucault, Michel; political subjectivity; subjectivity

subjectivity 16, 83; biopolitics/capital/ subjectivity in neoliberal governmentality 3, 20–22, 26, 28–55; 'critical ontology of the self' 20, 54, 137; *de-subjectified* individual 53, 128; ethical/entrepreneurial self 55; flexible subjectivity 83, 111, 126–27; Foucault, Michel 22, 40–41, 49, 125; neoliberal governmentality 3, 20–22, 125; neoliberal subjectivity 16, 30, 54, 132; 'normalization' 125; power 20; power/resistance struggle 16, 54; privilege 22; subject-as-capital 47–54; voluntourism 119, 121; *see also* Foucault, Michel; political subjectivity; subject formation

surveillance 24. 37, 42, 119, 120, 128

Terranova, Tiziana 45

terrorism 24, 81; biopolitics 37; War on Terror 37, 116, 119

tolerance 12, 74, 81, 84, 85, 110, 121, 123; multiculturalism 44, 76, 81, 123

Index 159

tourism industry 1, 3, 6, 15–16; affordable tourism 7, 72; alternative tourism 72–73; capitalism 72–73; Cook,Thomas 7, 72; mass tourism 72, 87 (criticism 2, 6–8, 56, 64); responsible tourism 8, 72, 82; *see also* voluntourism

travel writing 10, 11, 12

United Kingdom 135; Blair, Tony 35; British Volunteer Service Overseas 1; Cameron, David: International Citizen Service 131; higher education 97–98; neoliberalism 31, 35; Thatcher, Margaret 31, 130, 134

United States 30, 135; Clinton, Bill 35; higher education 92, 94, 98; neoliberalism 31, 35; Peace Corps 1, 59; Reagan, Ronald 31, 36, 43, 134; Travel Industry Association of America 1–2

utopia 49, 62, 75, 92, 134; retro-utopia 85; utopia within capitalism 43

violence 24, 26, 42, 80, 136

volunteer 5, 25, 135–36; Ghana 91, 95–96, 98, 117, 123–24; Guatemala 59, 60, 84; home, support/admiration 22, 28, 87, 91, 112–15, 118, 124; motivations 86, 119, 122, 133; number of 1–2; perception by host community 26 (racial tensions 15, 27, 87–88, 91, 104–12, 118, 123–24); slacking and local involvement/exploration 14, 28, 62, 64, 69–70, 80, 83, 86, 91, 102–3, 104, 112, 114, 118, 121–22; social capital 2, 3, 4, 9, 22, 52, 78, 112, 123, 130; volunteers are already workers 95–96, 114–15; *see also* voluntourism; white middle-class people

Volunteer Peten 14, 15, 57–62, 70, 121–23; apolitical organization 67–68; grassroots development work 56, 60, 67–68, 88, 121; ineffective leadership 61, 62, 64, 67; ineffective organizational structure 15, 62, 64, 121; mission/projects 59–60; Peters, Mateo 59, 60, 61–62, 67, 69–70; work routine 60–61, 64; *see also* Guatemala

Volunteer: A Traveller's Guide to Making a Difference Around the World 5

voluntourism 2, 15, 28, 86, 136; alternative tourism 72; anthropology 12, 22, 25, 80; capitalism 12, 15, 56–57, 119; colonialism 5, 9, 56–57, 79, 116; commodity 57, 68, 74, 78, 82, 119; depoliticization 67–68, 75; design destination 65; flexible citizenship 130; for-profit voluntourism 1, 2, 102, 131, 136; global politics 22; impact on host community 6, 9, 26, 53, 89, 99, 101–2, 103; IR research 22–26; limited understanding of 6, 8; neoliberalism 49–50, 120–21; origins 1, 73; paradox 22, 87; political subjectivity 130; poverty 2, 7; *raison d'être* 7; romanticism 56, 57, 69, 71–73, 78, 122–23; social responsibility 121; sociality 119, 121; subject formation 120–21; subjectivity 119, 121; theoretical framework 49–52; *see also following* voluntourism *entries*; volunteer

voluntourism, benefits 2, 3–4, 5, 7, 28–29, 72, 82, 87, 121, 130, 133; affective/entrepreneurial competence 4, 15, 26, 28, 56, 83, 91, 112, 118, 119, 121, 122, 123, 130, 132; education 1, 7, 15, 27, 50, 82, 86–87, 95, 104, 118, 121, 124, 132; employability 27, 95, 112, 118, 121, 133; Ghana 27, 87, 98–99, 114, 124; Guatemala 27, 82–84; host community 6, 9, 101; human capital 95, 96; intercultural competence 116–17; *kulturlos* subject 83; political subjectivity 4, 27, 29, 83, 84, 133; self-growth 72, 87, 99, 100, 111, 114, 118, 121, 125; skills acquisition/career development 8–9, 27, 29, 82–83, 84, 86–87, 95, 96–97, 103; social capital increase 52–53, 82–84, 112, 130; *see also* volunteer; voluntourism

voluntourism, criticism/shortcomings 3, 8–11, 15, 28, 56, 110, 121; bad-structured placements 3, 14, 15, 62, 64, 101, 102, 121; career development 8–9, 10, 53, 86, 96, 113; critical theory 10; deception 14, 28, 99; Ghana 87, 91, 97, 98–99, 101–2, 103, 114, 115, 118, 123; Guatemala 56, 62–64, 65, 67, 69, 83, 84, 122; 'hypocrisy charge' 8–9; ineffective leadership 61, 62, 64, 67; not feeling needed 3, 14, 26, 28, 62–63, 65, 67, 102, 114; one-sided exchange 100, 111, 112, 123; overpriced holiday 7,

160   *Index*

87, 88, 89, 91, 101, 102, 112, 114, 123, 124; self-indulgence 99; *see also* volunteer; voluntourism
voluntourism, effectiveness 4, 28–29, 103, 113, 118, 121; *see also* volunteer; voluntourism
voluntourism.org 1, 4–5
voluntourism, success 2, 4, 15, 28, 119; moral appeal 2, 4, 7, 15, 96, 113; personal attitude 5; *see also* volunteer; voluntourism

'We Are the 99%' 135
Weber, Max 42, 71

welfare 73; biopower 24, 30, 38; individual responsibility 32, 39, 46, 125, 129, 132; public welfare 30, 93; social welfare 37; weak welfare state 50, 93, 121, 129, 132; *see also* responsibility
white middle-class people 10, 15, 72, 83, 130; moral superiority 26, 57, 123, 130; norm-setting class 23; power 25; whiteness 27, 105, 106, 109–10, 111–12, 123–24 (provincializing whiteness 110, 112, 123–24); *see also* class

Zizek, Slavoj 43–44, 56, 83